Enrolled Agent University:

Individual Tax Law

Certifyible.com

ISBN: 9798825544809

ENROLLED AGENT UNIVERSITY

CONTENTS

TAX RETURN FOR INDIVIDUALS

Overview

Part one of the Special Enrollment Examination has six domains that you will be tested on which includes the following:

- Domain 1: Preliminary work and taxpayer data (14 questions)
- Domain 2: Income and assets (17 questions)
- Domain 3: Deductions and credits (17 questions)
- Domain 4: Taxation (15 questions)
- Domain 5: Advising the individual taxpayer (11 questions)
- Domain 6: Specialized returns for individuals (11 questions)

If you need more support check out the Enrolled Agent University online course and weekly live instructor training at www.certifyible.com.

This book as well as the online course is structured to cover all six domains above. The official prometric exam outline can be found here: https://www.prometric.com/test-takers/search/irs.

If you have any questions we are here to help. Feel free to reach out to us at hello@certifyible.com.

Use of prior year returns

There are many reasons to keep a copy of a tax return from a prior year. The IRS urges all taxpayers to keep copies of their tax returns for at least **three years**.

Copies of filed tax returns must be submitted to financial institutions, mortgage lenders, and brokers. Copies may also be needed whenever an individual wants to buy or refinance a home, get a loan for a business, or apply for federal aid for higher education.

Past due returns

File a past due return the same way and to the same location where you would file an on-time return.

Those who need a copy of their tax return should check with their software provider or tax preparer.

Taxpayers using a software product for the first time may need their Adjusted Gross Income (AGI) amount from their prior-year tax return to verify their identity.

Transcript Types

Taxpayers can get different types of transcripts from the IRS based upon their need.

Transcript types at no charge include the following:

- **Tax Return Transcript** - shows most line items from your original Form 1040-series tax return as filed, along with any forms and schedules. It doesn't show changes made after you filed your original return. This transcript is available for the current and three prior tax years. A tax return transcript usually meets the needs of lending institutions offering mortgages and student loans. **Note:** The secondary spouse on a joint return can use Get Transcript Online or Form 4506-T to request this transcript type. When using Get Transcript by Mail or calling 800-908-9946, the primary taxpayer on the return must make the request.
- **Tax Account Transcript** - shows basic data such as filing status, taxable income, and payment types. It also shows changes made after you filed your original return. This transcript is available for the current and nine prior tax years through Get Transcript Online, and the current and three prior tax years through Get Transcript by Mail or by calling 800-908-9946. These years and older tax years can be obtained by submitting Form 4506-T. **Note:** If you made estimated tax payments and/or applied an overpayment from a prior year return, you can request this transcript type a few weeks after the beginning of the calendar year to confirm your payments prior to filing your tax return.
- **Record of Account Transcript** - combines the tax return and tax account transcripts above into one complete transcript. This transcript is available for the current and three prior tax years using Get Transcript Online or Form 4506-T.
- **Wage and Income Transcript** - shows data from information returns we receive such as Forms W-2, 1098, 1099, and 5498 . If you see a message of "No Record of return filed" for the current tax year, it means information has not been added to the transcript yet. Check back in late May. Current tax year information may not be complete until July. This transcript is available for the current and nine prior tax years using Get Transcript Online or Form 4506-T.
- **Verification of Non-filing Letter** - states that the IRS has no record of a processed Form 1040-series tax return as of the date of the request. It

doesn't indicate whether you are required to file a return for that year. This letter is available after June 15 for the current tax year or anytime for the prior three tax years using Get Transcript Online or Form 4506-T. Use Form 4506-T if you need a letter for older tax years.

Note: A transcript isn't a photocopy of your return. If you need a copy of your original return, submit Form 4506, Request for Copy of Tax Return. Refer to the form for the processing time and fee.

TAXPAYER BIOGRAPHICAL INFORMATION

It's important to verify your clients so that you can ensure accuracy.

You must collect:

- Legal name, date of birth, marital status
- Residency status and or citizenship
- Dependents
- Taxpayer identification number which can include their SSN, ITIN or ATIN
- To prevent identity theft, you should collect the taxpayer's government identification.

You also want to collect copies of social security cards, ITIN letters to avoid putting the wrong taxpayer identification numbers on returns which is also one of the biggest reject returns.

Identity Protection Pin

Starting in 2021, taxpayers may voluntarily opt into the IP PIN program as a proactive way to protect themselves from tax-related identity theft. An Identity Protection PIN (IP PIN) is a six-digit number that prevents someone else from filing a tax return using the Social Security number.

The IP PIN is known only to the taxpayer and the IRS. It helps prevent identity thieves from filing fraudulent tax returns using a taxpayers' personally identifiable information.

Here are a few key things to know about the IP PIN Opt-In program:

- This is a voluntary program.
- Taxpayers must pass a rigorous identity verification process.
- Spouses and dependents of the taxpayers are eligible for an IP PIN if they can verify their identities.
- An IP PIN is valid for a calendar year.
- Taxpayers must obtain a new IP PIN each filing season.

- The online IP PIN tool is offline between November and mid-January each year.
- Correct IP PINs must be entered on electronic and paper tax returns to avoid rejections and delays.
- Taxpayers must never share their IP PIN with anyone but their trusted tax provider. The IRS will never call, text, or email requesting the IP PIN. Educate your clients of scams to steal their IP PIN.
- There currently is no opt-out option but the IRS is working on one for 2022.

In case of address changes, the taxpayers need to notify the IRS to ensure they'll receive any IRS refunds or correspondence.

If the address change happens before filing the tax return, enter the new address on the tax return when you file it. When the return is processed, the IRS will update their records. Always remind your clients to notify you in case of any address changes.

If the address change happens after filing the tax return, remind your client to notify the post office that serves the old address. Because not all post offices forward government checks, make sure to directly notify the IRS as described below.

To be able to change its address with the IRS, the taxpayer must complete a Form 8822, Change of Address, (For Individual, Gift, Estate, or Generation-Skipping Transfer Tax Returns) (PDF) and/or a Form 8822-B, Change of Address or Responsible Party — Business (PDF) and send them to the address shown on the forms

Taxpayers may also write to inform the IRS directly that their address is changing. For this to happen, they need to provide the following information to the IRS:

- full name
- old and new addresses
- social security number, individual taxpayer identification number, or employer identification number, and
- signature

Joint Filers - If they file a joint return, they should provide the information and signatures for both spouses. They need to send the written address change information to the IRS addresses listed in the instructions to the tax forms you filed.

Separated - If they file a joint return and they now have separate residences, each joint taxpayer should notify the IRS of the new, separate addresses.

It can take four to six weeks for a change of address request to be fully processed.

Your client got married and now is using a new spouse's last name or hyphenating a name? Or your client got divorced and is now back to using a former last name? Or your client is getting a New SS Card?

- A name change can have an impact on taxes. All the names on a taxpayer's tax return must match Social Security Administration records. A name mismatch can delay a tax refund.
- Taxpayers need to verify the SSA if a dependent had a name change.

CAUTION: IRS never calls or sends email or text messages asking taxpayers to provide information or log in to obtain a transcript or update their profile. Visit report phishing for instructions if you are unsure about the authenticity of any "unsolicited" communication between taxpayers and IRS, other than US mail, claiming to be from the IRS.

ITIN APPLICATIONS & RENEWALS

An ITIN is a 9-digit number issued by the U.S. Internal Revenue Service (IRS) to individuals who are required for U.S. federal tax purposes to have a U.S. taxpayer identification number but who do not have and are not eligible to get a social security number (SSN).

Form W-7 is used for applying for an IRS individual taxpayer identification number (ITIN). This form can also be used to renew an existing ITIN that is expiring or that has already expired.

An ITIN that hasn't been included on a U.S. federal tax return at least once in the last 3 consecutive tax years will expire. In addition, ITINs that were assigned before 2013 will expire according to an annual schedule based on the middle digits of the ITIN.

ITIN APPLICATION PROCEDURES

- Keep a copy of the application for your records.
- Applying for an ITIN for the first time. If your client had never applied for an ITIN before and are submitting an application for a new ITIN, include the following in the application package
- A completed Form W-7.
- The original tax return(s) for which the ITIN is needed. Attach Form W-7 to the front of the tax return. If the taxpayer is applying for more than one ITIN for the same tax return (such as for a spouse or dependent(s)), attach all Forms W-7 to the same tax return. Leave the area of the SSN blank on the tax return for each person who is applying for an ITIN. After the Form W-7 has been processed, the IRS will assign an ITIN to the return and process the return.

- There are exceptions to the requirement to include a U.S. federal tax return. If the taxpayer is claiming one of these exceptions, you must submit the documentation required instead of a tax return.
- Original documents, or certified copies of these documents from the issuing agency, required to support the information provided on Form W-7. The required supporting documentation must be consistent with the applicant's information provided on Form W-7. For example, the name, date of birth, and country(ies) of citizenship shown in the documentation must be the same as on Form W-7, lines 1a, 4, and 6a.

There are 13 acceptable documents, as shown in the following table. At least one document must contain a photograph, unless the applicant is a dependent under age 14 (under age 18 if a student). The applicant may later be required by the IRS to provide a certified translation of foreign-language documents.

Supporting Documentation	**Can be used to establish:**	
	Foreign status	**Identity**
Passport (the only stand-alone document*)	x	x
U.S. Citizenship and Immigration Services (USCIS photo identification	x	x
Visa issued by the U.S. Department of State	x	x
U.S. driver's license		x
U.S. military identification card		x
Foreign driver's license		x
Foreign military identification card	x	x
National identification card (must contain name, photograph, address, date of birth, and expiration date)	x	x
U.S. state identification card		x
Foreign voter's registration card	x	x
Civil birth certificate	x**	x
Medical records (valid only for dependents under age 6)	x**	x
School records (valid only for dependents under age 18, if student)	x**	x
* Applicants claimed as dependents who need to prove U.S. residency must provide additional original documentation if the passport doesn't have a date of entry into the United States. See *Proof of U.S. residency for applicants who are dependent* below. ** May be used to establish foreign status only if documents are foreign.		

Where To Apply

1. **By mail.**

- Mail Form W-7, the tax return (if applicable) or other documents required by an exception, and the documentation described under Supporting Documentation Requirements, earlier, to:

  Internal Revenue Service
  ITIN Operation
  P.O. Box 149342
  Austin, TX 78714-9342
- If you mail the application, don't use the mailing address in the instructions for the tax return.

2. **By private delivery services**

- If you use a private delivery service, submit the Form W-7, the tax return (if applicable) or other documents required by an exception, and the supporting documentation requirements to:

  Internal Revenue Service
  ITIN Operation
  Mail Stop 6090-AUSC
  3651 S. Interregional, Hwy 35
  Austin, TX 78741-0000

3. **In person**

- Taxpayers can apply for the ITIN by visiting designated IRS Taxpayer Assistance Centers (TACs). They can verify original documentation and certified copies of the documentation from the issuing agency for primary and secondary applicants and their dependents. For dependents, TACs can verify passports, national identification cards, and birth certificates. These documents will be returned to you immediately. Service at TACs is by appointment only. Appointments can be scheduled by calling 844-545-5640.

4. **Through an acceptance agent**

- Acceptance Agent (AA).
- Certifying Acceptance Agent (CAA).

Processing times

- Allow 7 weeks for the IRS to notify the applicant of the ITIN application status (9 to 11 weeks if the application is submitted during peak processing periods (January 15 through April 30) or if you're filing from overseas). If the applicant hasn't received the ITIN or correspondence at the end of that time, you can call the IRS to find out the status of the application.

ADOPTION TAXPAYER IDENTIFICATION NUMBER (ATIN)

An ATIN is an Adoption Taxpayer Identification Number issued by the Internal Revenue Service as a temporary taxpayer identification number for the child in a domestic adoption where the adopting taxpayers do not have and/or are unable to obtain the child's Social Security Number (SSN). The ATIN is to be used by the adopting taxpayers on their Federal Income Tax return to identify the child while final domestic adoption is pending.

The Form W-7A, Application for Taxpayer Identification Number for Pending Adoptions, is used by qualifying taxpayers to obtain an ATIN.

Taxpayers should apply as soon as the qualifying conditions are met, but at least 8 weeks before the due date of the individual federal income tax return, which is normally April 15.

People can apply for an ATIN only if they are in the process of adopting a child and they meet all of the following qualifications:

- The child is legally placed in their home for legal adoption by an authorized placement agency.
- The adoption is a domestic adoption OR the adoption is a foreign adoption and the child/children have a Permanent Resident Alien Card or Certificate of Citizenship.
- They cannot obtain the child's existing SSN even though they have made a reasonable attempt to obtain it from the birth parents, the placement agency, and other persons.
- They cannot obtain an SSN for the child from the SSA for any reason. (For example, the adoption is not final).
- They are eligible to claim the child as a dependent on the tax return.

Special Rule for a Deceased Child

A child who was born or died during the year is treated as having lived with the taxpayer more than half the year if the home was the child's home more than half the time he or she was alive during the year. The same is true if the child lived with the taxpayer more than half the year except for any required hospital stay following birth.

Taxpayers may be able to claim as a dependent a child born alive during the year, even if the child lived only for a moment. State or local law must treat the child as having been born alive. There must be proof of a live birth shown by an official document, such as a birth certificate. The child must be their qualifying child or qualifying relative, and all the other tests to claim the child as a dependent must be met.

Taxpayers cannot claim a stillborn child as a dependent.

TAX FORMS FOR INDIVIDUAL

1. 1040
2. 1040-ES
3. 1040-ES (NR)
4. 1040V
5. 1040X
6. 4868

Form 1040 - It's used by U.S. taxpayers to file an annual income tax return.

Schedule 1 - Is used for additional income and adjustments to income that are not reported directly on Form 1040 or Form 1040-SR such as capital gains, alimony, unemployment payments, or gambling winnings.

Schedule 2 - Is used for additional taxes owed such as self-employment tax, alternative minimum tax, or household employment taxes.

Schedule 3 – Is used to declare additional credits and payments such as capital gains or losses from real estate, shares, or mutual funds.

1040 SR - Is a simplified tax form created for seniors who have simple finances. The form helps report income from wages, salaries, and tips easily.

1040 NR – Is used by nonresident aliens who have earned income from U.S sources or engaged in business in the U.S throughout the tax year.

Example of 1040-NR:
Taxpayer A lives in Canada but owns stocks and real estate in the U.S. therefore he will file a 1040-NR tax return to report his US income.

FEDERAL INCOME TAX RATES

For the tax year 2021, the top tax rate remains 37% for individual single taxpayers with incomes greater than $523,601 ($628,301 for married couples filing jointly).

The other rates are:

- 37%, for incomes over $523,601 ($628,301 for married couples filing jointly);
- 35% for incomes over $209,426 ($418,851 for married couples filing jointly);
- 32% for incomes over $164,926 ($329,851 for married couples filing jointly);
- 24% for incomes over $86,376 ($172,751 for married couples filing jointly);
- 22% for incomes over $40,526 ($81,051 for married couples filing jointly).
- 12% for incomes over $9,951 ($19,901 for married couples filing jointly).
- The lowest rate is 10% for incomes of single individuals with incomes up to $9,875 (up to $19,750 for married couples filing jointly).

TAX RETURN DUE DATES & EXTENSIONS

April 15th each year is the due date for filing the Federal individual income tax return. The return is considered filed timely if the envelope is properly addressed and postmarked no later than April 15th. If the due date falls on a Saturday, Sunday, or legal holiday, the due date is delayed until the next business day.

If a taxpayer is unable to file the return within the automatic 2-month extension period, they may be able to get an additional 4-month extension of time to file the return, for a total of 6 months

If a taxpayer is not able to file the return by the due date, they generally can get an automatic 6-month extension of time to file. To get this automatic extension, they must file Form 4868 (PDF). Or, they can file Form 4868 electronically (e-file), using their own personal computer, or through a tax professional. Taxpayers do not have to explain why they are asking for the extension. They will be contacted only if the request is denied.

Definition of an Affected Taxpayer

A taxpayer does not have to be located in a federally declared disaster area to be an "affected taxpayer." Taxpayers are "affected" if records necessary to meet a filing or payment deadline postponed during the relief period are located in a covered disaster area.

An affected taxpayer can be:

- An individual
- Any business entity or sole proprietor
- Any shareholder in an S Corporation

Q: Does disaster relief apply to taxpayers if their tax preparer is in a disaster area but they're not?

Disaster relief applies to tax preparers who are unable to file returns or make payments on behalf of the client because of the disaster. Therefore, taxpayers outside of the disaster area can qualify for relief if:

- the tax preparer is in the disaster area, and
- the preparer is unable to file or pay on the client's behalf.
- To get the postponement for filing or payment, you must:
    - Call the Disaster Assistance Hotline at 1-866-562-5227.
    - Explain that the necessary records are located in a covered disaster area.
    - Provide the FEMA Disaster Number of the county where the tax preparer is located

JUNE 15 DEADLINES (AUTOMATIC TWO MONTH EXTENSION)

Taxpayers may be allowed an automatic 2-month extension of time to file the return and pay any federal income tax that is due. They will be allowed the extension if they are a U.S. citizen or resident alien and on the regular due date of the return:

- They are in military or naval service on duty outside the United States and Puerto Rico
- They are living outside of the United States and Puerto Rico and their main place of business or post of duty is outside the United States and Puerto Rico, or
- If they use a calendar year, the regular due date of the return is April 15, and the automatic extended due date would be June 15. If the due date falls on a Saturday, Sunday, or legal holiday, the due date is delayed until the next business day.
- Even if they are allowed an extension, they will have to pay interest on any tax not paid by the regular due date of the tax return.

To use this automatic 2-month extension, they must attach a statement to the return explaining which of the two situations listed earlier qualified for the extension.

PENALTIES & INTEREST

The IRS charges some penalties, such as the failure to pay the penalty, on a monthly basis, until the tax owed is paid in full.

Penalties and interest stop accruing as soon as the taxpayer pays the balance in full.

Common penalties include:

- **Failure to file**
  - when the taxpayer don't file the tax return by the return due date, April 15, or extended due date if an extension to file is requested and approved

- **Failure to pay**
  - when the taxpayer doesn't pay the taxes reported on the return in full by the due date, April 15. An extension to file doesn't extend the time to pay

- **Failure to pay proper estimated tax**
  - when the taxpayer don't pay enough taxes due for the year with the quarterly estimated tax payments, or through withholding, when required

- **Dishonored check**
  - when the bank doesn't honor the check or other form of payment.

Failure to file: Internal Revenue Code §6651(a)(1)

- 5% of unpaid tax required to be reported

- Reduced by the "failure to pay" penalty amount for any month where both penalties apply
- Charged each month or part of a month the return is late, up to 5 months
- Applies for a full month, even if the return is filed less than 30 days late
- Income tax returns are subject to a minimum late filing penalty when filed more than 60 days after the return due date, including extensions. The minimum penalty is the LESSER of two amounts – 100% of the tax required to be shown on the return that it's not paid on time, or a specific dollar amount that is adjusted annually for inflation. The specific dollar amounts are:
    - $435 for returns due on or after 1/1/2020*
    - $210 for returns due between 1/1/2018 and 12/31/2019
    - $205 for returns due between 1/1/2016 and 12/31/2017
    - $135 for returns due between 1/1/2009 and 12/31/2015
    - $100 for returns due before 1/1/2009

Failure to pay tax reported on return:

Internal Revenue Code §6651(a)(2)

- 0.5% of tax not paid by due date, April 15; 0.25% during approved installment agreement (if return was filed on time, and taxpayer is an individual); 1% if tax is not paid within 10 days of a notice of intent to levy
- Recurring charge on the remaining unpaid tax each month or part of a month following the due date, until the tax is fully paid or until 25% is reached
- Full monthly charge applies, even if the tax is paid before the month ends

Failure to pay tax not reported on original return and not paid in full within 21 days of the date of notice and demand;

10 Business days if the amount in the notice and demand equals or exceeds $100,000:

Internal Revenue Code §6651(a)(3)

- 0.5% of tax not paid by due date in notice - generally 21 calendar days from notice date, 10 business days if the balance equals or exceeds $100,000; 0.25% during approved installment agreement (if return was filed on time, and taxpayer is an individual); 1% if tax is not paid within 10 days of a notice of intent to levy
- Recurring charge on the remaining unpaid tax each month or part of a month following the due date, until the tax is fully paid
- Full monthly charge applies, even if the tax is paid before the month ends

Failure to pay proper estimated tax: Internal Revenue Code §6654

Estimated tax payments are generally required, if the taxpayer expects to owe $1,000 or more when the return is filed. If the income is received unevenly during the year, the taxpayer may be able to avoid or lower the penalty by annualizing his income and making unequal payments. Use Form 2210, Underpayment of Estimated Tax by Individuals, Estates and Trusts. The IRS calculates the penalty separately for each required installment. The number of days late is first determined and then multiplied by the effective interest rate for the installment period.

Dishonored check or other form of payment: Internal Revenue Code §6657

- For payments of $1,250 or more, the penalty is 2% of the amount of the payment.
- For payments less than $1,250, the penalty is the amount of the payment or $25, whichever is less.

RELIEF FROM JOINT TAX LIABILITY

Many married taxpayers choose to file a joint tax return because of certain benefits this filing status allows them.

When filing jointly, both taxpayers are jointly and severally liable for the tax and any additions to tax, interest, or penalties that arise from the joint return even if they later divorce. Joint and several liability means that each taxpayer is legally responsible for the entire liability. Thus, both spouses on a married filing jointly return are generally held responsible for all the tax due even if one spouse earned all the income or claimed improper deductions or credits.

This is also true even if a divorce decree states that a former spouse will be responsible for any amounts due on previously filed joint returns. In some cases, however, a spouse can get relief from being jointly and severally liable.

There are three types of relief from the joint and several liability of a joint return:

- **Innocent Spouse Relief** provides taxpayer relief from additional tax they owe if their spouse or former spouse failed to report income, reported income improperly or claimed improper deductions or credits.
- **Separation of Liability Relief** provides for the separate allocation of additional tax owed between the taxpayer and their former spouse or the current spouse they '"re legally separated from or not living with, when an item wasn't reported properly on a joint return. Taxpayers then are responsible for the amount of tax allocated to them. Refunds aren't available under separation of liability relief.
- **Equitable Relief** may apply when taxpayers don't qualify for innocent spouse relief or separation of liability relief for something not reported properly on a joint return and generally attributable to their spouse. They may also qualify for equitable relief if the amount of tax reported is correct on the joint return but the tax wasn't paid with the return.

Note: Taxpayers must request innocent spouse relief or separation of liability relief no later than 2 years after the date the IRS first attempted to collect the tax from them. For equitable relief, taxpayers must request relief during the period of time the IRS can collect the tax from them. If they're looking for a refund of tax they paid, then you must request it within the statutory period for seeking a refund, which is generally three years after the date the return is filed or two years following the payment of the tax, whichever is later.

INJURED SPOUSE CLAIMS

Taxpayers must meet all of the following conditions to qualify for innocent spouse relief:

- They filed a joint return that has an understatement of tax that's solely attributable to their spouse's erroneous item. An erroneous item includes income received by their spouse but omitted from the joint return. Deductions, credits, and property basis are also erroneous items if they're incorrectly reported on the joint return.
- They establish that at the time they signed the joint return they didn't know, and had no reason to know, that there was an understatement of tax and,
- Taking into account all the facts and circumstances, it would be unfair to hold the taxpayer liable for the understatement of tax.

REFUND CLAIMS & AMENDED RETURNS

If the taxpayer believes he has overpaid their tax, they have a limited amount of time in which to file a claim for a credit or refund. They can claim a credit or refund by filing Form 1040X. File the claim by mailing it to the IRS Service Center where they filed the original return. File a separate form for each year or period involved. Include an explanation of each item of income, deduction, or credit on which they are basing the claim.

1. Generally, the taxpayer must file a claim for a credit or refund within 3 years from the date they filed the original return or 2 years from the date they paid the tax, whichever is later. If they do not file a claim within this period, they may no longer be entitled to a credit or a refund.
2. If they file the claim within 3 years after filing the return, the credit or refund cannot be more than the part of the tax paid within the 3 years (plus the length of any extension of time granted for filing the return) before they file the claim.

Example:

John filed his return on October 31, 2003, 2 months after the extension period ended. He paid an additional $200 on that date. Three years later, on October 27, 2006, he filed an amended return and claimed a refund of $700. Although he filed the claim within 3 years from the date he filed the original return, the refund is limited to $200. The estimated tax of $1,000 was paid before the 3 years plus the 4-month extension period.

EXTENDED STATUTE FOR CLAIMING REFUNDS

- Taxpayers can take their case to the United States Tax Court if they disagree with the IRS.
- Taxpayers cannot take the case to the Tax Court before the IRS sends them a notice of deficiency. They can only appeal the case if they file a petition within 90 days from the date the notice is mailed to them (150 days if it is addressed to them outside the United States).
- Taxpayers can represent themselves before the Tax Court or they can be represented by anyone admitted to practice before that court.
- If the amount in the case is $50,000 or less for any 1 tax year or period, they can request that their case be handled under the small tax case procedure.
- Generally, the District Courts and the Court of Federal Claims hear tax cases only after taxpayers have paid the entire tax and penalties and filed a claim for a credit or refund.

STATUTE OF LIMITATIONS FOR IRS ASSESSMENT & COLLECTION

Generally, the IRS has 3 years from the date taxpayers file their return (or the date the return was due, if later) to assess any additional tax. However, if they file the return timely (including extensions), interest and certain penalties will be suspended if the IRS does not mail a notice to them, stating their liability and the basis for that liability, within a 36-month period beginning on the later of:

- The date on which they filed on the tax return, or
- The due date (without extensions) of their tax return.

If the IRS mails a notice after the 36-month period, interest and certain penalties applicable to the suspension period will be suspended.

ESTIMATED TAXES

Taxes must be paid as taxpayers earn or receive income during the year, either through withholding or estimated tax payments. If the amount of income tax withheld from their salary or pension is not enough, or if they receive income such as interest, dividends, alimony, self-employment income, capital gains, prizes and awards, they may have to make estimated tax payments. If taxpayers are in business for themselves, they generally need to make estimated tax payments. Estimated tax is used to pay not only income tax, but other taxes such as self-employment tax and alternative minimum tax.

If taxpayers don't pay enough tax through withholding and estimated tax payments, they may be charged a penalty. They also may be charged a penalty if the estimated tax payments are late, even if they are due a refund when they file the tax return.

Individuals, including sole proprietors, partners, and S corporation shareholders, generally have to make estimated tax payments if they expect to owe tax of $1,000 or more when their return is filed.

ESTIMATED TAX DUE DATES FOR MOST INDIVIDUALS

Estimated tax payments are due as follows:

- January 1 to March 31 – April 15
- April 1 to May 31 – June 15
- June 1 to August 31 - September 15
- September 1 to December 31 – January 15 of the following year

ESTIMATED TAXES FOR FARMERS & FISHERMAN

If your client is a farmer or fisherman, but their tax year does not start on January 1, they can either:

- Pay all estimated tax by the 15th day after the end of their tax year, or
- File the return and pay all the tax they owe by the 1st day of the 3rd month after the end of the tax year.

If at least two-thirds of your client's gross income for 2021 is from farming or fishing, their required annual payment is the smaller of:

- 66 ⅔% (rather than 90%) of your 2021 tax, or
- 100% of the tax shown on your 2020 return.

BACKUP WITHHOLDING

Taxpayers may be subject to backup withholding and the payers must withhold at a flat 24% rate when:

- They don't give the payer their TIN in the required manner.
- The IRS notifies the payer that the TIN they gave is incorrect.
- The IRS notifies the payer to start withholding on interest or dividends because they have underreported interest or dividends on the income tax return. The IRS will do this only after it has mailed them four notices over at least a 120-day period.
- They fail to certify that they're not subject to backup withholding for underreporting of interest and dividends.

Backup withholding can apply to most kinds of payments reported on Form 1099, including:

- Interest payments (Form 1099-INT);
- Dividends (Form 1099-DIV);
- Patronage dividends, but only if at least half of the payment is in money (Form 1099-PATR);
- Rents, profits, or other income (Form 1099-MISC);

- Commissions, fees, or other payments for work performed as an independent contractor (Form 1099-MISC);
- Payments by brokers and barter exchange transactions (Form 1099-B);
- Payments by fishing boat operators, but only the part that's in money and that represents a share of the proceeds of the catch (Form 1099-MISC);
- Payment Card and Third-Party Network Transactions (Form 1099-K); and
- Royalty payments (Form 1099-MISC).

FILING DEADLINE EXCEPTIONS

Section 7508A provides the Secretary of the Treasury or his delegate(Secretary)with authority to postpone the time for performing certain acts under the internal revenue laws for a taxpayer determined by the Secretary to be affected by a Federally declared disaster as defined in section 165(i)(5)(A).

Pursuant to section 7508A(a), a period of up to one year may be disregarded in determining whether the performance of certain acts is timely under the internal revenue laws.

RECORDKEEPING REQUIREMENTS FOR INDIVIDUALS

Taxpayers must keep records, such as receipts, canceled checks, and other documents that support an item of income, a deduction, or a credit appearing on a return as long as they may become material in the administration of any provision of the Internal Revenue Code, which generally will be until the period of limitations expires for that return.

- Keep records for 3 years from the date taxpayers filed the original return or 2 years from the date they paid the tax, whichever is later, if they file a claim for credit or refund after they file the return.
- Keep records for 7 years if they file a claim for a loss from worthless securities or bad debt deduction.
- Keep records for 6 years if they do not report income that they should report, and it is more than 25% of the gross income shown on the return.
- Keep records indefinitely if they do not file a return.
- Keep records indefinitely if individuals file a fraudulent return.
- Keep records relating to property until the period of limitations expires for the year in which they dispose of the property in a taxable disposition. Taxpayers must keep these records to figure the basis for computing gain or loss when they sell or otherwise dispose of the property.
- They should keep records of their own and their family members' health care insurance coverage. If they're claiming the premium tax credit, they'll need information about any advance credit payments they receive through the Health Insurance Marketplace and the premiums they paid.
- If they're in business, there's no particular method of bookkeeping they must use. However, they must use a method that clearly and accurately reflects the

gross income and expenses. The records should substantiate both the income and expenses. If they have employees, they must keep all employment tax records for at least 4 years after the tax becomes due or is paid, whichever is late.

POP QUIZ & ANSWER SHEET

TAX RETURN FOR INDIVIDUALS

POP QUIZ

Test your knowledge on *Tax Return for Individuals* by answering the questions below. The answer sheet may be found at the end of the Pop Quiz.

Q1: For how long should taxpayers need to keep their tax return as per the advice of the IRS?

A. At least one year
B. At least two year
C. At least three years
D. At least four years

Q2: A taxpayer who cannot obtain an SSN must apply for an ___ or an ___ in order to file a US tax return?

A. ITIN, ATIN
B. ITIN, AGI
C. SSN, ATIN
D. ITIN, SSN

Q3: Which of the following steps is incorrect on obtaining an actual copy of a tax return?

A. Pay $50
B. Mail Completed Form 4506
C. Both A & B
D. None of the Above

Q4: Newer ITINS will expire if not used within ___ year/s?

A. One Year
B. Two Years
C. Three Years
D. Four Years

Q5: What form is needed to apply or renew for an IRS Individual Taxpayer Identification Number (ITIN)?

A. Form W-7
B. Form 8962
C. Form 1095-A
D. Form 1040

Q6: An Adoption Taxpayer Identification Number (ATIN) issued for an adoptive child will expire after ___ years from the date it is issued.

A. 3 Years
B. 1 Year
C. 2 years
D. 4 Years

Q7: Which tax form is used to correct errors in a previously filed Form 1040?

A. Form 1040-X
B. Form 1040-Z
C. Form 1040 SR
D. Form 1040-NR

Q8: When is the due date for filing your Federal Individual Income Tax return each year?

A. January 15th
B. February 15th
C. March 15th
D. April 15th

Q9: What is the criteria for an automatic 2-month extension on filing the return and paying any federal income tax?

A. If you are a U.S. citizen or resident alien and on the regular due date of your return, you are living outside of the United States and Puerto Rico and your main place of business is outside the US or Puerto Rico
B. If you are a U.S. citizen or resident alien and on the regular due date of your return, you are in military or naval service on duty outside the United States and Puerto Rico.
C. Both A & B
D. None of the Above

Q10: What penalty could taxpayers potentially avoid if they file Form 4868, Application for Automatic Extension of Time To File U.S. Individual Income Tax Return?

A. Interest on the amount due
B. Failure-to-pay
C. Failure-to-file
D. Failure to pay proper estimated tax

Q11: Tax professionals should request the following in order to accurately prepare tax returns for taxpayers:

A. Prior Year Tax Return
B. Government Identification
C. Social Security cards or ITIN/ATIN Letters

D. All of the above

Q12: A taxpayer must generally make estimated tax payments if:

A. Taxpayer expects to owe at least $500 in tax (after subtracting withholding and tax credits)

B. Taxpayer expects to owe at least $1000 in tax (after subtracting withholding and tax credits)

C. Taxpayer expects to owe at least $600 in tax (after subtracting withholding and tax credits)

D. Taxpayer expects to owe at least $400 in tax (after subtracting withholding and tax credits)

Q13: The IRS will sometimes require backup withholding if a taxpayer has a delinquent tax debt, or if he or she fails to report all interest, dividends, and other income. What is the current backup withholding rate for 2021?

A. 15%

B. 24%

C. 30%

D. 35%

Q14: What is the statute of limitations for an assessment of tax if a taxpayer never files a return or a return is fraudulent?

A. 10 years

B. 15 years

C. 20 Years

D. There is no statute of limitation for an assessment of tax.

Q15: Robert & Margo's tax return was garnished by the State of New York due to Robert's unpaid child support from his first wife. To request her portion of the refund she should file:

A. As an Injured Spouse

B. As a Damaged Spouse

C. An Equitable Relief

D. As an Innocent Spouse

ANSWER SHEET

1. Answer is C – At least three years

2. Answer is A – ITIN, ATIN

3. Answer is D – None of the Above

4. Answer is C – Three Years

5. Answer is A – Form W-7

6. Answer is C – 2 years

7. Answer is A – Form 1040-X

8. Answer is D – April 15th

9. Answer is C – Both A & B

10. Answer is C – Failure-to-file

11. Answer is D – All of the above

12. Answer is B – Taxpayer expects to owe at least $1000 in tax (after subtracting withholding and tax credits)

13. Answer is B – 24%

14. Answer is D – There is no statute of limitation for an assessment of tax.

15. Answer is A – As an Injured Spouse

FILING STATUS & RESIDENCY

OVERVIEW

The taxpayer's filing status generally depends on whether they are single or married on Dec. 31 and that is their status for the whole year.

A taxpayer's status could change during the year.

Knowing the correct filing status can help taxpayers determine several things about filing their tax return:

- Is the taxpayer required to file a federal tax return or should they file to receive a refund?
- What is their standard deduction amount?
- Is the taxpayer eligible for certain credits?
- How much tax should they pay?

FILING STATUS

1. **Single**: Normally this status is for taxpayers who are unmarried, divorced or legally separated under a divorce or separate maintenance decree governed by state law.
2. **Married filing jointly**: If a taxpayer is married, they can file a joint tax return with their spouse. When a spouse passes away, the widowed spouse can usually file a joint return for that year.
3. **Married filing separately**: Alternatively, married couples can choose to file separate tax returns. It may result in less tax owed than filing a joint tax return.
4. **Head of household**: Unmarried taxpayers may be able to file using this status, but special rules apply. For example, the taxpayer must have paid more than half the cost of keeping up a home for themselves and a qualifying person living in the home for half the year.
5. **Qualifying widow(er) with dependent child**: This status may apply to a taxpayer if their spouse died during one of the previous two years and they have a dependent child.

SINGLE

- **Divorce and remarriage**
  If a person obtains a divorce for the sole purpose of filing tax returns as unmarried individuals, and at the time of divorce he intends to and do, in fact, remarry each other in the next tax year, the taxpayer and his/her spouse must file as married individuals in both years.
- **Annulled marriages**

If a person obtains a court decree of annulment, which holds that no valid marriage ever existed, he is considered unmarried even if he filed joint returns for earlier years.

- **Unmarried persons**
  An individual is considered unmarried for the whole year if, on the last day of the tax year, he is either:
  Unmarried, or Legally separated from his/her spouse under a divorce or separate maintenance decree. State law governs whether individuals are married or legally separated under a divorce or separate maintenance decree.
- **Divorced persons**
  If an individual is divorced under a final decree by the last day of the year, he is considered unmarried for the whole year.

MARRIED FILING JOINTLY

- **Married persons**
  If individuals are considered married, they can file a joint return or separate returns.
- **Considered Married**
  A person is considered married for the whole year if, on the last day of the tax year, he and his/her spouse meet any one of the following tests.
    - They are married and living together.
    - They are living together in a common law marriage recognized in the state where they now live or in the state where the common law marriage began.
    - They are married and living apart but not legally separated under a decree of divorce or separate maintenance.
    - They are separated under an interlocutory (not final) decree of divorce.
    - Individuals can choose married filing jointly as their filing status if they are considered married and both spouses agree to file a joint return.
    - On a joint return, the spouses report the combined income and deduct the combined allowable expenses. They can file a joint return even if one of the spouses had no income or deductions.
    - If the spouses decide to file a joint return, their tax may be lower than the combined tax for the other filing statuses. Also, the standard deduction (if they don't itemize deductions) may be higher, and they may qualify for tax benefits that don't apply to other filing statuses.
    - On Form 1040 or 1040-SR, spouses can show their filing status as married filing jointly by checking the "Married filing jointly" box on the Filing Status line at top of the form.
    - If each of the spouses have income, they may want to figure the tax both on a joint return and on separate returns (using the filing status of married filing separately). They can choose the method

that gives the two of them the lower combined tax unless they are required to file separately.

- **Spouse died**
    - If one of the spouses died during the year, the couple is considered married for the whole year and can choose married filing jointly as the filing status.
    - If a spouse died in 2021 before filing a 2021 return, the other spouse can choose married filing jointly as the filing status on the 2021 return.
- **Divorced persons**
  If a person is divorced under a final decree by the last day of the year, he is considered unmarried for the whole year and he can't choose married filing jointly as a filing status.

MARRIED FILING SEPARATELY

Spouses can choose married filing separately as their filing status if they are married. This filing status may be beneficial if the spouses want to be responsible only for their own tax or if it results in less tax than filing a joint return.

If the spouses don't agree to file a joint return, they must use this filing status unless they qualify for head of household status.

Taxpayers will generally pay more combined tax on separate returns than they would on a joint return.

Unless the spouses are required to file separately, they should figure their tax both ways (on a joint return and on a separate return). This way they can make sure they are using the filing status that results in the lowest combined tax.

How to file:

- If spouses file a separate return, they generally report only their own income, credits, and deductions.
- Select this filing status by checking the "Married filing separately" box on the Filing Status line at the top of Form 1040 or 1040-SR. Enter the spouse's full name and SSN or ITIN in the entry space at the bottom of the Filing Status section. If the spouse doesn't have and isn't required to have an SSN or ITIN, enter "NRA" in the space for the spouse's SSN.

SAME SEX SPOUSES

The IRS recognizes marriage of same-sex spouses that was validly entered into in a domestic or foreign jurisdiction whose laws authorize the marriage of two individuals of the same sex even if the married couple resides in a domestic or foreign jurisdiction that does not recognize the validity of same-sex marriages.

HEAD OF HOUSEHOLD

An individual may be able to file as head of household if he meets all of the following requirements.

- He is unmarried or considered unmarried on the last day of the year.
- He paid more than half the cost of keeping up a home for the year.
- A qualifying person lived with the individual in the home for more than half the year (except for temporary absences, such as school). However, if the qualifying person is the dependent parent, he or she doesn't have to live with the individual.

The tax rate will usually be lower than the rates for single or married filing separately. Individuals will also receive a higher standard deduction than if they file as single or married filing separately.

How to file:

- Indicate the choice of this filing status by checking the "Head of household" box on the Filing Status line at the top of Form 1040 or 1040-SR. If the child who qualifies the individual for this filing status isn't claimed as dependent in the Dependents section of Form 1040 or 1040-SR, enter the child's name in the entry space at the bottom of the Filing Status section.

CONSIDERED UNMARRIED FOR HOH STATUS

To qualify for head of household status, individuals must be either unmarried or considered unmarried on the last day of the year. People are considered unmarried on the last day of the tax year if they meet all the following tests.

- They file a separate return. A separate return includes a return claiming married separately, single, or head of household filing status.
- They paid more than half the cost of keeping up their home for the tax year.
- The home was the main home of the child, stepchild, or foster child for more than half the year.
- The spouse must be able to claim the child as a dependent.

HOH SPECIAL RULES

- To qualify for head of household status, the taxpayer must pay more than half of the cost of keeping up a home for the year.
- The qualifying person must live with the taxpayer for more than half of the year.
- Qualified person can be a qualifying child or relative.
- Special Rule for Parents: If the qualifying person is a father or mother, the taxpayer may be eligible to file as head of household even if the father or mother doesn't live with him. However, the individual must be able to claim his father or mother as a dependent. Also, he must pay more than half the cost of keeping up a home that was the main home for the entire year for his father or mother.

- If an individual pays more than half the cost of keeping his parent in a rest home or home for the elderly, that counts as paying more than half the cost of keeping up the parent's main home.

ANNULMENTS

If an individual obtains a court decree of annulment, which holds that no valid marriage ever existed, he is considered unmarried even if he filed joint returns for earlier years.

File amended returns (Form 1040-X) claiming single or head of household status for all tax years that are affected by the annulment and not closed by the statute of limitations for filing a tax return.

Example:

Taxpayer A and Taxpayer B married on March 13, 2018. While they were married, they filed a Married Filing Joint for the 2019 tax year and 2020 tax year. In 2021 Taxpayer A decides to get an annulment due to fraud and misrepresentation by Taxpayer B. As a result, the annulment was granted.

The tax years that the taxpayers filed (2019 and 2020) as married filing jointly must be amended using Form 1040x and filed with the appropriate filing status "single" or "head of household."

QUALIFYING WIDOW(ER) WITH DEPENDENT CHILD

If one of the spouses died in 2021, the other spouse can use married filing jointly as the filing status for 2021 if he or she otherwise qualifies to use that status.

The spouse may be eligible to use qualifying widow(er) as the filing status for 2 years following the year their spouse died. For example, if the spouse died in 2020 and the other spouse has not remarried, he or she may be able to use this filing status for 2021 and 2022.

This filing status entitles the spouse to use joint return tax rates and the highest standard deduction amount (if they don't itemize deductions). It doesn't entitle the spouse to file a joint return.

How to file:

Indicate the choice of this filing status by checking the "Qualifying widow(er)" box on the Filing Status line at the top of Form 1040 or 1040-SR. If the child who qualifies the individual for this filing status isn't claimed as a dependent in the Dependents section of Form 1040 or 1040-SR, enter the child's name in the entry space at the bottom of the Filing Status section.

DETERMINING RESIDENCY FOR TAX PURPOSES

An **Alien** is an individual who is not a U.S. citizen.

- **Resident Aliens**: generally are taxed on their worldwide income, the same as U.S. citizens. An individual is considered a resident alien for a calendar year if he meets the green card test or the substantial presence test for the year.
- **Non-Resident Aliens**: are taxed only on their income from sources within the United States and on certain income connected with the conduct of a trade or business in the United States. An individual is considered a nonresident alien for any period that he is neither a U.S. citizen nor a resident alien for tax purposes.

If an individual is both a nonresident and resident in the same year, he has a dual status.

TAX PURPOSES EXAMPLES:

- **Alien:** Lillian works for Amazon in Japan, but comes to the US for one week to train a unit in Palo Alto, California. Amazon Japan paid her normal wages plus travel for Lillian to provide the one time training.
- **Resident Alien:** Mark is from France but works part time as an Instructor in New York during the summer. He's going to report his income on form 1040. Mark will be generally taxed on his worldwide income, the same as US citizens.
- **Non-Resident Alien:** Emily is Canadian but purchases rental property in Michigan. Because she generates income in the US she must file and report her US based income on form 1040-NR. She rarely visits as she has a property management company to run her rental properties in the US.

DETERMINING RESIDENCY FOR TAX PURPOSES EXAMPLES:

- **Dual Status Alien:** Francesca lives and works in Canada and the US just about equal time. For the part of the year she is a U.S. resident alien, she is taxed on income from all sources. Income from sources outside the United States is taxable if she received it while she was a resident alien. For the part of the year she was a nonresident alien, she is taxed on income from U.S. sources only.

TAX RESIDENCY TESTS

Let's take a further look at the following:

- Green Card Test
- Substantial Presence Test

An alien taxpayer is automatically considered a US resident if he or she is a "lawful permanent resident" of the US at any time during the tax year. A taxpayer will have this status if they are a lawful immigrant and have been issued an alien registration card known as a "green card". An alien who has been present in the US any time during a calendar year as a lawful permanent resident may opt to be treated as a resident alien for the entire calendar year.

GREEN CARD TEST

An individual is a resident for tax purposes if he is a lawful permanent resident of the United States at any time during the calendar year, and this status hasn't been revoked or administratively or judicially determined to have been abandoned.

SUBSTANTIAL PRESENCE TEST

Taxpayers without a green card:

Individuals satisfy the substantial presence test, and are therefore treated as resident aliens for a calendar year, if they have been physically present in the United States for at least:

- 31 days during the current year, and
- 183 days during the 3-year period that includes the current year and the 2 years immediately preceding the current year.

To satisfy the 183-day requirement, count:

- All of the days individuals were **present in the current year**,
- One-third of the days individuals were **present in the first year before the current year, (4 months)** and
- One-sixth of the days individuals were **present in the second year before the current year. (2 months)**

If, at the end of the tax year, the individual is married and one spouse is a U.S. citizen or resident alien and the other is a nonresident alien, the spouses can choose to treat the nonresident as a U.S. resident.

If individuals make this choice, the following rules apply:

- The spouses are treated, for federal income tax purposes, as U.S residents for all tax years that the choice is in effect.
- The spouses must file a joint income tax return for the year they make the choice (but they can file joint or separate returns in later years).
- Each spouse must report his or her entire worldwide income for the year they make the choice and for all later years, unless the choice is ended or suspended.
- Generally, neither one of the spouses can claim tax treaty benefits as a resident of a foreign country for a tax year for which the choice is in effect.

EXEMPT INDIVIDUALS

Days of presence in the United States are not counted for purposes of the substantial presence test, if an individual falls into any of the following categories:

- An individual temporarily present in the United States as a foreign government-related individual under an A or G visa.
- A teacher or trainee temporarily present in the United States under a J or Q visa.
- A student temporarily present in the United States under an F, J, M, or Q visa.
- A professional athlete temporarily present in the United States to compete in a charitable sports event.

Even if the substantial presence test is met, individuals may still be treated as a nonresident alien if:

- They are present in the United States for fewer than 183 days during the current calendar year
- They maintain a tax home in a foreign country during the year
- They have a closer connection to that country than to the United States, and they timely file a Form 8840, Closer Connection Exception Statement for Aliens (PDF) claiming they have a closer connection to a foreign country or countries.

INTERNATIONAL STUDENTS

- Any individual who is temporarily in the United States on an "F," "J," "M," or "Q" visa and who substantially complies with the requirements of that visa.
- Also included are immediate family members of exempt students.
- Exempt from the substantial presence test for the first five calendar years they are in the US.

Gross Income Defined

Gross income is all income received in the form of money, goods, property, and services that isn't exempt from tax. If a person is married and lives with her or his spouse in a community property state, half of any income defined by state law as community income may be considered property of that person.

2021 Gross Income Filing Threshold

IF your filing status is...	AND at the end of 2021, you were...*	THEN file a return if the gross income was at least...**
	under 65	$ 12,550
	65 or older	$ 14,250
head of household	under 65	$ 18,800
	65 or older	$ 20,500
	under 65 (both spouses)	$ 25,100
	65 or older (one spouse)	$ 26,450
married filing jointly**	65 or older (both spouses)	$ 27,800
married filing separately	any age	$ 5
qualifying widow(er)	under 65	$ 25,100
	65 or older	$ 26,450

FILING REQUIREMENT FOR DEPENDENTS

Single Dependents not over age 65 or blind must file if:

- Unearned income was more than $1,100.
- Earned income was more than $12,550.
- Gross income was more than the larger of—$1,100, or earned income (up to $12,200) plus $350.

Single Dependents over age 65 or blind must file if:

- Unearned income was more than $2,750 ($4,400 if 65 or older and blind).
- Earned income was more than $14,250 ($15,950 if 65 or older and blind).
- Gross income was more than the larger of—$2,750 ($4,400 if 65 or older and blind) or earned income (up to $12,250) plus $2,000 ($3,650 if 65 or older and blind).

Married Dependents not over age 65 or blind must file if:

- Gross income was at least $5 and the spouse files a separate return and itemizes deductions.
- Unearned income was more than $1,100.
- Earned income was more than $12,400.
- The gross income was more than the larger of—$1,100 or earned income (up to $12,050) plus $350.

FILING REQUIREMENT FOR SELF-EMPLOYED

- Gross income from business is the total sales minus the cost of goods sold.
- Individuals must file a return if net earnings from self-employment is at least $400.
- Filing Schedule SE

ADDITIONAL FILING REQUIREMENTS

If any of the seven conditions listed below applied to a taxpayer for 2021, he must file a return.

1. He owes any special taxes, including any of the following.
    - Alternative minimum tax (Form 6251).
    - Additional tax on a qualified plan, including an individual retirement arrangement (IRA), or other tax- favored account. But if taxpayers are filing a return only because they owe this tax, they can file Form 5329 by itself.
    - Social security or Medicare tax on tips taxpayers didn't report to their employer or on wages they received from an employer who didn't withhold these taxes (Form 8919).
    - Write-in taxes, including uncollected social security, Medicare, or railroad retirement tax on tips taxpayers reported to their employer or on group-term life insurance and additional taxes on health savings accounts.
    - Household employment taxes. But if taxpayers are filing a return only because they owe these taxes, they can file Schedule H (Form 1040 or 1040-SR) by itself.
    - Recapture taxes. (See the Form 1040 and 1040-SR instructions for line 16 and the Schedule 2 (Form 1040) instructions for lines 7b and 8.)
2. An individual (or his or her spouse if filing jointly) received Archer MSA, Medicare Advantage MSA, or health savings account distributions.
3. An individual had net earnings from self-employment of at least $400. (See Schedule SE (Form 1040) and its instructions.)
4. An individual had wages of $108.28 or more from a church or qualified church-controlled organization that is exempt from employer social security and Medicare taxes. (See Schedule SE (Form 1040) and its instructions.)
5. Advance payments of the premium tax credit were made for the individual, his or her spouse, or a dependent who enrolled in coverage through the Health Insurance Marketplace. The individual should have received Form(s) 1095-A showing the amount of the advance payments, if any.
6. Advance payments of the health coverage tax credit were made for the individual, his or her spouse, or a dependent. The individual or whoever enrolled should have received Form(s) 1099-H showing the amount of the advance payments.
7. The individual is required to include amounts in income under section 965 or he has a net tax liability under section 965 that he is paying in installments under section 965(h) or deferred by making an election under section 965(i).

Although not required, consider filing if:

- The individual had income tax withheld from the pay.

- The individual made estimated tax payments for the year or had any of the overpayment for last year applied to this year's estimated tax.
- The individual qualifies for the earned income credit. He qualifies for the additional child tax credit.
- The individual qualifies for the refundable American opportunity education credit (Form 8863)
- The individual qualifies for the health coverage tax credit (Form 8885).
- The individual qualifies for the credit for federal tax on fuels (Form 4136).

POP QUIZ & ANSWER SHEET

FILING STATUS & RESIDENCY

POP QUIZ

Test your knowledge on *Filing Status & Residency* by answering the questions below. The answer sheet may be found at the end of the Pop Quiz.

Q1: The taxpayer's filing status generally depends on whether they are ___ or ___ on ___

A. Single or Married, Jan 1
B. Single or Married, April 15
C. Single or Married, June 1
D. Single or Married, December 31

Q2: What should the filing status of a taxpayer with no dependents be who is unmarried, divorced or legally separated under a divorce or separate maintenance decree governed by state law be?

A. Single
B. Head of Household
C. Married
D. Widow

Q3: Unmarried taxpayers who have paid more than half the cost of keeping up a home for themselves and a qualifying person living in the home for half the year should generally file if they qualify as:

A. Single
B. Head of Household
C. Married
D. Widow

Q4: There are some instances where a taxpayer can be "considered unmarried" for tax purposes. To be "considered unmarried" on the last day of the tax year the taxpayer must meet all of the following conditions, except:

A. File a separate return from the other spouse
B. Pay more than half the cost of keeping up a home for the tax year and maintain the home as the main residence of a qualifying child for more than half the year
C. Not live with a spouse in the home during the last three months of the year
D. Not live with a spouse in the home during the last six months of the tax year

Q5: Below are special rules for Head of Household, except:

A. You must pay more than half of the cost of keeping up a home for the year.
B. The qualifying person must live with you for more than half of the year.
C. Qualified person can be a qualifying child or relative.
D. You must pay more combined tax on separate returns than you would on a joint return.

Q6: If a taxpayer's qualifying person is a dependent parent, the dependent parent has to live with the taxpayer for how long to qualify the taxpayer for HOH?

A. The last 6 months of the year, if they provided more than half the cost of keeping up a home that was the parent's main home for the entire year
B. 12 months, if they provided more than half the cost of keeping up a home that was the parent's main home for the entire year
C. The dependent parent does not have to live with the taxpayer if they provided more than half the cost of keeping up a home that was the parent's main home for the entire year
D. None of the above

Q7: You satisfy the substantial presence test, and are therefore treated as a resident alien for a calendar year, if you have been physically present in the United States for at least:

A. 31 days during the current year and 183 days during the 3-year period that includes the current year and the 2 years immediately preceding the current year.
B. 31 days during the current year and 183 days during the 2-year period that includes the current year and the 1 year immediately preceding the current year.
C. 15 days during the current year and 180 days during the 3-year period that includes the current year and the 2 years immediately preceding the current year.
D. 15 days during the current year and 180 days during the 2-year period that includes the current year and the 1 year immediately preceding the current year.

Q8: A non-resident alien who does not meet the substantial presence test and does not have a green card may still elect to be treated as a resident for tax purposes if he or she meets all of the following, except:

A. Is married to a US Citizen or resident
B. Both spouses agree to file a joint return
C. Treat the nonresident alien as a resident alien on a joint return for the entire year
D. File a joint return with the US Citizen or Resident and write "NRA" for the social security number because they wouldn't have one being a non-resident alien

Q9: A taxpayer's divorce is final on November 12, 2021. The taxpayer has sole custody of a minor child aged nine who lived with the taxpayer the entire year and the taxpayer provided 100% of the cost of keeping up the home. What filing status should the taxpayer use?

A. Married Filing Separately
B. Single
C. Head of Household
D. Qualifying Widow(er)

Q10: All of the following individuals are required to file an income tax return, except:

A. A single taxpayer who earned $1800 for a W2 job
B. Married taxpayers who made $75,000 from their salaried jobs
C. Self-Employed taxpayer who earned $425 in self-employed earnings
D. Church employee who made $200

ANSWER SHEET

1. Answer is D – Single or Married, December 31

2. Answer is A – Single

3. Answer is B – Head of Household

4. Answer is C – Not live with a spouse in the home during the last three months of the year

5. Answer is D – You must pay more combined tax on separate returns than you would on a joint return.

6. Answer is C – The dependent parent does not have to live with the taxpayer if they provided more than half the cost of keeping up a home that was the parent's main home for the entire year

7. Answer is A –31 days during the current year and 183 days during the 3-year period that includes the current year and the 2 years immediately preceding the current year.

8. Answer is D – File a joint return with the US Citizen or Resident and write "NRA" for the social security number because they wouldn't have one being a non-resident alien

9. Answer is C – Head of Household

10. Answer is A – A single taxpayer who earned $1800 for a W2 job

DEPENDENTS

OVERVIEW

Dependent – A person, other than the taxpayer or the taxpayer's spouse, that can be claimed on a taxpayer's return. To be a dependent, a person must be a qualifying child or qualifying relative (both defined later) to the taxpayer.

A person who is a dependent may still have to file a return. It depends on his or her earned income, unearned income, and gross income.

The term "dependent" means:

- A qualifying child, or
- A qualifying relative.

PRIMARY TESTS FOR DEPENDENCY

- Taxpayers can't claim any dependents if they, or their spouse if filing jointly, could be claimed as a dependent by another taxpayer.
- Taxpayers can't claim a married person who files a joint return as a dependent unless that joint return is filed only to claim a refund of withheld income tax or estimated tax paid.
- Taxpayers can't claim a person as a dependent unless that person is a U.S. citizen, U.S. resident alien, U.S. national, or a resident of Canada or Mexico.
- Taxpayers can't claim a person as a dependent unless that person is their qualifying child or qualifying relative.

DEPENDENCY RELATIONSHIPS

Five tests must be met for a child to be a qualifying child.

- Relationship
- Age
- Residency Support
- Joint return

Four tests must be met for a person to be a qualifying relative.

- Not a qualifying child test
- Member of household or relationship test
- Gross income test
- Support test

TESTS FOR QUALIFYING CHILD

1. Relationship Test

To meet this test, a child must be:

- A son, daughter, stepchild, foster child, or a descendant (for example, a grandchild) of any of them; or
- A brother, sister, half brother, half sister, stepbrother, stepsister, or a descendant (for example, a niece or nephew) of any of them.

An adopted child is always treated as an individual's own child. The term "adopted child" includes a child who was lawfully placed with an individual for legal adoption.

A foster child is an individual who is placed with an individual by an authorized placement agency or by judgment, decree, or other order of any court of competent jurisdiction.

2. Age Test

To meet this test, a child must be:

- Under age 19 at the end of the year and younger than the individual (or the spouse if filing jointly),

Example 1—Your son turned 19 on December 10. Unless he was permanently and totally disabled or a student, he didn't meet the age test because, at the end of the year, he wasn't under age 19.

Example 2—Child younger than the spouse but not younger than you. The facts are the same as in Example 1 except your spouse is 25 years old. Because your brother is younger than your spouse and you and your spouse are filing a joint return, your brother is your qualifying child, even though he isn't younger than you.

- Permanently and totally disabled at any time during the year, regardless of age.
    - The child is permanently and totally disabled if both of the following apply.
    - He or she can't engage in any substantial gainful activity because of a physical or mental condition
    - A doctor determines the condition has lasted or can be expected to last continuously for at least a year or can lead to death.
- A student under age 24 at the end of the year and younger than the individual (or the spouse if filing jointly), or to qualify as a student, the child must be, during some part of each of any 5 calendar months of the year:
    - o A full-time student at a school that has a regular teaching staff, course of study, and a regularly enrolled student body at the school.

A full-time student is a student who is enrolled for the number of hours or courses the school considers to be full-time attendance.

- A student taking a full-time, on-farm training course given by a school described in (1), or by a state, county, or local government agency.
- The 5 calendar months don't have to be consecutive.
- A school can be an elementary school, junior or senior high school, college, university, or technical, trade, or mechanical school. However, an on-the-job training course, correspondence school, or school offering courses only through the Internet doesn't count as a school.
- Vocational high school students. Students who work on "co-op" jobs in private industry as a part of a school's regular course of classroom and practical training are considered full-time students.

3. Residency Test

To meet this test, the child must have lived with the individual for more than half the year. There are exceptions for temporary absences, children who were born or died during the year, kidnapped children, and children of divorced or separated parents.

Temporary absences - The child is considered to have lived with the individual during periods of time when the individual or the child, or both, are temporarily absent due to special circumstances such as:

- Illness, Education,
- Business, Vacation,
- Military service,
- Detention in a juvenile facility.

Death or birth of child - A child who was born or died during the year is treated as having lived with the individual more than half the year if the home was the child's home more than half the time he or she was alive during the year. The same is true if the child lived with the individual more than half the year except for any required hospital stay following birth.

4. Support Test

To meet this test, the child can't have provided more than half of his or her own support for the year

Example 1. Matt provided $4,000 toward his 16-year-old son's support for the year. He has a part-time job and provided $6,000 to his own support. He provided more than half of his own support for the year. He isn't Matt's qualifying child.

Example 2. Lauren, a foster child, lived with Mr. and Mrs. Smith for the last 3 months of the year. The Smiths cared for Lauren because they wanted to adopt her (although she had not been placed with them for adoption). They didn't care for her as a trade or business or to benefit the agency that placed her in their home. The Smiths' unreimbursed expenses aren't deductible as charitable contributions but are considered support they provided for Lauren.

5. Joint Return Test

To meet this test, the child can't file a joint return for the year.

Exception. An exception to the joint return test applies if the child and his or her spouse file a joint return only to claim a refund of income tax withheld or estimated tax paid.

Example 1—child files joint return. Megan supported her 18-year-old daughter, and she lived with Megan all year while her husband was in the Armed Forces. He earned $25,000 for the year. The couple files a joint return. Because Megan's daughter and her husband file a joint return, she isn't her qualifying child.

Example 2—child files joint return only as claim for refund of withheld tax. Sarah's 18-year-old son and his 17-year-old wife had $800 of wages from part-time jobs and no other income. They lived with Sarah all year. Neither is required to file a tax return. They don't have a child. Taxes were taken out of their pay so they filed a joint return only to get a refund of the withheld taxes. The exception to the joint return test applies, so her son may be her qualifying child if all the other tests are met.

RULES FOR QUALIFYING RELATIVE

1. Not a Qualifying Child Test

A child isn't the qualifying relative if the child is the qualifying child or the qualifying child of any other taxpayer.

> **Example 1** Sam's 22-year-old daughter, who is a student, lives with him and meets all the tests to be his qualifying child. She isn't his qualifying relative.
>
> **Example 2** Jordan's 13-year-old grandson lived with his mother for 3 months, with his uncle for 4 months, and with Jordan for 5 months during the year. He isn't Jordan's qualifying child because he doesn't meet the residency test. He may be his qualifying relative if the gross income test and the support test are met.

2. Member of Household or Relationship Test

To meet this test, a person must either:

- Live with the individual all year as a member of his or hers household, or
- Be related to the individual in one of the following ways:
    - The child, stepchild, foster child, or a descendant of any of them (for example, the grandchild). (A legally adopted child is considered a child.
    - The brother, sister, half-brother, half-sister, stepbrother, or stepsister.
    - The father, mother, grandparent, or other direct ancestor, but not foster parent.
    - The stepfather or stepmother.
    - A son or daughter of a brother or sister.
    - A son or daughter of the half-brother or half-sister.
    - A brother or sister of the father or mother.
    - The son-in-law, daughter-in-law, father-in-law, mother-in-law, brother-in- law, or sister-in-law. Any of these relationships that were established by marriage aren't ended by death or divorce.

If at any time during the year the person was the spouse, that person can't be the qualifying relative.

Joint return. If an individual files a joint return, the person can be related to either the individual or his or her spouse. Also, the person doesn't need to be related to the spouse who provides support.

Temporary absences. A person is considered to live with the individual as a member of the household during periods of time when either of the household members, or both, are temporarily absent due to special circumstances.

Cousin. A cousin meets this test only if he or she lives with the individual all year as a member of the household. A cousin is a descendant of a brother or sister of the father or mother.

Death or birth. A person who died during the year, but lived with the individual as a member of the household until death, will meet this test. The same is true for a child who was born during the year and lived with the individual as a member of the household for the rest of the year.

The test is also met if a child lived with the individual as a member of the household except for any required hospital stay following birth. If the dependent died during the year and the individual otherwise qualifies to claim that person as a dependent, he or she can still claim that person as a dependent.

3. **Gross Income Test**

To meet this test, a person's gross income for the year must be less than $4,200.

Gross income is all income in the form of money, property, and services that isn't exempt from tax.

In a manufacturing, merchandising, or mining business, gross income is the total net sales minus the cost of goods sold, plus any miscellaneous income from the business.

Gross receipts from rental property are gross income. Don't deduct taxes, repairs, or other expenses to determine the gross income from rental property.

Gross income includes a partner's share of the gross (not net) partnership income.

Gross income also includes all taxable unemployment compensation, taxable social security benefits, and certain scholarship and fellowship grants.

Scholarships received by degree candidates and used for tuition, fees, supplies, books, and equipment required for particular courses aren't generally included in gross income.

1. Support Test

To meet this test, the individual must generally provide more than half of a person's total support during the calendar year.

How to determine if support test is met:

- Individuals figure whether they have provided more than half of a person's total support by comparing the amount they contributed to that person's support with the entire amount of support that person received from all sources. This includes support the person provided from his or her own funds.
- Year support is provided. The year individuals provide the support is the year they pay for it, even if they do so with borrowed money that they repay in a later year. If they use a fiscal year to report the income, they must provide more than half of the dependent's support for the calendar year in which the fiscal year begins.

Total Support

To figure out if the individual provided more than half of a person's support, he or she must first determine the total support provided for that person. Total support includes amounts spent to provide food, lodging, clothing, education, medical and dental care, recreation, transportation, and similar necessities.

The following items aren't included in total support.

- Federal, state, and local income taxes paid by persons from their own income.
- Social security and Medicare taxes paid by persons from their own income.

- Life insurance premiums.
- Funeral expenses.
- Scholarships received by the child if the child is a student.
- Survivors' and Dependents' Educational Assistance payments used for the support of the child who receives them.

SPECIAL RULES FOR DIVORCED AND SEPARATED PARENTS

In most cases, a child of divorced or separated parents (or parents who live apart) will be a qualifying child of one of the parents. However, if the child doesn't meet the requirements to be a qualifying child of either parent, the child may be a qualifying relative of one of the parents.

Custodial parent and noncustodial parent.

The custodial parent is the parent with whom the child lived for the greater number of nights during the year. The other parent is the noncustodial parent. If the parents divorced or separated during the year and the child lived with both parents before the separation, the custodial parent is the one with whom the child lived for the greater number of nights during the rest of the year.

A child will be treated as being the qualifying relative of his or her noncustodial parent if all four of the following statements are true.

- The parents:
    - Are divorced or legally separated under a decree of divorce or separate maintenance,
    - Are separated under a written separation agreement, or
    - Lived apart at all times during the last 6 months of the year, whether or not they are or were married.
- The child received over half of his or her support for the year from the parents (and the rules on multiple support agreements, explained earlier, don't apply).
- The child is in the custody of one or both parents for more than half of the year.
- Either of the following statements is true.
    - The custodial parent signs a written declaration, discussed later, that he or she won't claim the child as a dependent for the year, and the noncustodial parent attaches this written declaration to his or her return.
    - A pre-1985 decree of divorce or separate maintenance or written separation agreement that applies to 2021 states that the noncustodial parent can claim the child as a dependent, the decree or agreement wasn't changed after 1984 to say the non-custodial parent can't claim the child as a dependent, and the noncustodial parent provides at least $600 for the child's support during the year.

(If the decree or agreement went into effect after 1984 and before 2009, see Post-1984 and pre-2009 divorce decree or separation agreement. If the decree or agreement went into effect after 2008, see Post-2008 divorce decree or separation agreement.)

Tiebreaker rules:

To determine which person can treat the child as a qualifying child to claim these five tax benefits, the following tiebreaker rules apply.

- If only one of the persons is the child's parent, the child is treated as the qualifying child of the parent.
- If the parents file a joint return together and can claim the child as a qualifying child, the child is treated as the qualifying child of the parents.
- If the parents don't file a joint return together but both parents claim the child as a qualifying child, the IRS will treat the child as the qualifying child of the parent with whom the child lived for a longer period of time during the year. If the child lived with each parent for the same amount of time, the IRS will treat the child as the qualifying child of the parent who had the higher adjusted gross income (AGI) for the year.
- If no parent can claim the child as a qualifying child, the child is treated as the qualifying child of the person who had the highest AGI for the year.
- If a parent can claim the child as a qualifying child but no parent does so claim the child, the child is treated as the qualifying child of the person who had the highest AGI for the year, but only if that person's AGI is higher than the highest AGI of any of the child's parents who can claim the child.

Subject to these tiebreaker rules, both individuals may be able to choose which of them can claim the child as a qualifying child.

MULTIPLE SUPPORT AGREEMENTS

Sometimes no one provides more than half of the support of a person. Instead, two or more persons, each of whom would be able to claim the person as a dependent but for the support test, together provide more than half of the person's support.

When this happens, both individuals can agree that any one of them who individually provides more than 10% of the person's support, but only one, can claim that person as a dependent. Each of the others must sign a statement agreeing not to claim the person as a dependent for that year. The person who claims the person as a dependent must keep these signed statements for his or her records. A multiple support declaration identifying each of the others who agreed not to claim the person as a dependent must be attached to the return of the person claiming the person as a dependent. Form 2120, Multiple Support Declaration, can be used for this purpose.

Both individuals can claim someone as a dependent under a multiple support agreement for someone related to them or for someone who lived with them all year as a member of the household.

POP QUIZ & ANSWER SHEET

DEPENDENTS

POP QUIZ

Test your knowledge on *Dependents* by answering the questions below. The answer sheet may be found at the end of the Pop Quiz.

Q1: Which among the examples below meet the age test for a dependent?

A. At the end of the filing year, your child was younger than you (or your spouse if filing a joint return) and younger than 19.

B. At the end of the filing year, your child was younger than you (or your spouse if filing a joint return) and younger than 20.

C. At the end of the filing year, your child was younger than you (or your spouse if filing a joint return), younger than 24, and a full-time student.

D. At the end of the filing year, your child was younger than you (or your spouse if filing a joint return), younger than 25, and a full-time student.

Q2: What are the tests to be fulfilled for a child to be considered your qualifying child?

A. Relationship, Age, Dependency, Citizenship, TIN, Joint Return

B. Relationship, Age, Support, Residency, Tiebreaker

C. Residency, Dependency, Citizenship, TIN, Age, Joint Return

D. Residency, Relationship, Dependency, Citizenship, Age

Q3: For a taxpayer to qualify for the Residency Test to claim a qualifying child, how long must the child live with the taxpayer to qualify?

A. The Entire Year

B. 5 Months of the Year

C. More than 6 months of the Year

D. At least until May of that year

Q4: Ernest, a 23 year old full time college student lives in his college dorm the whole year. He works part time at Arby's making about $200 per week. His parents are paying for his college dorm, college tuition and other living expenses. Is he still considered a dependent of his parents?

A. Yes, because being away from college is considered a temporary absence.

B. Yes, because his parents are paying for his college dorm.

C. No, because he has been away from home for more than 6 month.

D. No, because he works part time and can live independently.

Q5: A Taxpayer provided $2,000 toward their 18 year old son's support for the year. He works part time and provided $5,000 to his own support. Is he still considered their qualifying child?

A. Yes, because he is only 18 years old.

B. Yes, because he is only working part time and will need more financial support in the future.
C. No, because he provided more than half of his support for the year.
D. No, because his income is more than what you can provide for him.

Q6: Which among the examples qualify as your dependent child:
A. You supported your 19 year old daughter, and she lived with you the whole year while her husband was deployed in Iraq. He earned $25,000 for the year. The couple files a joint return.
B. Your 19-year-old son and his 18-year-old wife had $1,700 of wages from part-time jobs and no other income. They lived with you all year. Neither is required to file a tax return. They don't have a child. Taxes were taken out of their pay so they filed a joint return only to get a refund of the with-held taxes.
C. You supported your 19 year old daughter, and she lived in your basement while her husband was away in a fishing vessel. He earned $17,000 for the year. They filed a joint return together.
D. You supported your 18 year old son and his 19 year old wife, they are living with you the whole year. They are both earning and their total earning for the year is $20,000. At the end of the year they filed for a joint return.

Q7: A taxpayer's cousin who worked part-time and earned $2900 for the entire year lives with the taxpayer all year round and doesn't have to pay rent or any bills. The cousin was only required to buy his own food. Is he a qualifying relative or a qualifying child? Why or why not?
A. He is not the taxpayers qualifying child because he is the taxpayers cousin.
B. He is not the taxpayers qualifying relative because he is the son of their mom's half brother.
C. He is a qualifying child because he lives with the taxpayer and is part of his/her household.
D. He is a qualifying relative because he lives with the taxpayer for the entire year and didn't provide more than half of his/her own support.

Q8: If two or more people want to claim a child as a dependent, all are considered valid tie-breakers to claim a qualifying child, except:
A. Parents who file joint
B. Be the parent the child lived with the longest during the year
C. Be the parent with the highest AGI if the child lived with each parent for the same length of time during the tax year
D. Parents who file separately

Q9: Jerry, age 44 is permanently blind and disabled and he lived with his mother Susan for the entire year. Susan, 63 years old is single and provides all of the support for herself and Jerry. What type of dependent could Susan claim Jerry as?
A. Jerry will be a qualifying relative since he is over the age of 19
B. Jerry will be a qualifying child since he is permanently and totally disabled

C. Jerry will be a qualifying "other dependent" since he is 44 years old
D. Jerry can not be claimed as a dependent

Q10: When would form 2120, Multiple Support Declaration be used?
A. When a son is taking care of his grandmother in a nursing home
B. When two sisters is equally taking care of their Mother who has Alzheimer's
C. When three siblings are splitting the household bills equally
D. When a mother is taking care of her two children since divorce

ANSWER SHEET

1. Answer is C – At the end of the filing year, your child was younger than you (or your spouse if filing a joint return), younger than 24, and a full-time student.

2. Answer is B – Relationship, Age, Support, Residency, Tiebreaker

3. Answer is C – More than 6 months of the Year

4. Answer is A – Yes, because being away from college is considered a temporary absence.

5. Answer is C – No, because he provided more than half of his support for the year.

6. Answer is B – Your 19-year-old son and his 18-year-old wife had $1,700 of wages from part-time jobs and no other income. They lived with you all year. Neither is required to file a tax return. They don't have a child. Taxes were taken out of their pay so they filed a joint return only to get a refund of the with-held taxes.

7. Answer is D – He is a qualifying relative because he lives with the taxpayer for the entire year and didn't provide more than half of his/her own support.

8. Answer is D – Parents who file separately

9. Answer is B – Jerry will be a qualifying child since he is permanently and totally disabled

10. Answer is B – When two sisters are equally taking care of their mother who has Alzheimer's.

TAXABLE & NON-TAXABLE INCOME

OVERVIEW

The Internal Revenue Code (IRC) describes types of income that are taxable and non-taxable. Federal tax law sets forth that all income is taxable unless it is specifically excluded. An exclusion is not the same as a deduction, and it is important to understand the distinction because some deductions and credits are phased out as a taxpayer's gross income increases.

Excluded income, on the other hand, retains its character without regard to the amount of the taxpayer's gross income.

Most types of excluded income do not have to be reported on a tax return.

Example:

Adam is a best-selling author who made more than $1,500,000 of taxable income last year. Because of his high income, some deductions and credits are phased out for Adam. However, later that year Adam is involved in an auto accident and sustains major injuries. Adam sues the other driver and receives an insurance settlement of $95,000 related to his injuries resulting from the accident. The settlement is excluded from his gross income because compensation for physical injuries is not taxable to the recipient, regardless of his taxable income level. Adam does not even have to report the injury settlement on his tax return.

CALCULATING TAXABLE INCOME

For a taxpayer to figure out how much tax he owes, he first needs to determine his gross income. Gross income is all income a taxpayer receives in the form of money, goods, property, and services that are not exempt from tax. In addition to wages, salaries, commissions, tips, and self-employment income, gross income includes other forms of compensation, such as interest, dividends, capital gains, taxable fringe benefits, and stock options.

Next, the taxpayer calculates his adjusted gross income (AGI) by subtracting from gross income certain specific deductions or adjustments. These deductions include IRA contributions, certain expenses for self-employed individuals, alimony payments," and moving expenses.

The amount of a taxpayer's AGI is important because it helps determine eligibility for certain deductions and credits. Finally, the taxpayer calculates his taxable income by subtracting additional deductions (standard or itemized) from AGI.

How to Calculate Taxable Income & Tax Liability

1. Start with Gross Income
2. Subtract adjustments to income ("above the line" deductions)
3. = Adjusted Gross Income (AGI)
4. Subtract greater of itemized deductions or standard deduction
5. = Taxable Income x Tax Rate = Gross Tax Liability – Subtracts Credits
6. = Net tax liability or refund receivable (based on the amount of prepaid tax if any

EARNED INCOME VS. UNEARNED INCOME

Earned income such as wages, salaries, tips, professional fees, or self-employment income is received for services performed.

Unearned income includes interest, dividends, retirement income, alimony, and disability benefits.

Earned income is generally subject to Social Security and Medicare taxes (also called FICA taxes).

Investment income and other unearned income are generally not subject to FICA taxes. The amount of taxable income is used to determine the taxpayer's gross income tax liability before applicable credits

CONSTRUCTIVE RECEIPT OF INCOME

The doctrine of constructive receipt requires that cash-basis taxpayers be taxed on income when it becomes available and is not subject to substantial limitations or restrictions, regardless of whether it is in their physical possession. Income received by an agent for a taxpayer is constructively received in the year the agent receives it.

Example:

Keith is a landlord who owns several rental properties. On December 30, 2021, a customer delivered a $500 rent check to Keith's payment lockbox. Keith does not collect the rental deposits in the lockbox on December 30 and instead leaves town later that day to celebrate New Year's Eve. Keith does not take physical possession of the check until January 5, 2022, the same day he deposits the check in his bank account. He is considered to have constructive receipt in 2021 and must include the $500 of gross income on his 2021 tax return because the check was available to Keith at that time without any substantial limitations or restrictions.

Constructive Receipt of Income

Most individuals are cash-basis taxpayers who report income when it is actually or constructively received during the tax year. This concept of constructive receipt would not apply to accrual-basis taxpayers who recognize income when it is earned rather than when it is received.

Funds must be available without substantial limitations under the constructive receipt rules. If there are significant restrictions on the income, or if the income is not accessible to the taxpayer, it is not considered to have been constructively received. Income is also not considered to have been "constructively received" if a taxpayer declines it, as in the case of a prize or an award.

Example:

Mia won concert tickets valued at $1,200 from a local radio station. Mia would be required to pay taxes based on the fair market value of the tickets. However, on the day of the concert, the concert is canceled and Mia is not able to attend the concert. Since she never received the tickets, the prize is not taxable to her because she never had constructive receipt of it.

Definitions:

The IRS defines fair market value (FMV) as:

- The price at which a property would change hands between a buyer and a seller when both have reasonable knowledge of all the necessary facts, and neither is being forced to buy or sell.
- If parties with adverse interests place a value on property in an arms-length transaction, that is strong evidence of FMV. If there is a stated price for services, this price is treated as the FMV unless there is evidence to the contrary.

THE "CLAIM OF RIGHT" DOCTRINE

Under the "claim of right" doctrine, income received without restriction (over which the taxpayer has complete control) must be reported in the year received, even if there is a possibility it may have to be repaid in a later year.

If there is a dispute and income is later repaid, the repayment is deductible in the year repaid. As a result, the taxpayer is not required to amend his reported gross income for the earlier year.

Example

In 2021, Antoinette sold an NFT for $20,000. She properly includes $20,000 in her gross income and pays taxes on the income for the 2021 tax year. On March 2, 2022, the customer discovers the nft is a forgery and returns it for a full refund of $20,000. Since Antoinette pays back the $20,000 in 2022, she is entitled to deduct the amount from her gross income in 2022. She does not have to amend her 2021 tax return.

WORKER CLASSIFICATION

For federal tax purposes, the IRS classifies workers in two broad categories: employees or independent contractors. These workers are taxed in different ways, and it is critical for businesses to identify the correct classification for everyone to whom it makes payments for services.

In general, a business must withhold and remit income taxes, Social Security and Medicare taxes, and pay unemployment tax on salaries and wages paid to an employee.

A business generally does not have to withhold or pay taxes on payments to independent contractors.

SELF-EMPLOYED TAXPAYERS

Self-employment income is earned by taxpayers who work for themselves. A taxpayer who has self-employment income of $400 or more in a year must file a tax return and report the earnings to the IRS.

Taxpayers who are independent contractors usually receive Forms 1099-NEC or 1099-MISC from their business clients showing the income they were paid. The amounts from the Forms 1099-NEC or 1099-MISC, along with any other business income payments, are reported by most self-employed individuals on Schedule C, Profit or Loss from Business, of Form 1040.

Self-employed farmers or fishermen report their earnings on Schedule F, Profit or Loss from Farming, of Form 1040. Self-employment income also includes:

- Income of ministers, priests, and rabbis for the performance of services such as baptisms and marriages
- The distributive share of trade or business income allocated by a partnership to its general partners or by a limited liability company to its members. The income is reported on IRS Schedule K-1 (Form 1065).
- A taxpayer does not have to conduct regular full-time business activities to be considered self-employed. A taxpayer may have a side business in addition to a regular job, and this is also considered self-employment.

FICA TAX (PAYROLL TAXES)

The Federal Insurance Contributions Act (FICA) tax includes two separate taxes:

- Social Security tax and
- Medicare tax.

The current rate for Social Security is 6.2% for the employer and 6.2% for the employee, or 12.4% total. The current rate for Medicare is 1.45% for the employer and 1.45% for the employee, or 2.9% total.

The combined FICA tax rate for 2021 is 15.3% and applies up to $142,800 of a taxpayer's combined earned income, including wages, tips, and net earnings from self-employment.

If the taxpayer's combined earned income exceeds $142,800, a rate of 2.9%, representing only the Medicare portion, applies to any excess earnings over $142,800.

There is no cap on earnings subject to the 2.9% Medicare tax. An additional Medicare surtax of 0.9% is applied to wages and self-employment income above certain thresholds.

The 7.65% tax rate is the combined rate for Social Security and Medicare. The Social Security portion (also called "OASDI") is 6.2% of earnings up to the applicable taxable maximum amount ($142,800 in 2021).

Remember: the Medicare portion is 1.45% on all earned income. There is no yearly maximum for Medicare tax.

SELF-EMPLOYMENT TAX

For the 2021 tax year, the self-employment tax rate is 15.3%. Social Security represents 12.4% of this tax and Medicare represents 2.9% of itSelf-employment tax (SE tax) is imposed on self-employed individuals in a manner like the Social Security and Medicare taxes that apply to wage earners.

Self-employed individuals are responsible for paying the entire amount of Social Security and Medicare taxes applicable to their net earnings from self-employment.

Self-employment tax is calculated on IRS Schedule SE, Self-Employment Tax.

If a taxpayer has wages in addition to self-employment earnings, the Social Security tax on the wages is paid first.

There are two adjustments related to the self-employment tax that reduce overall taxes for a taxpayer with self-employment income.

First, the taxpayer's net earnings from self-employment are reduced by 7.65%. Just as the employer's share of Social Security tax is not considered wages to the employee, this reduction removes a corresponding amount from the net earnings before the SE tax is calculated.

Second, the taxpayer can deduct the employer-equivalent portion of his self-employment tax in determining his adjusted gross income.

If a taxpayer owns more than one business, he must net the profit or loss from each business to determine the total earnings subject to SE tax. However, married taxpayers cannot combine their income or loss from self-employment to determine their individual earnings subject to SE tax.

EMPLOYEE COMPENSATION

Wages, salaries, bonuses, tips, and commissions are compensation received by employees for services performed. This compensation is taxable income to the employee and a deductible expense for the employer. Employers are required by January 31 to issue Forms W-2, which show the amounts of wages paid to employees for the previous year.

Employers are required by law to withhold Social Security and Medicare taxes from an employee's wages. If the employer fails to withhold these taxes, the employee is required to file Form 8919, Uncollected Social Security and Medicare Tax on Wages.

If a taxpayer has more than one employer and his total compensation is over the $142,800 Social Security base limit for 2021, too much Social Security tax may have been withheld. In this case, a taxpayer can claim the excess as a credit against his income tax.

Advance Wages: If an employee receives advance wages, commissions, or other earnings, he must recognize the income in the year it is constructively received, regardless of whether he has earned the income. If the employee is later required to pay back a portion of the earnings, the amount would be deducted from his taxable wages at that time.

Example:

Salary Advances received in 2021 will be taxable income in 2021 even though the worker will not earn the advance until 2022.

SUPPLEMENTAL WAGES

Supplemental wages are compensation paid to an employee in addition to his regular pay. These amounts are listed on the employee's Form W-2 and are taxable just like regular wages, even if the pay is not actually for work performed. Vacation pay and sick pay are examples of supplemental wages that are taxable just like any other wage income, even though the employee has not technically "worked" for the income. Supplemental wages may also include:

- Bonuses, commissions, prizes
- Severance pay, back pay, and holiday pay
- Payment for nondeductible moving expenses

GARNISHED WAGES

An employee may have his wages garnished for various reasons, such as when he owes child support, back taxes due, or other debts. Regardless of the amounts garnished from the employee's paycheck, the full amount of his gross wages must be included in his taxable wages at year end.

PROPERTY OR SERVICES IN LIEU OF WAGES

Wages paid in any form other than cash are measured by their fair market value. An employee who receives property for services performed must generally recognize the fair market value of the property when it is received as taxable income.

However, if an employee receives stock or other property that is restricted, the property is not included in income until it is available to the employee without restriction.

Another common arrangement is when colleges offer tuition reduction and/or free on campus housing in lieu of wages to student teachers. Any portion of a grant or scholarship that is compensation for services is taxable as wages,

TIP INCOME

Tips received by food servers, baggage handlers, hairdressers, and others for performing services are taxable income.

An individual who receives $20 or more per month in tips must report the tip income to his employer.

An employee who receives less than $20 per month in tips while working one job does not have to report the tip income to his employer.

Tips of less than $20 per month are exempt from Social Security and Medicare taxes, but are still subject to federal income tax.

An employee who does not report all her tips to her employer generally must report the tips and related Social Security and Medicare taxes on her Form 1040.

Form 4137, Social Security and Medicare Tax on Unreported Tip Income, is used to compute the additional tax.

Non-cash tips (for example, concert tickets, or other items) do not have to be reported to the employer, but they must be reported and included in the taxpayer's income at their fair market value.

Taxpayers who are self-employed and receive tips must include their tip income in gross receipts on Schedule C.

TAXABLE FRINGE BENEFITS FOR EMPLOYEES

Employers often offer fringe benefits to employees; common fringe benefits include health insurance, retirement plans, and parking passes. Although most employee fringe benefits are nontaxable, some benefits must be reported on the employee's Form W-2 and included in his taxable income. Examples of taxable fringe benefits include:

- Off-site athletic facilities and health club memberships,
- Concert and athletic event tickets
- The value of employer-provided life insurance over $50,000,
- Any cash benefit or benefits in the form of a credit card or gift card (an exception applies for occasional meal money or transportation fare to allow an employee to work beyond normal hours),
- Transportation benefits, if the value of a benefit for any month is more than a specified non taxable limit,
- Employer-provided vehicles, if they are used for personal purposes.
- The nontaxable benefit for both mass transit and parking for 2021 is $270 per month, although the amounts are no longer deductible by the employer, they are still non-taxable to the employee if the employer continues to provide the benefit. Any expense over that amount is included in the employee's taxable income as wages. An employee can receive both parking and transit benefits in the same month.

NON-TAXABLE FRINGE BENEFITS FOR EMPLOYEES

This section discusses the exclusion rules that apply to fringe benefits. These rules exclude all or part of the value of certain benefits from the recipient's pay.

In most cases, the excluded benefits aren't subject to federal income tax withholding, social security, Medicare, federal unemployment (FUTA) tax, or Railroad Retirement Tax Act (RRTA) taxes and aren't reported on Form W-2.

Exclusion rules for the following fringe benefits.

- Accident and health benefits.
- Achievement awards.
- Adoption assistance.
- Athletic facilities.
- De minimis (minimal) benefits.
- Dependent care assistance.
- Educational assistance.
- Employee discounts.
- Employee stock options.
- Employer-provided cell phones.
- Group-term life insurance coverage.
- HSAs.
- Lodging on your business premises.
- Meals.
- No-additional-cost services.

- Retirement planning services.
- Transportation (commuting) benefits.
- Tuition reduction.
- Working condition benefits.

Retirement Plans

Employer contributions on behalf of their employees' qualified retirement plans are not taxable to the employees when they are made.

When an employee receives distributions from a retirement plan, the amounts received are taxable income.

Retirement plans may also allow employees to contribute part of their pre-tax compensation to the plan. This type of contribution is called an elective deferral and is excluded from taxable compensation for income tax purposes but subject to Social Security and Medicare taxes.

CAFETERIA PLANS

A cafeteria plan is a separate written plan maintained by an employer for employees that meets the specific requirements of and regulations of section 125 of the Internal Revenue Code.

It provides participants an opportunity to receive certain benefits on a pretax basis. Participants in a cafeteria plan must be permitted to choose among at least one taxable benefit (such as cash) and one qualified benefit.

A qualified benefit is a benefit that does not defer compensation and is excludable from an employee's gross income under a specific provision of the Code, without being subject to the principles of constructive receipt. Qualified benefits include the following:

1. Accident and health benefits (but not Archer medical savings accounts or long-term care insurance)
2. Adoption assistance
3. Dependent care assistance
4. Group-term life insurance coverage
5. Health savings accounts, including distributions to pay long-term care services
    - The written plan must specifically describe all benefits and establish rules for eligibility and elections.
    - A section 125 plan is the only means by which an employer can offer employees a choice between taxable and nontaxable benefits without the choice causing the benefits to become taxable. A plan offering only a choice between taxable benefits is not a section 125 plan.

Employee contributions are usually deducted based upon salary reduction agreements (i.e., the money is withheld directly from the employee's paycheck and deposited into an account).

Salary reduction contributions are not considered actually or constructively received by the employee and therefore are not treated as taxable wages.

Therefore, they are generally not subject to income tax withholding, FICA (Social Security and Medicare taxes), or FUTA (unemployment tax).

An employer may choose to make benefits available to employees, their spouses, and dependents.

FLEXIBLE SPENDING ARRANGEMENTS (FSAS)

An FSA is a form of cafeteria plan benefit that reimburses employees for expenses incurred for certain qualified benefits, such as health care and daycare expenses. The benefits are subject to annual maximum limits and are typically subject to an annual "use-it-or-lose-it" rule, with a short (two-and-a-half-months) grace period after year end to use any remaining balance.

In 2021, employee salary reduction contributions to a health-care FSA are capped at $2,750. The Dependent Care FSA (also known as Dependent Care Assistance Plan) limit is at $10,500 in 2021.

Both employer and employee may contribute to an employee's health-care FSA, but contributions from all sources combined must not exceed the annual maximum.

If a taxpayer over-contributes to their health-care FSA, the taxpayer must pay income tax, plus a 6% excise tax, on any excess contributions and related earnings for each tax year the excess contributions remain in the account. In order to avoid the excise tax on excess contributions, the taxpayer must remove the year's excess contributions and related investment earnings before the last day to file federal income taxes for the pertinent tax year, generally April 15.

Up to $500 of unused FSA money per account may be carried over to the following year. An employer must choose between either the grace period or the carryover option.

Adoption Assistance in a "Cafeteria Plan": An employee can exclude amounts paid or reimbursed by an employer under a qualified adoption assistance program ($14,440 for 2021).

Dependent Care Assistance Program

This is also sometimes called a Dependent Care FSA, or Dependent Care Flexible Spending Account (DCFSA). An employee can exclude up to $10,500 in 2021 ($5,250 if MFS) of benefits received under a qualified dependent care assistance program each year. The amounts can be used to pay for eligible daycare services, before or after school programs, including child or adult daycare. Amounts paid directly to the taxpayer or to a daycare provider qualify for exclusion.

HIGHLY COMPENSATED EMPLOYEES (HCES) & KEY EMPLOYEES

A cafeteria plan cannot have rules that favor eligibility for highly compensated employees to participate, contribute, or benefit from a cafeteria plan. If a benefit plan favors HCEs, the value of their benefits may become taxable. This is to discourage companies from offering excellent tax-free benefits to their top executives while ignoring the needs of lower-paid employees.

For purposes of a cafeteria plan, an HCE is any of the following:

- An owner of more than 5% of the interest in the business at any time during the year or the preceding year, regardless of how much compensation that person received
- An employee with gross compensation in excess of $120,000 in the current or previous year
- An officer of the company
- A family member of one of these employees.

The IRS uses a process called 'family attribution" in order to make the determination of who qualifies as an HCE, which means that an employee can be determined to be an HCE merely by familial relationship.

An employee who's a spouse, child, grandparent or parent of someone who is a 5% (or greater) owner of the business, is also automatically considered an owner under the family attribution rules.

HCEs hired in the middle of the year will not receive HCE status until the start of the following year when they are eligible to collect the entirety of their salary. For example, an HCE hired in March 2021 does not qualify as an HCE until January 1, 2022, regardless of their salary level

Highly Compensated" Employees and "Key Employees" have similar-sounding names, but the rules for defining Key Employees are slightly different. Employer-provided benefits also cannot favor "key employees."

IRS guidelines define "Key Employees" as any of the following:

- A company officer of the employer with annual compensation greater than $185,000 in the current or previous year, or
- A 5% owner of the company, or
- A 1% owner of the company with annual compensation of more than $150,000.
- Although the compensation threshold is lower for HCEs than Key Employees, ($120,000 versus $180,000), an employee can be classified as a

"key employee" without having any ownership in the company at all.

A plan is considered to have improperly "favored" HCEs and key employees if more than 25% of all the benefits are given to those employees.

If a cafeteria plan or a retirement plan fails to pass IRS non-discrimination testing, highly compensated employees and key employees may lose the tax benefits of participating in the plan.

If this happens, then the plans can lose their tax-favored status, and the HCEs or key employees must include the value of these benefits as taxable compensation.

These types of "corrections" often take the form of taxable distributions to plan participants.

OTHER TYPES OF EMPLOYEE FRINGE BENEFITS

Educational Assistance

An employer can offer employees educational assistance for the cost of tuition, fees, books, supplies, and equipment. The payments may be for either undergraduate or graduate-level courses, and do not have to be work-related.

In 2021, $5,250 in educational assistance may be excluded per year per employee. If an employer pays more than $5,250, the excess is generally taxed as wages to the employee. The cost of courses involving sports, games, or hobbies is not covered unless they are related to the business or are required as part of a degree program. The cost of lodging, meals, and transportation is also not included.

Tuition Fee Reduction Benefits

An educational organization can exclude the value of a qualified undergraduate tuition reduction to an employee, his spouse, or a dependent child. A tuition reduction is "qualified" only if the taxpayer receives it from, and uses it at, an eligible educational institution.

Graduate education only qualifies if it is for the education of a graduate student who performs teaching or research activities for the educational organization.

There is an exception for job-related education. If the education is directly job related, amounts in excess of the $5,250 limit may qualify for exclusion as a working condition fringe benefit.

EMPLOYER-PROVIDED MEALS & LODGING

An employer may exclude the value of meals and lodging provided to employees if they are provided:

- On the employer's business premises, and
- For the employer's convenience.

For lodging, there is an additional rule: it must be required as a condition of employment. Lodging can be provided for the taxpayer, the taxpayer's spouse, and the taxpayer's dependents and still not be taxable to the employee.

Supplemental Wages

The exclusion from taxation does not apply if the employee can choose to receive additional pay instead of lodging. Meals may be provided to employees for the convenience of the employer on the employer's business premises for several reasons, such as when:

- Police officers and firefighters need to be on call for emergencies during the meal period
- Eating facilities are not available in areas near the workplace
- Meals furnished to restaurant employees before, during, or after work hours are also considered furnished for the employer's convenience and are not taxable to the employee.
- The nature of the business requires short meal periods
- Meals are furnished immediately after working hours because the employee's duties prevented him from obtaining a meal during working hours

TRANSPORTATION FRINGE BENEFITS

Employers may provide transportation benefits to their employees up to certain amounts without having to include the benefits in the employees' taxable income.

Qualified transportation benefits include transit passes, paid parking, and a ride in a commuter highway vehicle between the employee's home and workplace. The nontaxable benefit for both mass transit and parking for 2020 is $270 per month.

Due to the TCJA, the amounts are no longer deductible by the employer, but transportation benefits are still non-taxable to the employee if the employer continues to provide the benefit (with the notable exception of bicycle commuting benefits, which became taxable to the employee in 2018 under the TCJA).

Any expense over that amount is included in the employee's taxable income as wages. An employee can receive both parking and transit benefits in the same month. The use of a company car for commuting purposes or other personal use is generally a taxable benefit. Therefore, the value of the vehicle's use for either of these purposes is considered taxable wages to the employee.

There is an exception in IRS regulations that exempts the personal-use of certain types of vehicles. Qualified nonpersonal use vehicles, such as police or fire vehicles, school buses, and ambulances are exempt from fringe benefit reporting, even if the vehicles are used for commuting purposes, if the employer is requiring their use for the employees to do their jobs.

Example:

Selena was offered a lucrative new job in New York City as a computer programmer. As part of her employment contract, she negotiates a parking space for her car. Her new employer agrees to pay the cost of the space at the garage across the street from her work. Monthly parking is quite expensive in New York City, and the monthly parking fee at the garage is $550. Since this amount exceeds the allowable limit for parking fringe benefits, a portion of the parking costs will be taxable to Selena as wages. In 2018, the allowable transportation benefit for parking is $260. Therefore, an additional $290 ($550-$260) would be taxable to Selena each month.

Cellphones

The value of the business use of an employer- provided cell phone may be excluded from an employee's income to the extent that, if the employee paid for its use, the payment would be deductible. There must be substantial "non compensatory" reasons for the use of a phone that relate to the employer's business.

Legitimate reasons include the employer's need to contact the employee in the event of work-related emergencies and the employee's need to be available to speak with clients when away from the office. If a cell phone is provided simply to promote goodwill, to boost an employee's morale, or to attract a prospective employee, the value of the cell phone must be added to the employee's wages.

Group-Term Life Insurance Coverage

Up to $50,000 of life insurance coverage may be provided as a nontaxable benefit to an employee. The cost of insurance coverage on policies that exceed $50,000 is a taxable benefit. If an employer provides more than $50,000 of coverage, the amount included in the taxpayer's income is reported as part of their taxable wages on their Form W-2. Also, the taxable amount is shown separately in box 12 of their Form W-2 with code C.

Work-Related Moving Expense Reimbursements

Starting in 2018, moving expenses are no longer deductible for most taxpayers, except for members of the armed forces. Therefore, moving expenses that are reimbursed or paid by an employer must be included in the employee's taxable income as wages. This is true even if the moving expenses are paid under an accountable plan.

Moving Expenses

An "accountable" plan is an employee reimbursement allowance arrangement or a method for reimbursing employees for business expenses that complies with IRS regulations.

There is an exception for qualified moving expenses that were incurred in 2017, but only reimbursed by the employer in 2018. These moving expenses reimbursements may be excluded from the employee's wages and are not subject to federal income or employment taxes.

Example:

Kamryn was offered a new job in another state on December 1, 2017. Her new employer offered to reimburse her qualified moving expenses as a condition of her employment. She accepted the position and moved on December 26, 2017. Kamryn submits the paperwork and her employer reimburses her moving expenses on January 15, 2018. Even though the reimbursement occurred in 2018, none of the amounts would be taxable to Kamryn, because her moving expenses were actually incurred in the previous year, when moving expenses were still deductible by most taxpayers. She does not have to include the amounts on her 2018 return, and the expenses are still fully deductible by the employer as a business expense.

No-Additional-Cost Services

Non-taxable fringe benefits also include services provided to employees that do not impose any substantial additional cost to the employer because the employer already offers those services in the ordinary course of doing business. Employees do not need to include these no-additional-cost services in their income. Typically, no-additional cost services are excess capacity services, such as unused airline seat tickets for airline employees or open hotel rooms for hotel employees.

Health Club

If an employee is provided with the free or low-cost use of a health club on the employer's premises, the value is not included in the employee's compensation. The gym must be used primarily by employees, their spouses, and their dependent children. However, if the employer pays for a fitness program or use of a facility at an off-site location, the value of the program is included in the employee's compensation.

Example:

Dalilah is a flight attendant with Starlight Airlines. She can fly for free on standby flights when there is an extra seat. This fringe benefit is allowed at no additional cost to the employer and is therefore non-taxable to Dalilah.

Employee Achievement Awards

If an employee is provided with the free or low-cost use of a health club on the employer's premises, the value is not included in the employee's compensation. The gym must be used primarily by employees, their spouses, and their dependent children. However, if the employer pays for a fitness program or use of a facility at an off-site location, the value of the program is included in the employee's compensation.

Example:

An emergency happens at work and asks Thomas to work overtime in order to get the situation under control. The employer gives $20 in cash in order to purchase a meal during this unusual overtime shift. The cash can be excluded as a de minimis benefit because it is for the benefit of his employer that Thomas is working overtime, and it is an unusual and infrequent situation.

Employers may generally exclude from an employee's taxable wages the value of awards given for length of service or safety achievement. The tax-free amount is limited to the following:

- $400 for awards that are not qualified plan awards. A qualified plan award is one that does not discriminate in favor of highly compensated employees.
- $1,600 for all awards, whether or not they are qualified plan awards
- The exclusion for employee awards does not apply to awards of cash, gift cards, or items such as vacations or tickets to sporting events.
- De Minimis (Minimal) Benefits: This is a property or service an employer provides that has so little value that accounting for it would be impractical. Examples of de minimis benefits include the following:
- Occasional personal use of a company copying machine
- Holiday gifts with a low fair market value
- Beverages such as coffee or soft drinks for employees
- Cash and gift cards are not excludable as de minimis benefits unless they are for occasional meal money or transportation fare. The benefit must be provided so that an employee can work an unusual, extended schedule.

Employee Discounts

Employers may exclude the value of employee discounts from wages up to the following limits:

- For services, a 20% discount of the price charged to nonemployee customers for merchandise, the company's gross profit percentage multiplied by the price nonemployee customers pay

REIMBURSEMENT OF EMPLOYEE BUSINESS EXPENSES

When a business reimburses its employees for certain business expenses, such as meals and travel, reimbursements are not taxable income if employees meet all the following requirements of an accountable plan:

- Have incurred the expenses while performing services as employees

- Adequately account for travel, meals, and lodging
- Provide evidence of their employee business expenses, such as receipts or other records
- Return any excess reimbursement within a reasonable period

Under an accountable plan, a business may advance money to employees. The cash advance must be reasonably calculated to equal the anticipated expenses, and it must be advanced within a reasonable period. If any expenses reimbursed under this arrangement are not substantiated, they are considered taxable income for the employee.

Qualifying expenses for travel are excludable from an employee's income if they are incurred for temporary travel on business away from the area of the employee's tax home.

Travel expenses paid in connection with an indefinite work assignment cannot be excluded from income. Any work assignment in excess of one year is considered "indefinite." Travel expense reimbursements include:

- Costs of travel to and from the business destination (such as flights and mileage reimbursements)
- Transportation costs while at the business destination (such as taxi fares and shuttles)
- Lodging, meals, and incidental expenses
- Cleaning, laundry, and other miscellaneous expenses

Example:

Dane works for an agency in Atlanta. He flies to Boston to conduct business for an entire week. His employer pays the cost of the flight to and from Boston, as well as lodging and meals while there. The reimbursements for substantiated travel expenses are excluded from Dane's income.

TAXATION OF CLERGY MEMBERS

There are special rules regarding the taxation of clergy members, defined as individuals who are ordained, commissioned, or licensed by a religious body or church denomination. A clergy member's salary is reported on Form W-2 and is taxable. Offerings and fees received for performing marriages, baptisms, and funerals must also be reported as self-employment income on Schedule C.

Housing Allowance for Clergy: A clergy member who receives a housing allowance may exclude the allowance from gross income to the extent it is used to pay the expenses of providing a home. The exclusion for housing is limited to the. lesser of:

- Fair market rental value (including utilities), or
- The actual cost to provide the home.

The housing allowance cannot exceed reasonable pay and must be used for housing in the year it is received. Salary, other fees, and housing allowances must be included in income for purposes of determining self-employment tax.

Even if a minister is considered an employee, churches cannot withhold Social Security and Medicare taxes from his wages. They are treated as self-employed for purposes of these taxes.

Examples:

Solomon is an ordained minister who receives $35,000 in salary from his church. He receives an additional $5,000 for performing marriages and baptisms. His housing allowance is $500 per month, for a total of $6,000 per year, and is excluded from his gross income. Solomon must report the $35,000 as salary and the $5,000 as self-employment income. The $6,000 housing allowance is subject to self-employment tax, but not to income tax.

Doris is a full-time ordained minister. Her church allows her to use a house that has a rental value of $8,000. She is paid a salary of $22,000, and her church does not withhold Social Security or Medicare taxes. Her income for self-employment tax purposes is $30,000 ($22,000 + $8,000).

A clergy member may apply for an exemption from self-employment tax if he is conscientiously opposed to public insurance because of religious principles.

For a clergy member or a minister to claim an exemption from SE tax, the minister must file IRS Form 4029, Application for Exemption from Social Security and Medicare Taxes and Waiver of Benefits The sect or religious order must also complete part of the form. The exemption does not apply to federal income tax, only to self-employment tax.

If the exemption is granted, the clergy member will not pay Social Security or Medicare taxes on his earnings, and he will not receive credit toward those benefits in retirement.

If a clergy member is a member of a religious order that has taken a vow of poverty, he is exempt from paying SE tax on his earnings for qualified services. The earnings are tax-free because they are considered the income of the religious order, rather than of the individual clergy member.

COMBAT PAY & VETERANS BENEFITS

Wages earned by military personnel are generally taxable. However, there are a number of special rules for military personnel regarding taxable income. Combat zone wages (combat pay) are not taxable income.

Hazardous duty pay is also excludable for certain military personnel. Enlisted personnel who serve in a combat zone for any part of a month may exclude their pay from tax. For officers, pay is excluded up to a certain amount, depending on the branch of service.

Veterans' benefits paid by the Department of Veterans Affairs to a veteran or his family are not taxable if they are for education (the GI Bill), training, disability compensation, work therapy, dependent care assistance, or other benefits or pension payments given to the veteran because of disability.

DISABILITY PAYMENTS

There are several types of disability payments, and the taxability of the income depends on several factors. There are also some types of disability-related payments that are given to workers that are not taxable at all. Worker's compensation is one such example.

Worker's compensation should not be confused with disability insurance, sick pay, or unemployment compensation; it is a type of benefit that only pays workers who are injured on the job Worker's compensation is paid to a taxpayer under a worker's compensation act or another state statute. The amounts are always exempt from tax.

Workers' compensation is a type of mandatory insurance, meaning most large and mid-sized employers are required to have coverage for their employees.

Example:

Harrison is a construction worker. In 2019, he was struck by a falling brick on a construction site. The brick crushes his arm, causing serious injuries and a long hospital stay. Worker's compensation covers Harrison's medical costs as well as a portion of his lost wages while he is recovering from the injury. The amounts are not taxable to Harrison and do not need to be reported on his tax return.

DISABILITY INSURANCE BENEFITS

A taxpayer may also receive long-term disability payments as a result of an insurance policy. Generally, long-term disability payments from an insurance policy are excluded from income if the taxpayer pays the premiums for the policy.

If an employer pays the insurance premiums, the employee must report the payments as taxable income.

If both an employee and his employer have paid premiums for a disability policy, only the employer's portion of the disability payments would be reported as taxable income.

Example:

Maggie became disabled in 2018 and began to receive a long-term disability benefit of

$4,200 a month. The original insurance policy was paid for by both her employer and herself. Before Maggie became disabled, her employer paid 80% of the disability insurance premiums. Maggie paid the remaining premium amount (20%) with post-tax dollars. In this case, because the employer paid 80% of the policy premiums, 80% of the benefits received would be taxable to Maggie. This means that $3,360 ($4,200 x 80%) would be taxable. The remaining benefits of $840 (20% x $4,200) would not be taxable since Maggie paid that portion of the insurance premium with her own post-tax dollars.

Disability Insurance Benefits

Disability Insurance Premium	Taxability of Benefits
The employer pays 100%	100% taxable
The employer pays a portion and employee pays the balance with post-tax dollars	Partially Taxable; the taxable percentage is based on the premiums paid by the employer
The employer pays portion and employee pays the balance with pretax dollars	Not taxable
The employee pays 100% with post-tax dollars	100% taxable
The employee pays 100% with pretax dollars	100% taxable

Disability Retirement Benefits

Disability retirement benefits are taxable as wages if a taxpayer retired on disability before reaching the minimum retirement age. The benefit is usually based on the employee's final average earnings and their years of actual service. Once the taxpayer reaches retirement age, the payments are no longer taxable as wages. They are taxable as pension income. This type of disability retirement benefit is offered to most Federal government workers and U.S. Postal Service employees. In order to apply for this benefit, the employee's disability generally must have caused them to discontinue working.

Social Security Disability Insurance (SSDI) benefits is a separate benefit from disability retirement benefits that are offered to federal and postal service employees.

Do not confuse sick pay with disability pay. Sick pay, or sick leave, is always taxable as wages, just like vacation pay and holiday pay.

POP QUIZ & ANSWER SHEET

TAXABLE & NON-TAXABLE INCOME

POP QUIZ

Test your knowledge on Taxable & Non-Taxable Income by answering the questions below. The answer sheet may be found at the end of the Pop Quiz.

Q1: A key employee during 2021 is generally an employee who is either of the following, except:

A. An officer having annual pay of more than $185,000.
B. A shareholder who owns more than 5% of the voting power of all classes of the company's stock.
C. A 1% owner of your business whose annual pay is more than $150,000.
D. All of the Above

Q2: Which of the following is not an example of unearned income?

A. Social Security
B. Alimony
C. Interest & Dividends
D. Tips

Q3: Which of the following statements is true?

A. An employer must withhold income taxes, withhold and pay Social Security and Medicare taxes, and pay unemployment tax on wages paid to an employee.
B. An employer must withhold or pay taxes on payments to independent contractors.
C. Both A & B
D. None of the Above

Q4: Which of the following is considered as self-employment?

A. You carry on a trade or business as a sole proprietor or an independent contractor.
B. You are a member of a partnership that carries on a trade or business.
C. You are otherwise in business for yourself (including a part-time business).
D. All of the Above

Q5: What is the rate for self-employment tax?

A. 15.5% = 12.6% for social security and 2.9% for Medicare taxes
B. 15.3% = 12.4% for social security and 2.9% for Medicare taxes
C. 18.8% = 12.6% for social security and 6.2% for Medicare taxes

D. 18.6% = 12.4% for social security and 6.2% for Medicare taxes

Q6: The IRS can seize part of an employee's wages each pay period until:
A. No arrangements are made to pay the overdue taxes
B. The amount of overdue taxes is paid
C. The levy is not released
D. All of the above

Q7: The following are the steps to report tip income, except:
A. Keep a daily tip record (Form 4070-A)
B. Report tips to the employer (Form 4070)
C. Report total tips for any 1 month from any one job including those that are less than $20
D. Report all your tips on the income tax return (as wages on Form 1040)

Q8: Which of the following is not taxable?
A. Medical Benefits
B. Commissions
C. Vacation Pay
D. Sick-Pay

Q9: All of the following about Retirement Plans are true, except:
A. Contributions by employers to a qualified plan for employees aren't included in income.
B. When an employee receives distributions from a retirement plan, the amounts received are taxable income.
C. Retirement plans typically allow employees to contribute part of their pre-tax compensation to the plan.
D. When an employee receives distributions from a retirement plan, the amounts received are not taxable income.

Q10: The following are the benefits of Flexible Spending Arrangements (FSA), except:
A. Contributions made by your employer will be included in your gross income.
B. No employment or federal income taxes are deducted from the contributions. Reimbursements may be tax free if you pay qualified medical expenses.
C. Reimbursements may be tax free if you pay qualified medical expenses.
D. You can use an FSA to pay qualified daycare expenses.

ANSWER SHEET

1. Answer is B – A shareholder who owns more than 5% of the voting power of all classes of the company's stock.

2. Answer is D – Tips

3. Answer is A – An employer must withhold income taxes, withhold, and pay Social Security and Medicare taxes, and pay unemployment tax on wages paid to an employee.

4. Answer is D – All of the Above

5. Answer is B – 15.3% = 12.4% for social security and 2.9% for Medicare taxes.

6. Answer is B – The amount of overdue taxes is paid.

7. Answer is C – Report total tips for any 1 month from any one job including those that are less than $20.

8. Answer is A – Medical Benefits

9. Answer is D – When an employee receives distributions from a retirement plan, the amounts received are not taxable income.

10. Answer is A – Contributions made by your employer will be included in your gross income.

INVESTMENT INCOME & EXPENSES

OVERVIEW

Investment income and expenses, includes information for individual shareholders of mutual funds or other regulated investment companies, such as money market funds. It explains:

- What investment income is taxable and what investment expenses are deductible.
- When and how to show these items on the tax return.
- How to determine and report gains and losses on the disposition of investment property.
- Information on property trades and tax shelters.

INTEREST INCOME

It is the amount paid to an individual for lending its money or letting another individual use its funds.

On a larger scale, it is the amount earned by an investor wherein he placed his money in an investment or project.

Penalties paid by customers on overdue accounts receivable can be considered interest income, since these payments are created on the use of the company's funds.

It is recorded within the interest income account in the general ledger.

It is usually taxable; the ordinary income tax rate is relevant to this form of income.

INTEREST EARNED: CERTIFICATE OF DEPOSIT

Interest that is received or that is credited to an account that can be withdrawn from without penalty is taxable income in the year it becomes available. The taxpayer should receive Copy B of Form 1099-INT reporting payments of interest and/or tax-exempt interest of $10 or more. The taxpayer may receive these forms as part of a composite statement from a broker and must report all taxable and tax-exempt interest on your federal income tax return, even if they don't receive a Form 1099-INT or Form 1099-OID.

TAX-EXEMPT INTEREST

Interest on a bond that is used to finance government operations generally is not taxable if the bond is issued by a state, the District of Columbia, a U.S. possession, or any of their political subdivisions. Political subdivisions include:

- Port authorities,
- Toll road commissions,
- Utility services authorities,
- Community redevelopment agencies, and
- Qualified volunteer fire departments (for certain obligations issued after 1980).

Obligations that are not bonds - Interest on a state or local government obligation may be tax exempt even if the obligation is not a bond. For example, interest on a debt evidenced only by an ordinary written agreement of purchase and sale may be tax exempt. Also, interest paid by an insurer on default by the state or political subdivision may be tax exempt.

Indian tribal governments - Bonds issued after 1982 by an Indian tribal government are treated as issued by a state. Interest on these bonds is generally tax exempt if the bonds are part of an issue of which substantially all of the proceeds are to be used in the exercise of any essential government function. However, interest on private activity bonds (other than certain bonds for tribal manufacturing facilities) is taxable.

Original issue discount (OID) on tax-exempt state or local government bonds is treated as tax-exempt interest

Recap:

Tax interest is not subject to income taxes, it is not part of AGI (adjusted gross income) for taxation purposes.

Issuers or lenders that pay more than $10 in tax exempt interest must report the income interest to the taxpayer and IRS on Form 1099 – NT.

Taxpayers or borrowers, must report this tax-exempt interest on Form 1040.

To determine the amount of taxpayer's Social Security benefits is taxable, the amount received as tax-exempt interest is used by the IRS.

INTEREST ON U.S. TREASURY BILLS, NOTES & BONDS

Treasury bonds, Treasury bills, and Treasury notes are all government-issued fixed income securities that are considered safe and secure.

T-bonds mature in 30 years and give investors the highest interest payments bi-annually.

T-notes mature from two up to 10 years, with bi-annual interest payments, but lower earnings.

T-bills have the shortest maturity terms—from four weeks to a year.

These investments are auctioned off regularly on the U.S. Treasury's website.

Treasury Bonds

Often times referred to as: long bonds

- Take the longest to mature
  - Maturity of 30 years
  - A fixed interest payment every 6 months for the purchasers.
  - Issued at monthly online auctions held directly by the US Treasury
- The price and its yield are determined during the auction
  - Investors expect a high degree of safety and steady
  - Individual investors often use T-bonds to keep a part of their retirement savings risk-free, to provide a steady income in retirement.

Also known as T- notes.

- Similar to T bonds but offered in 2 years up to 10 years Produce interest payments twice a year.
- Give lower yields because the terms offered are lower than T-bonds.
- A closely watched government bond is the 10-year T-note
  - It is also auctioned and sold in $100 increments by the US Treasury
  - The price may fluctuate based on the result of the auction

T-bills have the shortest terms:

- Have a maturity date of 4, 8, 13, 26 and 52 weeks
- Auctioned off to investors at a discount to par or face value.
- The return is the difference between the par value and the discount price paid at purchase.
- CMB (Cash Management Bill) is a short-term security offered by the US Treasury
  - Has much shorter maturity date between 7 days to 3 months
  - Can be purchased in $100 increments

THE EDUCATION SAVINGS BOND PROGRAM

1. An education savings bond program lets taxpayers exempt some or all of the interest earned upon redemption of eligible savings bonds from their annual gross income.
2. When the bond is purchased, the bond owner must be at least 24 years old
3. The bond must be used exclusively for tuition associated expenses
4. The bonds cannot be used to pay for textbooks, room and board, or sports programs

Investors must comply with the following rules:
- At the time of purchase, the bond owner must be 24 years of age.

- When savings bonds are redeemed, funds must be used to pay off education expenses for the owners, spouse and their dependents.
- Funds can only be used on tuition related expenses.
- Funds on redeemed bonds can be used to make tax-free contributions to a Coverdell Education Savings Account.
- Eligible education expenses must be acquired during the same tax year as the redemption of the bond.
- Non taxable educational payments must be subtracted from eligible expenses.
- The total proceeds from the bonds equal less than the amount of eligible expenses, all of the interest accrued on the bond remains tax-free.
- The amount of tax exempt interest is based on the owner's modified adjusted gross income (MAGI).
- All payments made with bond proceeds must be reported to the IRS together with a detailed receipt.

DIVIDEND INCOME

Dividend income refers to any dispersal of a company earnings to shareholders from stocks or mutual funds owned.

The tax treatment of dividend income rests on whether the income meets the definition of a "qualified dividend" and if it is held in a retirement account, like an IRA.

How companies use their profits:

1. Companies can keep earnings within the business, for purposes such as to expand their operations, pay down debt, or to build up a stockpile of cash.
2. Company can elect to allocate some of its profits to shareholders, in cash or stock, which is known as a dividend
3. Some companies are obliged to pay out most of their income as dividends.

What is a qualified dividend?

To qualify for a lower tax rate, a received dividend must meet these two criteria:

- The dividend must be paid by a US corporation or a qualified foreign corporation.
- The individual must have held the stock for more than 60 days during the 121-day period starting 60 days before the ex-dividend date.

STOCK DIVIDENDS AND STOCK DISTRIBUTIONS

Distributions by a corporation of its own stock are commonly known as stock dividends. Stock rights (also known as "stock options") are distributions by a corporation of rights to acquire its stock. Distributions of stock dividends and stock rights are generally tax-free to shareholders. However, if any of the following apply to their distribution, stock and stock rights are treated as property, as discussed under Money or Property Distributions.

- Any shareholder has the choice to receive cash or other property instead of stock or stock rights.
- The distribution gives cash or other property to some shareholders and an increase in the percentage interest in the corporation's assets or earnings and profits to other shareholders.
- The distribution is in convertible preferred stock and has the same result as in (2).
- The distribution gives preferred stock to some common stock shareholders and gives common stock to other common stock shareholders.
- The distribution is on preferred stock. (An increase in the conversion ratio of convertible preferred stock made solely to take into account a stock dividend, stock split, or similar event that would otherwise result in reducing the conversion right is not a distribution on preferred stock.)

The term "stock" includes rights to acquire stock and the term "shareholder" includes a holder of rights or convertible securities.

Money or Property Distributions

Most distributions are in money, but they may also be in stock or other property. For this purpose, "property" generally does not include stock in the corporation or rights to acquire this stock. However, see Distributions of Stock or Stock Rights, later.

A corporation generally does not recognize a gain or loss on the distributions covered by the rules in this section. However, see Gain from property distributions below.

Gain from property distributions

A corporation will recognize a gain on the distribution of property to a shareholder if the FMV of the property is more than its adjusted basis.

This is generally the same treatment the corporation would receive if the property were sold.

However, for this purpose, the FMV of the property is the greater of the following amounts.

- The actual FMV.
- The amount of any liabilities the shareholder assumed in connection with the distribution of the property.

If the property was depreciable or amortizable, the corporation may have to treat all or part of the gain as ordinary income from depreciation recapture. For more information on depreciation recapture and the sale of business property, see Pub. 544.

DIVIDEND REINVESTMENT PLANS (DRIP)

DRIP is a type of Direct Investment Plan, instead of buying shares on the stock market, individuals can purchase shares directly to the company.

Dividends automatically go towards purchasing additional shares either as a regular basis or one time purchase.

DRIPS are like mutual funds, beneficial for investors starting with very little capital.

With very little investment, individuals can purchase stocks in small quantities with little or no fees. When they purchase, they own the stock of one company.

Individuals can invest at their own pace. Enable individuals to make additional investments It also eliminates the middleman (Broker) since individuals purchase stocks directly from the company. The movement of the market has very little effect since individuals build their wealth slowly and surely. Every penny in dividends is automatically reinvested so that individuals will purchase additional shares in the company.

MUTUAL FUND DISTRIBUTIONS

A mutual fund is a regulated investment company that pools funds of investors allowing them to take advantage of a diversity of investments and professional asset management.

Individuals own shares in the mutual fund but the fund owns capital assets, such as shares of stock, corporate bonds, government obligations, etc. One of the ways the fund makes money for the investors is to sell these assets at a gain.

If the mutual fund holds the capital asset for more than one year, the nature of the income is capital gain, and the mutual fund passes it on as a capital gain distribution. These capital gain distributions are usually paid to the investors or credited to the mutual fund account, and are considered income to the investors. Form 1099-DIV, Dividends and Distributions distinguishes capital gain distributions from other types of income, such as ordinary dividends.

Consider capital gain distributions as long-term capital gains no matter how long the shares are owned in the mutual fund.

Capital Gain Distributions

Regulated investment companies (RICs) (mutual funds, exchange traded funds, money market funds, etc.) and real estate investment trusts (REITs) may pay capital gain distributions.

Capital gain distributions are always reported as long-term capital gains. Individuals must also report any undistributed capital gain that RICs or REITs have designated in a written notice.

They report these undistributed capital gains to the individuals on Form 2439, Notice to Shareholder of Undistributed Long-Term Capital Gains (PDF).

For information on how to report qualifying dividends and capital gain distributions, refer to the Instructions for Form 1040 and 1040-SR (PDF).

Return of principal payments affects Mutual Funds

The return of principal payments is often called either a return of capital or a non dividend distribution.

As a return of the original investment (cost), it reduces the basis. However, the basis can't be adjusted below zero.

This information may be reported to the individual on a Form 1099-DIV, Dividends and Distributions in box 3.

Once the basis is adjusted to zero, report any additional returns or distributions (other than dividend distributions) on Schedule D (Form 1040 or 1040- SR), Capital Gains and Losses and Form 8949, Sales and Other Dispositions of Capital Assets.

How to compute the average basis of Mutual Funds

To figure the gain or loss using an average basis, individuals must have acquired the shares at various times and prices.

To calculate average basis:

- Add up the cost of all the shares owned in the mutual fund.
- Divide that result by the total number of shares owned. This gives the average amount per share.
- Multiply the average per share by the number of shares sold.

Individuals may no longer use the double-category method for figuring the average basis. If they were using that method for shares acquired before April 1, 2011 and they sell, exchange, or otherwise dispose of those shares on or after April 1, 2011, those investors must figure the average basis of those shares by averaging together all identical shares in the account on April 1, 2011, without regard for the holding period.

If the investors wish to use the average basis to figure the gain on the sale of mutual fund shares, they must elect to do so.

To choose the election, there are two separate processes for making the election for average basis method for covered and non covered securities.

CONSTRUCTIVE DISTRIBUTIONS

The following sections discuss transactions that may be treated as distributions:

1. **Below-market loans**
    a. If a corporation gives a shareholder a loan on which no interest is charged or on which interest is charged at a rate below the applicable federal rate, the interest not charged may be treated as a distribution to the shareholder.
2. **Corporation cancels shareholder's debt**
    a. If a corporation cancels a shareholder's debt without repayment by the shareholder, the amount canceled is treated as a distribution to the shareholder.
3. **Transfers of property to shareholders for less than FMV**
    a. A sale or exchange of property by a corporation to a shareholder may be treated as a distribution to the shareholder.
    b. For a shareholder who is not a corporation, if the FMV of the property on the date of the sale or exchange exceeds the price paid by the shareholder, the excess may be treated as a distribution to the shareholder.
4. **Unreasonable rents**
    a. If a corporation rents property from a shareholder and the rent is unreasonably more than the shareholder would charge to a stranger for use of the same property, the excessive part of the rent may be treated as a distribution to the shareholder.
5. **Unreasonable salaries**
    a. If a corporation pays an employee who is also a shareholder a salary that is unreasonably high considering the services actually performed by the shareholder-employee, the excessive part of the salary may be treated as a distribution to the shareholder-employee.

POP QUIZ & ANSWER SHEET

INVESTMENT INCOME & EXPENSES

POP QUIZ

Test your knowledge on *Investment Income & Expenses* by answering the questions below. The answer sheet may be found at the end of the Pop Quiz.

Q1: Which of the following is considered as interest income?

A. It is the amount paid to an individual for lending its money or letting another individual use its funds.

B. It is the amount earned by an investor wherein he placed his money in an investment or project.

C. It is the penalties paid by customers on overdue accounts receivable.

D. All of the Above

Q2: Taxpayer A has $85,000 in wage income and $2800 in municipal bond interest that was reported to him on Form 1099-INT. How much income will Taxpayer A be taxed on their tax return?

A. $85,000

B. $87,800

C. $82,800

D. $82,200

Q3: Qualified Dividends are reported on which of the following forms?

A. 1099-NEC

B. 1099-INT

C. 1099-DIV

D. 1099-MISC

Q4: The examples below are all tax-exempt interest, except:

A. Interest on private activity bonds (other than certain bonds for tribal manufacturing facilities).

B. Interest on a debt evidenced only by an ordinary written agreement of purchase and sale

C. Interest paid by an insurer on default by the state or political subdivision.

D. Bonds issued after 1982 by an Indian tribal government are treated as issued by a state.

Q5: Taxpayer A received $100 for opening up a new checking account with her local bank. What form is used to report this transaction? Is this considered taxable or non-taxable income to Taxpayer A?

A. 1099-NEC, Non-Taxable Income
B. 1099-INT, Taxable Income
C. 1099-INT, Non-Taxable Income
D. 1099-MISC, Taxable Income

Q6: Taxpayer A receives 1000 shares as a stock dividend from Corporation B that can be sold after three years of employment. The stock's value is $10 per share. How much must Taxpayer A report as taxable income if any on their tax return?

A. $10,000
B. $1,000
C. $0
D. $10

Q7: Capital gain distributions from a mutual fund are always treated as ___?

A. Short Term Capital Gains
B. Long Term Capital Gains
C. Dividend Reinvestment Plans (DRIP)
D. Taxpayers Basis

Q8: Taxpayer A is using educational savings bonds to help pay for college expenses. Which of the following is a "qualified expense" for educational savings bond exclusion?

A. Required Textbooks
B. Room and Board
C. College Tuition
D. Transportation

Q9: The following are the purpose of Education Savings bond, except:

A. It allows taxpayers to exempt some or all of the interest earned upon redemption of eligible savings bonds from their annual gross income.
B. It is used for tuition associated expenses.
C. It is used to pay for textbooks, room and board, or sports programs.
D. It is used for lab fees.

Q10: It refers to any dispersal of a company earnings to shareholders from stocks or mutual funds you own.

A. Dividend Income
B. Stock Options
C. Bartering Income
D. Business Income

ANSWER SHEET

1. Answer is D – All of the Above

2. Answer is A – $85,000

3. Answer is C – 1099-DIV

4. Answer is A – Interest on private activity bonds (other than certain bonds for tribal manufacturing facilities).

5. Answer is B – 1099-INT, Taxable Income

6. Answer is C – $0

7. Answer is B – Long Term Capital Gains

8. Answer is C – College Tuition

9. Answer is C – It is used to pay for textbooks, room and board, or sports programs.

10. Answer is A – Dividend Income

OTHER TAXABLE INCOME

OVERVIEW

Other Income is generally taxable income that is not common income. It is reported on Line 8 of Schedule 1.

Self-employment income is not reported as Other Income. Even if your clients get a 1099-MISC or 1099-NEC in the mail, make sure you don't confuse self-employment income with Other Income.

Non-taxable income is also not considered Other Income. Income that falls into the category of Other Income is always taxable.

TAXABLE RECOVERIES

If a deduction for medical expenses, mortgage interest, casualty and theft losses, or other deductible costs and later receive money back from an insurance company, a lawsuit, a bank, or other source, these must be reported as an income.

The amount of income is figured under the "tax benefit rule." This means you pick up the income to the extent that the original deduction gave the individual a tax benefit. As in the case of a refund of state and local income tax, if the individual didn't itemize, then the insurance recovery isn't taxable. But if the individual did itemize, you must figure the portion of the recovery that represents a tax benefit to the individual.

If an interest on a recovery is received, the interest is reported separately as interest income.

ALIMONY RECEIVED

For a divorce or separation instrument entered prior to 2019, alimony received is reported as taxable income, and the person making the alimony payment may claim a deduction in the year of payment.

For a divorce or separation instrument entered after 2018, including modifications, alimony received is not reported as taxable income, and the person making the alimony payment may not deduct it in the year paid.

Alimony received is entered on Form 1040, Schedule 1, line 2a.

Payments are alimony if ALL the following are true:

- Payments are required by a divorce or separation instrument.

- Payer and recipient spouse do not file a joint return.
- Payment is in cash, check, or money order.
- Payment is not designated in the instrument as "not alimony."
- Divorced and legally separated spouses are not members of the same household when payment is made.
- Payments are not required after the death of the recipient spouse.
- Payment is not treated as child support.

GOVERNMENT BENEFITS

- Unemployment benefits are fully taxable as regular income.
- Disaster relief payments under the disaster relief and emergency assistance act can't be included in income if they're to help meet necessary expenses for medical, dental, transportation, personal property or funeral expenses.
- Medicare – the costs for medical care under Medicare are tax free, and the premiums are tax deductible (if deductions are itemized).
- Jury duty pay is taxable.
- Food stamps are not taxable.

SOCIAL SECURITY INCOME

If taxpayers receive Social Security benefits, they may have to pay federal income tax on part of those benefits. Below are the base amounts when social security is NOT taxable, however if a client has earned income above the base amounts a portion of their social security will become taxable.

Below the base amount, your Social Security benefits are not taxable. Between the base and maximum amount, your Social Security income is taxable up to 50%. Above the maximum amount, your Social Security benefits are taxable up to 85%.

Base Amounts include:

- $25,000 base and maximum of $34,000 if the individual is single, head of household, or qualifying widow(er);
- $32,000 if the individual is married filing jointly; or
- $0 if the individual is married filing separately and lived with his or her spouse at any time during 2021.

OTHER INCOME

Individuals can receive income in the form of money, property, or services. This section discusses many kinds of income that are taxable or nontaxable. It includes discussions on employee wages and fringe benefits, and income from bartering, partnerships, S corporations, and royalties. The information on this page should not be construed as all-inclusive.

Generally, an amount included in the income is taxable unless it is specifically exempted by law. Income that is taxable must be reported on the return and is subject to tax. Income that is nontaxable may have to be shown on the tax return but is not taxable.

A list is available in Publication 525, Taxable and Nontaxable Income.

The IRS requires you to declare all income on the return. This can include:
- Wages
- Salaries
- Commissions
- Unemployment compensation
- Strike pay
- Rental income
- Alimony (for divorce decrees finalized before 2019)
- Royalty payments
- Stock options, dividends, and interest
- Self-employment income

Income from Fringe Benefits

If individuals receive fringe benefits for rendered services, they are usually considered taxable income, even if someone else receives them, such as the individuals' spouse. These taxable benefits and perks may include:
- A company-paid off-site gym membership
- A company vehicle for personal use
- Holiday gifts in the form of cash or gift certificates from the employer
- A certain portion of employer-paid dependent care
- Company-paid tuition fees over a certain amount
- Company-paid financial counseling fees
- Employer-paid group life insurance over a certain amount

Miscellaneous income
- Income that may not be readily identified as taxable but generally must be included on the tax return includes:
- Employer contributions to an unqualified retirement plan
- The fair-market value of property received for the services
- Disability retirement payments from an employer-paid plan
- Money and income from offshore accounts
- The remaining amount of a debt or loan that is canceled or forgive

GAMBLING WINNINGS

A payer is required to issue the taxpayer a Form W-2G, Certain Gambling Winnings if he or she receives certain gambling winnings or have any gambling winnings subject to federal income tax withholding.

Taxpayers must report all gambling winnings as "Other Income" on Form 1040 or Form 1040-SR (use Schedule 1 (Form 1040 or 1040-SR), including winnings that aren't reported on a Form W-2G.

When individuals have gambling winnings, they may be required to pay an estimated tax on that additional income. For more information on withholding on gambling winnings, refer to Publication 505, Tax Withholding and Estimated Tax.

CANCELLATION OF DEBT INCOME

In general, if individuals have cancellation of debt income because the debt is canceled, forgiven, or discharged for less than the amount that must be paid, the amount of the canceled debt is taxable and individuals must report the canceled debt on their tax return for the year the cancellation occurs.

The canceled debt isn't taxable, however, if the law specifically allows individuals to exclude it from gross income.

Forms

After a debt is canceled, the creditor may send a Form 1099-C, Cancellation of Debt.

Report any taxable amount of a canceled debt as ordinary income from the cancellation of debt on Form 1040, U.S. Individual Income Tax Return (PDF), Form 1040-SR, U.S. Tax Return for Seniors (PDF) or Form 1040-NR, U.S. Nonresident Alien Income Tax Return as "other income" if the debt is a nonbusiness debt, or on an applicable schedule if the debt is a business debt.

Example:

Matt has bought a boat for personal use for $20,000, paying $2,000 down and signing a recourse note for $18,000.

After paying down $4,000 on the note, he is no longer able to make payments. The boat dealer repossesses the boat, which is now worth $11,000.

He will have ordinary income from cancellation of debt of $3,000 ($14,000 remaining debt owed minus $11,000 FMV of boat).
He will have a $9,000 loss on disposition of the boat, the difference between the boat's FMV of $11,000 (the amount realized on repossession) minus $20,000 (the adjusted basis in the boat).

The facts are the same except that he signed a non-recourse note when buying the boat. When the dealer repossesses the boat, Matt will have a loss of $6,000, the difference between the $14,000 amount realized (the face amount of the remaining debt) and $20,000 (the adjusted basis in the boat). Matt has no ordinary income from cancellation of the debt.

Exclusions from Gross Income:

- Debt canceled in a Title 11 bankruptcy case
- Debt canceled to the extent insolvent
- Cancellation of qualified farm indebtedness
- Cancellation of qualified real property business indebtedness
- Cancellation of qualified principal residence indebtedness that is discharged subject to an arrangement that is entered into and evidenced in writing before January 1, 2021.

NON-TAXABLE CANCELED DEBT

Exceptions to Cancellation of Debt Income:

- Amounts canceled as gifts, bequests, devises, or inheritances
- Certain qualified student loans canceled under the loan provisions that the loans would be canceled if you work for a certain period of time in certain professions for a broad class of employers
- Certain other education loan repayment or loan forgiveness programs to help provide health services in certain areas.
- Amounts of canceled debt that would be deductible if you, as a cash basis taxpayer, paid it
- A qualified purchase price reduction given by the seller of property to the buyer
- Amounts from student loans discharged on the account of death or total and permanent disability of the student.

Amounts that meet the requirements for any of the following exclusions aren't included in income, even though they're cancellation of debt income.

CANCELLATION OF STUDENT LOANS

1099 C is a tax document that outlines how much of the debt was forgiven so the taxpayer can report it on the taxes. Similar to a W-2, the taxpayer and the IRS will receive a 1099-C in the mail for the year in which the debt was canceled.

When Do You Pay Taxes on Forgiven Student Loan Debt?

Only programs that require applicants to work in public service or high need areas as teachers, lawyers, or medical professionals offer tax-free assistance. This includes the popular Public Service Loan Forgiveness, as well as Teacher Loan Forgiveness and the National Health Service Corps Loan Repayment Program. There are many state programs that provide similar student loan forgiveness.

How Will Forgiveness Affect The Taxes?

The 1099-C will report how much student debt was forgiven. First, check this amount against the records. If it's wrong, contact the creditor, whose contact info will be provided in the form.

On the form, box 2 shows the amount of debt discharged — you'll need to put that in the "Other income" line on the 1040 tax form. That amount will essentially be added to the adjusted gross income on the taxes and will be taxed as income.

The federal government counts any canceled debt as a lump sum of money handed to taxpayers to pay off the rest of the debt.

What To Do If Extra Taxes Cannot Be Paid?

If taxpayers applied for student loan forgiveness because they couldn't pay off their loan, it's likely they won't be able to pay the taxes on the debt that was forgiven. The IRS usually expects to receive those taxes all at once.

Alternatively individuals may qualify for an installment agreement to pay the tax debt off over a specific period of time.

HOBBY INCOME

Taxpayers who make money from a hobby must report that income on their tax return.

If someone has a business, they operate the business to make a profit. In contrast, people engage in a hobby for sport or recreation, not to make a profit. Taxpayers should consider nine factors when determining whether their activity is a business or a hobby. They should base their determination on all the facts and circumstances of their activity.

If a taxpayer receives income for an activity that they don't carry out to make a profit, the expenses they pay for the activity are miscellaneous itemized deductions and can no longer be deducted. The taxpayer must still report the income they receive on Schedule 1, Form 1040, line 21.

COURT AWARDS AND DAMAGES

To determine if settlement amounts individuals receive by compromise or judgment must be included in the income, individuals must consider the item that the settlement replaces. The character of the income as ordinary income or capital gain depends on the nature of the underlying claim. Include the following as ordinary income.

Court Awards and Damages Ordinary Income:

- Interest on any award.
- Compensation for lost wages or lost profits in most cases.

- Punitive damages, in most cases. It does not matter if they relate to a physical injury or physical sickness.
- Amounts received in settlement of pension rights (if the taxpayer did not contribute to the plan).
- Damages for:
    - Patent or copyright infringement,
    - Breach of contract, or
    - Interference with business operations.
- Back pay and damages for emotional distress received to satisfy a claim under Title VII of the Civil Rights Act of 1964.
- Attorney fees and costs (including contingent fees) where the underlying recovery is included in gross income.

- Attorney fees and costs relating to whistleblower awards where the underlying recovery is included in gross income.

Court Awards and Damages Excluded from income:

The Internal Revenue Service has consistently held that compensatory damages, including lost wages, received on account of a personal physical injury are excludable from gross income with the exception of punitive damages.

Example:

Assume that a taxpayer is in an automobile accident, is injured, and as a result of that injury suffers:

- medical expenses
- lost wages, and
- pain, suffering, and emotional distress that cannot be measured with precision.
- If the taxpayer settles a resulting lawsuit for $30,000 (and if the taxpayer has not previously deducted her medical expenses, the entire $30,000 would be excludable under § 104(a)(2).
- The medical expenses for injuries arising out of the accident clearly constitute damages received "on account of personal injuries."
- Similarly, the portion of the settlement intended to compensate for pain and suffering constitutes damages "on account of personal injury.
- Finally, the recovery for lost wages is also excludable as being "on account of personal injuries," as long as the lost wages resulted from time in which the taxpayer was out of work as a result of her injuries

PRIZES & AWARDS

Generally, if an individual accepts a prize or award, he or she must include it as income. Where the income is reported on the tax return depends on why the individual receives the prize or award.

If an individual receives the prize or award in the capacity as an employee, the income should be included with the W-2 wages.

Employee achievement awards of tangible personal property, like a watch or trophy, for length of service or safety achievement are not usually taxable. However, the non-taxable amount is limited to the employer's cost and can't be more than $1,600 ($400 for awards that aren't qualified plan awards) for all awards received during the year.

Awards of cash, cash equivalents, vacations, meals, lodging, tickets to an event, stocks or other securities cannot be excluded from the income under this rule and may be taxable.

The exclusion doesn't apply to the following awards.

- A length-of-service award if it's received for less than 5 years of service or if another length-of-service award is received during the year or the previous 4 years.
- A safety achievement award if the individual is a manager, administrator, clerical employee, or other professional employee or if more than 10% of eligible employees previously received safety achievement awards during the year.
- The fair market value should be used for non-cash prizes and awards. Individuals should receive Form 1099-MISC they received prizes and awards of at least $600 though they may still have to report the prizes and awards won even if they did not receive a 1099-MISC. If individuals received the prize or award for services performed as a contractor or non-employee, the income should be reported as part of the Schedule C.

EDUCATIONAL ASSISTANCE

The educational assistance can be for a primary or secondary school, a college or university, or a vocational school.

- Scholarships;
- Fellowship grants;
- Need-based education grants, such as a Pell grant; and
- Qualified tuition reductions

Many types of educational assistance are tax free if they meet the requirements discussed here.

Types of Educational Assistance:

Scholarships and Fellowship

- A scholarship is generally an amount paid or allowed to, or for the benefit of, a student (whether an undergraduate or a graduate) at an educational institution to aid in the pursuit of his or her studies.

- A fellowship grant is generally an amount paid for the benefit of an individual to aid in the pursuit of study or research.
- A scholarship or fellowship grant is tax free (excludable from gross income) only if the taxpayer is a candidate for a degree at an eligible educational institution

A scholarship or fellowship grant is tax free only to the extent:

- It doesn't exceed the qualified education expenses;
- It isn't designated or earmarked for other purposes (such as room and board), and doesn't require (by its terms) that it can't be used for qualified education expenses; and
- It doesn't represent payment for teaching, research, or other services required as a condition for receiving the scholarship. For exceptions, see Payment for services, later

Example:

John receives a scholarship of $2,500. The scholarship wasn't received under any of the exceptions mentioned above. As a condition for receiving the scholarship, John must serve as a part-time teaching assistant. Of the $2,500 scholarship, $1,000 represents payment for teaching. The provider of the scholarship gives him a Form W-2 showing $1,000 as income. The qualified education expenses were at least $1,500. Assuming that all other conditions are met, the most he can exclude from his gross income is $1,500. The $1,000 received for teaching must be included in his gross income.

Other Types of Educational Assistance

Fulbright Grants

A Fulbright grant is generally treated as a scholarship or fellowship grant in figuring how much of the grant is tax free.

Pell Grants and Other Title IV Need-Based Education Grants

These need-based grants are treated as scholarships for purposes of determining their tax treatment. They are tax free to the extent used for qualified education expenses during the period for which a grant is awarded.

Veterans' Benefits

Payments received for education, training, or subsistence under any law administered by the Department of Veterans Affairs (VA) are tax free. Don't include these payments as income on the federal tax return.

Qualified Tuition Reduction

If a person is allowed to study tuition free or for a reduced rate of tuition, he may not have to pay tax on this benefit. This is called a "tuition reduction." He doesn't have to include a qualified tuition reduction in the income. A tuition reduction is qualified only if a person receives it from, and uses it at, an eligible educational institution.

Individuals don't have to use the tuition reduction at the eligible educational institution from which they received it. In other words, if they work for an eligible educational institution and the institution arranges for them to take courses at another eligible educational institution without paying any tuition, they may not have to include the value of the free courses in their income.

Example:

Emily has returned to college and is receiving two education benefits under the latest GI Bill: (1) a $1,534 monthly basic housing allowance (BHA) that is directly deposited to her checking account, and (2) $3,840 paid directly to her college for tuition.

Neither of these benefits is taxable and she doesn't report them on her tax return. She also wants to claim an American opportunity credit on the return.

Her total tuition charges are $5,000. To figure the amount of credit, she must first subtract the $3,840 from the qualified education expenses because this payment under the GI Bill was required to be used for education expenses. She doesn't subtract any amount of the BHA because it was paid to her and its use wasn't restricted.

QUALIFIED TUITION PROGRAMS

A qualified tuition program (QTP), also referred to as a section 529 plan, is a program established and maintained by a state, or an agency or instrumentality of a state, that allows a contributor either to prepay a beneficiary's qualified higher education expenses at an eligible educational institution or to contribute to an account for paying those expenses. Eligible educational institutions can also establish and maintain QTPs but only to allow prepaying a beneficiary's qualified higher education expenses. Qualified higher education expenses include tuition, up to a total amount of $10,000 per year from all of the designated beneficiary's QTPs. It also includes expenses for fees, books, supplies, and equipment required for the participation in an apprenticeship program registered and certified with the Secretary of Labor and qualified education loan repayments in limited amounts.

An eligible educational institution is generally any college, university, vocational school, or other postsecondary educational institution eligible to participate in a student aid program administered by the Department of Education.

The benefits of establishing a QTP are:

- Earnings accumulate tax free while in the account.

- The beneficiary doesn't generally have to include the earnings from a QTP as income.
- Distributions aren't taxable when used to pay for qualified higher education expenses (including tuition at an elementary or secondary public, private, or religious school). However, if the amount of a distribution is greater than the beneficiary's qualified higher education expenses (including tuition at an elementary or secondary public, private, or religious school), a portion of the earnings is taxable.

Distributions:

Individuals should receive a Form 1099-Q from each of the programs from which they received a QTP distribution. The amount of the gross distribution (box 1) shown on each form will be divided between the earnings (box 2) and the basis or return of investment (box 3). Form 1099-Q should be made available by January 31, 2021.

COVERDELL EDUCATION SAVINGS ACCOUNT (ESA)

A Coverdell education savings account (Coverdell ESA) is a trust or custodial account set up in the United States solely for paying qualified education expenses for the designated beneficiary of the account. This benefit applies not only to qualified higher education expenses, but also to qualified elementary and secondary education expenses. There are certain requirements to set up a Coverdell ESA:

- When the account is established, the designated beneficiary must be under the age of 18 or be a special needs beneficiary.
- The account must be designated as a Coverdell ESA when it is created.
- The document creating and governing the account must be in writing, and it must meet certain requirements.

Contributions

Individuals may be able to contribute to a Coverdell ESA to finance the beneficiary's qualified education expenses. Contributions must be made in cash, and they're not deductible. Any individual whose modified adjusted gross income is under the limit set for a given tax year can make contributions.

Organizations, such as corporations and trusts can also contribute regardless of their adjusted gross income. Contributors must contribute by the due date of their tax return (not including extensions).

There's no limit to the number of accounts that can be established for a particular beneficiary; however, the total contribution to all accounts on behalf of a beneficiary in any year can't exceed $2,000.

Distributions

In general, the designated beneficiary of a Coverdell ESA can receive tax-free distributions to pay qualified education expenses. The distributions are tax-free to the extent the amount of the distributions doesn't exceed the beneficiary's qualified education expenses. If a distribution exceeds the beneficiary's qualified education expenses, a portion of the earnings is taxable to the beneficiary. Amounts remaining in the account must be distributed when the designated beneficiary reaches age 30, unless the beneficiary is a special needs beneficiary. Certain transfers to members of the beneficiary's family are permitted.

Individuals should receive a Form 1099-Q, Payments From Qualified Education Programs (Under Sections 529 and 530) from each of the Coverdell ESAs from which is received a distribution. Form 1099-Q should be made available by January 31, 2021.

MISCELLANEOUS OTHER INCOME

The money taxpayers dole out at their business doesn't just go toward employee wages. They might hire an independent contractor or attorney to do work for their company. Or, they might make rental payments for office space. When individuals make payments like these, they need to report them as miscellaneous income.

Miscellaneous income is any income received outside of typical employee wages. These payments are not reported on Form W-2.

File Form 1099-MISC for each person to whom you have paid during the year:

- At least $10 in royalties or broker payments in lieu of dividends or tax-exempt interest.
- At least $600 in:
  - Rents.
  - Prizes and awards.
  - Other income payments.
  - Medical and health care payments.
  - Crop insurance proceeds.
  - Cash payments for fish (or other aquatic life) you purchase from anyone engaged in the trade or business of catching fish.
  - Generally, the cash paid from a notional principal contract to an individual, partnership, or estate.
  - Payments to an attorney.
  - Any fishing boat proceeds.

In addition, use Form 1099-MISC to report that you made direct sales of at least $5,000 of consumer products to a buyer for resale anywhere other than a permanent retail establishment.

1099-NEC, Nonemployee Compensation

The PATH Act, accelerated the due date for filing Form 1099 that includes nonemployee compensation (NEC) from February 28 to January 31 and eliminated the automatic 30-day extension for forms that include NEC. Use form 1099-NEC to report nonemployee compensation.

POP QUIZ & ANSWER SHEET

OTHER TAXABLE INCOME

POP QUIZ

Test your knowledge on Other Taxable Income by answering the questions below. The answer sheet may be found at the end of the Pop Quiz.

Q1: Which of the following is considered as "Other Income"?
A. Self-Employment Income
B. Dividend Income
C. Gambling Winnings
D. Stock Distribution

Q2: The following payments are considered as alimony, except:
A. Payments treated as child support.
B. Payments are required by a divorce or separation instrument.
C. Payer and recipient spouse do not file a joint return.
D. Payment is not designated in the instrument as "not alimony."

Q3: The list below shows the requirements to set up a Coverdell Education Savings Account. Which of the requirements below are not true?
A. When the account is established, the designated beneficiary must be under the age of 21 or be a special needs beneficiary.
B. The account must be designated as a Coverdell ESA when it is created.
C. The document creating and governing the account must be in writing, and it must meet certain requirements.
D. Magi in 2021 must be below $190,000-$220,000 for joint fillers, or $95,000-$110,000 for all other filing statuses.

Q4: Which of the following court awards and damages is excluded from income?
A. Compensation for lost wages or profits.
B. Compensatory damages from personal physical injury.
C. Interest on any award.
D. Amounts received in settlement of pension rights (if you did not contribute to the plan).

Q5: What tax document outlines how much of your debt was forgiven so you can report it on your taxes?
A. 1099-C

B. 1099-MISC
C. 1099-NEC
D. 1099-D

Q6: Which of the following is not tax free?
A. Educational Assistance
B. Scholarship and Fellowship
C. Prizes and Awards
D. Tangible Employee Achievement Awards

Q7: A scholarship or fellowship grant is tax free only to the extent:
A. It exceeds your qualified education expenses.
B. It isn't designated or earmarked for other purposes (such as room and board).
C. It represents payment for teaching, research, or other services required as a condition for receiving the scholarship.
D. All of the above

Q8: Taxpayer A defaults on a non-recourse motorcycle loan that he purchased for $16,000 and has a FMV of $17,500. What is true of the lender?
A. The lender will issue a 1099-C Cancellation of Debt for $17,500 that the taxpayer must include as income
B. The lender will repo the motorcycle and send the Taxpayer $1500 as 1099-Interest Income because the FMV is more than what the taxpayer owes
C. The lender will issue a 1099-C Cancellation of Debt for $16,000 that must be included in the taxpayers income
D. The lender can repo the motorcycle but will not issue a 1099-C Cancellation of Debt because the FMV is more than what the taxpayer owes

Q9: State and local income tax refunds are reported as taxable income in the year received if the taxpayer:
A. Took the Standard Deduction
B. Itemized deductions in the prior year
C. Paid more than $1000 in taxes
D. Paid medical and dental expenses

Q10: All of the following Miscellaneous Other Income is taxable and reported on line 8 of Sch 1, except:
A. Jury Duty Pay that was turned over to the taxpayers employer and deducted as an adjust to income
B. Strike Benefits
C. Compensatory damages for personal physical injury
D. Fees paid by an estate to a personal representative

ANSWER SHEET

1. Answer is C – Gambling Winnings

2. Answer is A – Payments treated as child support.

3. Answer is A – When the account is established, the designated beneficiary must be under the age of 21 or be a special needs beneficiary.

4. Answer is B – Compensatory damages from personal physical injury.

5. Answer is A – 1099-C

6. Answer is C – Prizes and Awards

7. Answer is B – It isn't designated or earmarked for other purposes (such as room and board).

8. Answer is D – The lender can repo the motorcycle but will not issue a 1099-C Cancellation of Debt because the FMV is more than what the taxpayer owes.

9. Answer is B – Itemized deductions in the prior year

10. Answer is C – Compensatory damages for personal physical injury

ADJUSTMENTS TO GROSS INCOME

OVERVIEW

Adjusted Gross Income (AGI) is defined as gross income minus adjustments to income.

Gross income includes the wages, dividends, capital gains, business income, retirement distributions as well as other income.

Adjustments to Income include such items as Educator expenses, Student loan interest, Alimony payments or contributions to a retirement account.

The AGI will never be more than the Gross Total Income on the return and, in some cases, may be lower.

Above-the-line deductions

Are expenses that are deducted to calculate an individual's adjusted gross income (AGI). These differ from itemized deductions, which are the dollar amounts deducted from the determined AGI.

The following examples represent above-the-line expenses:

Domestic Production Activities, Retirement Plan Contributions, HSA, MSA Contributions, Health Insurance premiums, Self-Employed Business Expenses & SE Tax, Alimony, Educator Expenses, Early Withdrawal Penalties, Student Loan Interest, Tuition and Fees

Below-the-line deductions (Itemized Deductions)

Include any deduction reported on a line that comes after the AGI calculation on a return.

While both deductions ultimately reduce your taxable income, some can have a more favorable impact on your tax bill than others. In most cases, above-the-line deductions are the better choice for the following reasons.

- You can take above-the-line deductions even if you don't itemize
- Above-the-line deductions reduce your adjusted gross income

(SCHEDULE 1) COMMON ADJUSTMENTS TO GROSS INCOME

To identify the adjustments to income that taxpayers can claim, you will need to ask the taxpayers if they had the types of expenses listed on the Adjustments to Income section of Schedule 1. Review the taxpayers' answers on their intake and interview sheet.

During the tax year did the taxpayer or spouse:

- Pay qualified educator expenses?
- Receive income from self-employment?
- Have self-employed health insurance?
- Pay a penalty for early withdrawal of savings?
- Pay alimony?
- Make contributions to a traditional IRA?
- Contribute to a health savings account?
- Pay student loan interest?
- Receive income from jury duty that was turned over to an employer?

LINE 11: EDUCATOR EXPENSE DEDUCTION

If the taxpayer is an eligible educator, he or she can deduct up to $250 ($500 if married filing jointly and both spouses are eligible educators, but not more than $250 each) of unreimbursed educator expenses. Qualified expenses are amounts paid or incurred for participation in professional development courses, books, supplies, computer equipment (including related software and services), other equipment, and supplementary materials that a taxpayer uses in the classroom.

For courses in health or physical education, the expenses for supplies must be for athletic supplies.

Teachers can make this deduction even if they do not itemize

Individuals are considered eligible educators if, for the tax year they are a kindergarten through grade 12 teacher, instructor, counselor, principal or aide for at least 900 hours a school year in a school that provides elementary or secondary education (college educators do not qualify)

Note: Sometimes called the "educator expense deduction" or "teacher credit".

Covid Note: Educator expenses include personal protective equipment (ppe) such as masks, hand sanitizer purchased after March 12, 2020 to help prevent the spread of COVID-19.

LINE 12: CERTAIN BUSINESS EXPENSES OF RESERVISTS, PERFORMING ARTISTS, AND FEE-BASIS GOVERNMENT OFFICIALS

Individuals can no longer claim any miscellaneous itemized deductions that are subject to the 2% of adjusted gross income limitation, including unreimbursed employee expenses. However, taxpayers may be able to deduct certain unreimbursed employee business expenses if they fall into one of the following categories of employment listed:

- Armed Forces reservists.
- Qualified performing artists.
- Fee-basis state or local government officials.
- Employees with impairment-related work expenses.

An ordinary expense is one that is common and accepted in the field of trade, business, or profession.

A necessary expense is one that is helpful and appropriate for the business. An expense doesn't have to be required to be considered necessary.

Armed Forces reservist (member of a reserve component).

Members of a reserve component of the Armed Forces of the United States that are in the Army, Navy, Marine Corps, Air Force, or Coast Guard Reserve; the Army National Guard of the United States; or the Reserve Corps of the Public Health Service.

Armed Forces reservists traveling more than 100 miles from home.

Members of the reserved component of the Armed Forces of the United States and individuals who travel more than 100 miles away from home in connection with the performance of services as a member of the reserves, individuals can deduct some of the travel expenses as an adjustment to gross income. The amount of expenses that can be deducted as an adjustment to gross income is limited to the regular federal per diem rate (for lodging, meals, and incidental expenses) and the standard mileage rate (for car expenses) plus any parking fees, ferry fees, and tolls. The balance, if any, is reported on Schedule A.

Qualified performing artist

Individuals are considered qualified performing artist if they:

- Performed services in the performing arts as an employee for at least two employers during the tax year,
- Received from at least two of the employers wages of $200 or more per employer,
- Had allowable business expenses attributable to the performing arts of more than 10% of gross income from the performing arts, and
- Had adjusted gross income of $16,000 or less before deducting expenses as a performing artist.

If the individuals are a qualified performing artist, they can deduct the employee's business expenses as an adjustment to income rather than as a miscellaneous itemized deduction. For example, musicians and entertainers can deduct the cost of theatrical clothing and accessories that aren't suitable for everyday wear. If the taxpayer is an employee, complete Form 2106.

Example:

Elsie performs around the world with the organization Shen Yun. She works exclusively with the performing arts company year- round. Elsie earns $50,000 per year performing. She must pay for her own performing arts coach and supplies which costs her $7,500 per year. Her AGI is $23,000..

How much of the $7,500 Elsie paid out of pocket can she deduct on her taxes?

Elsie Shi can not deduct the $7,500 on her taxes.

Here's why:

- She only worked for one employer; she must have had to work for at least two employers.
- She DID have expenses over 10% of her adjusted gross income however,
- Her AGI was more than the allowable $16,000 before deducting expenses.

Elsie simply does not meet all the QUALIFIED PERFORMING ARTIST requirements therefore she can not deduct any of the $7,500 as employee business expenses.

Fee-basis state or local government official

Individuals are considered qualifying fee-basis officials if they are employed by a state or political subdivision of a state and are compensated, in whole or in part, on a fee basis.

If they are a fee-basis official, taxpayers can claim the expenses in performing services in that job as an adjustment to income rather than as a miscellaneous itemized deduction.

Employee with impairment-related work expenses.

Impairment-related work expenses are the allowable expenses of an individual with physical or mental disabilities for attendant care at his or her place of employment. They also include other expenses in connection with the place of employment that enable the employee to work.

If individuals have a physical or mental disability that limits their being employed, or substantially limits one or more of their major life activities, such as performing manual tasks, walking, speaking, breathing, learning, and working, individuals can deduct the impairment-related work expenses.

Impairment-related work expenses are ordinary and necessary business expenses for attendant care services at the place of work and other expenses in connection with the place of work that are necessary for the individual to be able to work.

Unreimbursed employee expenses for individuals in these categories of employment are deducted as adjustments to gross income. Qualified employees listed in one of the categories above must complete Form 2106 to take the deduction. Certain qualified educator expenses are also deducted as an adjustment to gross income but they are not required to complete Form 2106.

Individuals can deduct only unreimbursed employee expenses that are:

- Paid or incurred during the tax year,
- For carrying on the trade or business of being an employee, and
- Ordinary and necessary.

LINE 13: HEALTH SAVINGS ACCOUNT DEDUCTION (HSAS)

A Health Savings Account (HSA) is a tax-exempt trust or custodial account that individuals can set up with a qualified HSA trustee to pay or reimburse certain medical expenses they incur.

No permission or authorization from the IRS is necessary to establish an HSA. Individuals can set up an HSA with a trustee. A qualified HSA trustee can be a bank, an insurance company, or anyone already approved by the IRS to be a trustee of individual retirement arrangements (IRAs) or Archer MSAs. The HSA can be established through a trustee that is different from the health plan provider.

To be an eligible individual and qualify for an HSA, individuals must meet the following requirements.

- Individuals need to be covered under a high deductible health plan (HDHP) on the first day of the month.
- Individuals cannot have any other health coverage except what is permitted under Other health coverage, later.
- Individuals cannot be enrolled in Medicare.
- Individuals cannot be claimed as a dependent on someone else's 2021 tax return.

The amount a taxpayer can contribute to an HSA depends on the type of HDHP coverage they have, age, the date they become an eligible individual, and the date they cease to be an eligible individual.

LINE 14: MOVING EXPENSES FOR MEMBERS OF THE ARMED FORCES

Individuals may be able to exclude from income the value of government-provided services and reimbursement. If the individuals are not reimbursed, they may be able to deduct expenses incurred when they moved.

To deduct moving expenses, individuals must be a member of the Armed Forces on active duty and, due to a military order, the move must be the result of a permanent change of station.

What constitutes a permanent change of station?

- A permanent change of station includes:
- A move from the home to the first post of active duty,
- A move from one permanent post of duty to another, and
- A move from the last post of duty to the home or to a nearer point in the United States. The move must occur within 1 year of ending the active duty or within the period allowed under the Joint Travel Regulations.

If the taxpayer is the spouse or dependent of a member of the Armed Forces who deserts, is imprisoned, or dies, a permanent change of station for him or her includes a move to:

- The member's place of enlistment or induction;
- The taxpayer's home, or the member's home of record; or
- A nearer point in the United States.

If the military moves the individuals to or from a different location than the member, the moves are treated as a single move to the new main job location.

If the individual moves because of a permanent change of station, he or she can deduct the reasonable unreimbursed expenses of moving for them and for members of the household.

A member of the household is anyone who has both the former home and the new home as his or her main home. It doesn't include a tenant or employee unless he or she can claim that person as a dependent on their tax return.

Individuals can deduct expenses (if not reimbursed or furnished in kind) for:

- Moving household goods and personal effects,
- Storing and insuring household goods and personal effects, and
- Travel.

How To Report Moving Expenses

Figure moving expense deductions on Form 3903. The Form 3903 instructions provide information on how to figure the deduction for qualified expenses that exceed the reimbursements and allowances (including dislocation allowances, temporary lodging expenses, temporary lodging allowances, or move-in housing allowances that are excluded from gross income).

If the individual qualifies to deduct expenses for more than one move, use a separate Form 3903 for each move.

Carry the moving expense deduction from Form(s) 3903, line 5, to Schedule 1 (Form 1040 or 1040-SR), line 13. For more information, see Form 3903 and its instructions.

LINE 15: DEDUCTIBLE PART OF SELF- EMPLOYMENT TAX

Individuals are considered self-employed for this purpose if they are sole proprietors (including independent contractors), a partner in a partnership (including a member of a multi-member limited liability company (LLC) that is treated as a partnership for federal tax purposes) or are otherwise in business for themselves.

The term sole proprietor also includes the member of a single member LLC that's disregarded for federal income tax purposes and a member of a qualified joint venture.

Individuals usually must pay self-employment tax if they had net earnings from self-employment of $400 or more. Generally, the amount subject to self-employment tax is 92.35% of the net earnings from self-employment.

You calculate net earnings by subtracting ordinary and necessary trade or business expenses from the gross income derived from the trade or business.

Individuals can be liable for paying self-employment tax even if they currently receive social security benefits. The law sets a maximum amount of net earnings subject to the social security tax.

This amount changes annually. All of the net earnings are subject to the Medicare tax.

LINE 16: SELF- EMPLOYED SEP, SIMPLE AND QUALIFIED PLANS

If a person is self-employed, he or she may qualify for a tax deduction for contributions made to a qualified retirement plan.

The person must have self-employment income to qualify. Self-employment income consists of net profits from Schedule C or Schedule F. The deduction is the total plan contributions that can be subtracted from the gross income on the federal income tax return. Limits apply to the amount deductible. Self-employed individuals can avoid examinations and additional assessments by making sure they qualify for the deduction.

The self-employed retirement plan deduction may not be allowable if:

- Form 1040, Schedule SE, Section A (if applicable), Line 4, is less than the amount on Form 1040, Line 28.
- Form 1040, Schedule SE, Section B (if applicable), Line 6, is less than the amount on Form 1040, Line 28.
- Form W-2 indicates an individual is a Statutory Employee and the amount in Box 1 is less than Form 1040, Line 28.

Simplified Employee Pension (SEP)

If individuals contribute to a SEP-IRA, they must make a special computation to figure the maximum deduction for these contributions.
When figuring the deduction for contributions made to the SEP-IRA, compensation is the net earnings from self-employment which takes into account both of the following deductions:

- Deduction for one-half of the self-employment tax.
- Deduction for contributions to the SEP-IRA.

Use the rate table or worksheets in chapter 5 of IRS Publication 560, "Retirement Plans for Small Business" for figuring the allowable contribution rate and tax deduction for the SEP-IRA plan contributions.

When to deduct contributions for a year depends on the tax year on which the SEP is maintained. If the SEP is maintained on a calendar year basis, deduct the yearly contributions on the tax return for the year within which the calendar year ends.

If individuals file a tax return and maintain the SEP using a fiscal year or short tax year, deduct contributions made for a year on the tax return for that year.

For example, a fiscal year taxpayer whose tax year ends June 30 and maintains a SEP on a calendar year basis. Deduct SEP contributions made for calendar year 2008 on the tax return for the tax year ending June 30, 2009.

The allowable deduction is reported on the Form 1040 Line 28.

SIMPLE Plan

Individuals can make salary deferrals (salary reduction contributions) of up to $13,500 to a SIMPLE IRA plan in 2021. If they are age 50 or over, they can contribute an additional $3,000 in catch-up contributions.

If individuals participate in more than one retirement plan that allows them to make salary deferrals (such as a 401(k) or a 403(b) plan), the total annual employee contributions to all the plans can't exceed the personal limit of $19,500 in 2021plus an additional $6,500 in 2021 if aged 50 or older. However, because the SIMPLE IRA plan limits the contributions to $12,500, plus an additional $3,000 catch-up contribution, this is the maximum amount that can be contributed to the SIMPLE IRA plan.

There are two basic kinds of qualified plans—defined contribution plans and defined benefit plans—and different rules apply to each. Individuals can have more than one qualified plan, but the contributions to all the plans must not total more than the overall limits

A defined contribution plan provides an individual account for each participant in the plan. It provides benefits to a participant largely based on the amount contributed to that participant's account. Benefits are also affected by any income, expenses, gains, losses, and forfeitures of other accounts that may be allocated to an account. A defined contribution plan can be either a profit-sharing plan or a money purchase pension plan.

- **Profit-sharing plan.** Although it is called a "profit-sharing plan," individuals don't actually have to make a business profit for the year in order to make a contribution. A profit-sharing plan can be set up to allow for discretionary employer contributions, meaning the amount contributed each year to the plan isn't fixed. An employer may even make no contribution to the plan for a given year. The plan must provide a definite formula for allocating the contribution among the participants and for distributing the accumulated funds to the employees after they reach a certain age, after a fixed number of years, or upon certain other occurrences. In general, individuals can be more flexible in making contributions to a profit-sharing plan than to a money purchase pension plan (discussed next) or a defined benefit plan.
- **Money purchase pension plan.** Contributions to a money purchase pension plan are fixed and aren't based on the business profits. For example, a money purchase pension plan may require that contributions be 10% of the participants' compensation without regard to whether individuals have profits (or the self-employed person has earned income)

The deduction for contributions to a defined contribution plan (profit-sharing plan or money purchase pension plan) can't be more than 25% of the compensation paid (or accrued) during the year to the eligible employees participating in the plan. If the individuals are self-employed, they must reduce this limit in figuring the deduction for contributions made for the account.

A defined benefit plan is any plan that isn't a defined contribution plan. Contributions to a defined benefit plan are based on what is needed to provide definitely determinable benefits to plan participants. Actuarial assumptions and computations are required to figure these contributions. Generally, individuals will need continuing professional help to have a defined benefit plan.

The deduction for contributions to a defined benefit plan is based on actuarial assumptions and computations. Consequently, an actuary must figure out the deduction limit.

LINE 17: SELF- EMPLOYED HEALTH INSURANCE DEDUCTION

Self-employed taxpayers who reported a net profit on Schedule C for the year may be able to deduct the cost of their health insurance paid as a deduction to their adjusted gross income. The insurance plan must be established under the trade or business and the deduction cannot be more than the earned income from that trade or business. If filing Schedule C, the policy can be either in the taxpayer's name, the spouse's name (if Married Filing Jointly), or in the name of the business.

Medicare premiums voluntarily paid to obtain insurance in the taxpayer's name that is similar to qualifying private health insurance can be used to figure the deduction. The spouse's Medicare premiums qualify for the deduction when Married Filing Jointly even though paid from the spouse's benefits. Include health, dental, vision, supplemental, limited coverage, and long-term care (LTC) premiums. LTC is limited to the deduction cap for Schedule A, based on age.

Self-employed taxpayers cannot deduct payments for medical insurance for any month in which they were eligible to participate in a health plan subsidized by their employer, a spouse's employer, or an employer of the taxpayer's dependent or child under age 27 at the end of the tax year. Taxpayers cannot deduct payments for a qualified long-term care insurance contract for any month in which they were eligible to participate in an employer- subsidized long-term care insurance plan.

For this purpose, health coverage can be for the taxpayer, spouse, dependents, or the taxpayer's child under the age of 27 even though the child is not the taxpayer's dependent. A child includes a son, daughter, stepchild, adopted child, or foster child.

The self-employed health insurance deduction is limited to the net self-employment profit shown on the return reduced by the deduction for one-half of the self-employment tax.

Carson is single and has his own business. During the year, he paid qualified health insurance premiums of $3,000. His Schedule C shows a profit of $5,500 and his self-employment tax deduction is $389 for a net of $5,111 ($5,500 – $389). The full $3,000 premium paid is deductible as self-employment health insurance because it is less than the net profit.

Self-employed taxpayers who purchased their coverage from the Marketplace and are eligible for the Premium Tax Credit are out of scope for the VITA/TCE program.

LINE 18: PENALTY ON EARLY WITHDRAWAL OF SAVINGS

Most retirement plan distributions are subject to income tax and may be subject to an additional 10% tax. Generally, the amounts an individual withdraws from an IRA or retirement plan before reaching age 59½ are called "early" or "premature" distributions. Individuals must pay an additional 10% early withdrawal tax unless an exception applies.

Taxpayers can adjust their income to deduct penalties they paid for withdrawing funds from a deferred interest account before maturity. Ask if the taxpayer and/or spouse made any early withdrawals during the tax year. If so, ask to see Form 1099-INT, Interest Income, or Form 1099-OID, Original Issue Discount, documenting the penalty. The penalty is reported on Form 1040, Schedule 1.

Example:

Gloria withdrew $5,000 early from a one-year, deferred interest certificate of deposit. She had to pay a penalty of three months' interest. She can claim this penalty amount as an adjustment to income.

LINE 19A: ALIMONY PAID

Pre-2019 Divorces

Alimony is a payment to a spouse or former spouse under a divorce or legal separation instrument. The payments do not have to be made directly to the ex-spouse. For example, payments made on behalf of the ex-spouse for expenses specified in the instrument, such as medical bills, housing costs, and other expenses can qualify as alimony. Alimony does not include child support or voluntary payments outside the instrument. The person paying alimony can subtract it as an adjustment to income; the person receiving alimony must treat it as income. A summary of the alimony requirements can be found in Tab E, Adjustments, in the Volunteer Resource Guide.

When you conduct the interview, ask if the taxpayer paid alimony under a divorce or separation instrument. If so, explain that you need the exact amount, as well as the Social Security number of the recipient, because the recipient must report the payment to the IRS as income and the two amounts must agree.

Post-2018

Divorces For divorce or separation agreement (or amendments) executed after 2018, the deduction for alimony payments and the inclusion of alimony in income are eliminated.

Example:

Anthony was divorced in 2017. Under his divorce instrument, he paid his ex-wife $8,000 during the tax year. As a favor, he also made $4,000 in payments to cover part of her vehicle lease so she could keep steady employment. He can take the $8,000 as an adjustment to income. He cannot count the lease payments because those were payments not required by the divorce instrument.

LINE 20: IRA DEDUCTION

Individual Retirement Arrangements (IRAs) are personal savings plans that offer tax advantages to set aside money for retirement.

Taxpayers may be able to deduct some or all of their contributions to the IRA (depending on circumstances).

Generally, amounts in an IRA, including earnings and gains, are not taxed until distributed.

Contributions may be eligible for the retirement savings contribution credit. Although contributions to a Roth IRA cannot be deducted, the taxpayer may be eligible for the retirement savings contribution credit, discussed in the lesson on Miscellaneous Credits.

Example:

George has a traditional IRA account and a Roth IRA account. During the tax year, George contributed $2,200 to his traditional IRA and $1,000 to his Roth IRA. The most George will be able to deduct is the $2,200 contribution to his traditional IRA

Eligibility Requirements for An IRA Contribution

The taxpayer, and the taxpayer's spouse if applicable, must meet these eligibility requirements in order to make an IRA contribution:

- Types of IRAs: Verify the types of IRAs to which the taxpayer and spouse contributed.
- Only contributions to traditional IRAs are deductible.
- Age limit: Taxpayers can contribute to a traditional IRA only if they are under 70½ years of age at the end of the tax year. Check the taxpayer's birth date (and spouse's if applicable) indicated on the intake and interview sheet. There is no age limit for Roth IRA contributions.
- Compensation: Individuals must have taxable compensation (i.e., wages, self-employment income, commissions, taxable alimony, or taxable scholarships or fellowships, but only if shown in box 1 of Form W-2).
- Time limits: Contributions must be made by the due date for filing the return, not including extensions. Verify with the taxpayer and spouse that they made the contribution(s) (or will make them) by the due date of the return.

How much can a taxpayer deduct for an IRA contribution?

Generally, individuals can deduct the lesser of:

- The contributions to the traditional IRA for the year, or
- The general limit reduced for Roth IRA contributions made for the same tax year.
- If taxpayers file a joint return, and one spouse's compensation is less than the other spouse's compensation, the most that can be contributed for that spouse is the lesser of:
    - The general limits, or
    - The total compensation includible in the gross income of both spouses for the year, reduced by:
        - Traditional IRA contributions for the spouse with the greater compensation
        - Any contribution for the year to a Roth IRA for the spouse with the greater compensation

In other words, as long as they file a joint return, married taxpayers' combined IRA contributions cannot exceed their combined compensation, and neither spouse can contribute more than the general IRA limit to their own IRA.

When can IRA contributions be deducted?

Deductions can be taken for contributions to traditional IRAs for returns that are in scope. The taxpayer's deduction for IRA contributions may be "phased out" (i.e., reduced or eliminated) depending on their income, filing status, and whether the taxpayer is covered by a retirement plan at work. The difference between the permitted contributions and the IRA deduction, if any, is the taxpayer's non-deductible contribution. Form 8606, Non-deductible IRAs, must be completed for any non-deductible traditional IRA contributions.

If taxpayers do not report non-deductible contributions, all of the contributions to a traditional IRA will be treated as having been deducted. This means all distributions will be taxed when withdrawn unless the taxpayer can show, with satisfactory evidence, that non- deductible contributions were made.

Example:

Thomas and Amber are married and are both over 50 years old.

Thomas earned $70,000 and Amber earned $1,500. During the tax year, Thomas contributed $3,500 to his traditional IRA and $2,000 to a Roth IRA, making his total contributions $5,500. To figure the maximum contribution to Amber's IRA, use a total compensation of $66,000 (i.e., $71,500 – $5,500). If Thomas and Amber file jointly, they can contribute up to the IRA limit to Amber's IRA even though her own compensation was just $1,500.

LINE 21: STUDENT LOAN INTEREST DEDUCTION

The student loan interest deduction is generally the smaller of $2,500 or the interest payments paid that year on a qualified student loan. This amount is gradually reduced (phased out) or eliminated based on the taxpayer's filing status and MAGI. Generally, student loan interest is paid during the year on a loan for qualified higher education expenses. The loan must meet all three of these conditions:

- It was for the taxpayer, the taxpayer's spouse, or a person who was the taxpayer's dependent when the loan was obtained
- The qualified higher education expenses were paid within a reasonable period of time before or after obtaining the loan
- It was for an eligible student

Interest does not qualify if the loan was from a related person, a qualified employer plan, or if the taxpayer is not legally liable for the loan.

What are the exceptions?

For purposes of the student loan interest deduction, the following are exceptions to the general rules for dependents:

- An individual can be a dependent even for someone that is the dependent of another taxpayer
- An individual can be a dependent even if the individual files a joint return with a spouse
- An individual can be the dependent even if the individual had gross income for the year that was equal to or more than the threshold amount for the year.

Where can I get the information?

If the taxpayer paid $600 or more in interest to a single lender, the taxpayer should receive Form 1098-E, Student Loan Interest Statement, or another statement from the lender showing the amount of interest paid. This information will assist you in completing the student loan interest deduction. The taxpayer should keep documentation of all qualified student loan interest paid during the tax year.

Line 22: Reserved For Future Use

This line is left blank.

Line 23: Archer MSA Deduction

Contributions to an MSA

- Contributions to an Archer MSA must be made in cash. You can't contribute stock or other property to an Archer MSA.

Who can contribute to my Archer MSA?

If you are an employee, your employer may make contributions to your Archer MSA. (You don't pay tax on these contributions.) If your employer doesn't make contributions to your Archer MSA, or you are self-employed, you can make your own contributions to your Archer MSA. You and your employer can't make contributions to your Archer MSA in the same year. You don't have to make contributions to your Archer MSA every year.

Reporting Contributions on Your Return

Report all contributions to your Archer MSA on Form 8853 and file it with your Form 1040, 1040-SR, or 1040-NR. You should include all contributions you or your employer made for 2021, including those made from January 1, 2022, through April 15, 2022, that are designated for 2021.

Line 24: Other Adjustments

a. Jury duty pay

b. Deductible expenses related to income reported on line 8k from the rental of personal property engaged in for profit

c. Nontaxable amount of the value of Olympic and Paralympic medals and USOC prize money reported on line 8

d. Reforestation amortization and expenses

e. Repayment of supplemental unemployment benefits under the Trade Act of 1974

f. Contributions to section 501(c)(18)(D) pension plans

g. Contributions by certain chaplains to section 403(b) plans

h. Attorney fees and court costs for actions involving certain unlawful discrimination claims

i. Attorney fees and court costs for actions involving certain unlawful discrimination claims

j. Housing deduction from Form 2555

k. Excess deductions of section 67(e) expenses from Schedule

K-1

z. Other adjustments. List type and amount

POP QUIZ & ANSWER SHEET

ADJUSTMENTS TO GROSS INCOME

POP QUIZ

Test your knowledge on Adjustments to Gross Income by answering the questions below. The answer sheet may be found at the end of the Pop Quiz.

Q1: Taxpayer A is a part time elementary teacher who worked 827 hours during the year and had qualified educator expenses of $450. How much could Taxpayer A claim as an Educator Expense Deduction on Line 10, Sch 1?

A. $250
B. $450
C. $0
D. $300

Q2: You're an eligible educator if:

A. For the tax year you're a kindergarten through grade 12 teacher, instructor, counselor, principal or aide for at least 800 hours a school year in a school that provides elementary or secondary education as determined under state law.
B. For the tax year you're a kindergarten through grade 12 teacher, instructor, counselor, principal or aide for at least 900 hours a school year in a school that provides elementary or secondary education as determined under state law.
C. For the tax year you're a kindergarten through grade 12 teacher, instructor, counselor, principal or aide for at least 1000 hours a school year in a school that provides elementary or secondary education as determined under state law.
D. For the tax year you're a kindergarten through grade 12 teacher, instructor, counselor, principal or aide for at least 1100 hours a school year in a school that provides elementary or secondary education as determined under state law.

Q3: Taxpayers can no longer claim any miscellaneous itemized deductions that are subject to the 2% of adjusted gross income limitation, including unreimbursed employee expenses. However, taxpayers may be able to deduct certain unreimbursed employee business expenses if they fall into one of the following categories of employment listed, except:

A. Fee-basis federal government officials

B. Employees with related work expenses
C. Qualified performing artists
D. Armed forces reservists

Q4: Elsa performs around the world with the organization Shen Yun. She works exclusively with the performing arts company year-round. Elsa earns $50,000 per year performing. She must pay for her own performing arts coach and supplies which costs her $7,500 per year. Her AGI is $23,000. How much of the $7,500 Elsa paid out of pocket can she deduct on her taxes?

A. Elsa can deduct $5,000 on her taxes.
B. Elsa can deduct $2,500 on her taxes.
C. Elsa cannot deduct the $7,500 on her taxes.
D. Elsa cannot deduct the $7,500 on her taxes and instead can file it as an exemption.

Q5: Taxpayer A is 66, single and has an HSA through his employer. In 2021 the taxpayer withdraws $2500 from his HSA to pay for home repairs. How would this withdrawal be treated?

A. As taxable income with no penalty
B. As non-taxable income because the Taxpayer is over 65 years old
C. As non-taxable income because it is an HSA
D. As non-taxable income, No 20% additional penalty because the taxpayer is over 65

Q6: Taxpayer A is self-employed as an Artist and grosses $42,000 for 2021 but after expenses only had a net profit of $2300. How much can Taxpayer A contribute to their SEP Plan?

A. $42,000
B. $2,300
C. $6,000
D. $7,000

Q7: What constitutes a permanent change of station for moving members of the Armed Forces?

A. A move from your home to their first post of active duty.
B. A move from one permanent post of duty to a temporary duty.
C. Within 2 years of ending your active duty or within the period allowed under the Joint Travel Regulations.
D. All of the Above

Q8: Married Taxpayers divorce was final by a court decree on December 15, 2019 that ordered Taxpayer A to pay Taxpayer B $2500 per month in alimony for 2021. How much can Taxpayer A deduct as an alimony deduction on their 2021 tax return?

A. $30,000
B. $2,500
C. $0

D. $15,000

Q9: Taxpayer A, unmarried earned $180,000 in 2021 and paid $5700 in student loan interest. How much can taxpayer A write off as a student loan interest deduction?

A. $5,700
B. $2,500
C. $1,000
D. $0

Q10: All are miscellaneous write-in adjustments on Line 22, except:

A. Jury duty pay remitted to an employer
B. Archer MSA deduction
C. Attorney fees and course costs for unlawful discrimination claims (only to the amount of income from such actions)
D. IRA contribution

ANSWER SHEET

1. Answer is C – $0

2. Answer is B – For the tax year you're a kindergarten through grade 12 teacher, instructor, counselor, principal, or aide for at least 900 hours a school year in a school that provides elementary or secondary education as determined under state law.

3. Answer is B – Employees with related work expenses

4. Answer is C – Elsa cannot deduct the $7,500 on her taxes.

5. Answer is A – As taxable income with no penalty

6. Answer is B – $2,300

7. Answer is A – A move from your home to their first post of active duty.

8. Answer is C – $0

9. Answer is D – $0

10. Answer is D – IRA contribution

INDIVIDUAL TAX CREDITS

OVERVIEW

- Subtract tax credits from the amount of tax owed.
- There are two types of tax credits:

A **nonrefundable** tax credit means the taxpayer gets a refund only up to the amount owed. Any amount that remains from the credit is automatically forfeited by the taxpayer.

A **refundable** tax credit means the taxpayer gets a refund, even if it's more than the amount owed.

COMMON NON-REFUNDABLE CREDITS

- Adoption credit
- American opportunity tax credit (partially refundable)
- Child and dependent care credit (refundable for 2021 only)
- Child tax credit
- Lifetime learning credit
- Foreign tax credit
- Retirement savings contributions credit or the saver's credit
- The credit for other dependent

REFUNDABLE TAX CREDIT

A refundable tax credit means getting a refund, even if it's more than the amount owed.

Common types of refundable credits are:

- Additional child tax credit
- American opportunity tax credit (partially non-refundable)
- Credit for excess social security and RRTA tax withheld
- Earned Income tax credit
- Premium tax credit
- 2021 Recovery rebate credit

CHILD AND DEPENDENT CARE CREDIT

The American Rescue Plan Act of 2021, was enacted on March 11, 2021, making the Child and Dependent Care credit substantially more generous and potentially refundable (up to $4,000 for one qualifying person and $8,000 for two or more qualifying persons) only for the tax year 2021. This means an eligible taxpayer can receive this credit even if they owe no federal income tax. Your federal income tax may be reduced by claiming the Credit for Child and Dependent Care expenses on your tax return.

Individuals may be able to claim the credit if they pay someone to care for their dependent who is under age 13 or for their spouse or dependent who isn't able to care for himself or herself.

To qualify, individuals must pay expenses so they can work or look for work.

If individuals receive any dependent care benefits from their employer during the year, they may be able to exclude all or part of them from the income. Individuals must complete Form 2441, Part III, before they can figure the amount of the credit. See Dependent Care Benefits under How To Figure the Credit, later.

To be able to claim the credit for child and dependent care expenses, individuals must file Form 1040, 1040-SR, or 1040-NR, not Form 1040-NR-EZ, and meet all the tests.

The amount of a taxpayer's adjusted gross income determines the percentage of their work-related expenses that they are allowed as a credit. For this purpose, your income is your "adjusted gross income" shown on your Form 1040, 1040-SR, or 1040-NR.

For 2021, the 50-percent amount begins to phase out if your adjusted gross income is more than $125,000, and completely phases out if your adjusted gross income is more than $438,000.

To be able to claim the credit for child and dependent care expenses, individuals must meet all the following tests.

1. Qualifying Person Test. The care must be for one or more qualifying persons who are identified on Form 2441. (See Who Is a Qualifying Person, later)
2. Earned Income Test. individuals (and their spouses if filing jointly) must have earned income during the year.
3. Work-Related Expense Test. Individuals must pay child and dependent care expenses so they (and their spouses if filing jointly) can work or look for work.
4. Individuals must make payments for child and dependent care to someone they (and their spouse) can't claim as a dependent. If they make payments to the child, he or she can't be the dependent and must be age 19 or older by the end of the year. Individuals can't make payments to:
    - Their spouse, or
    - The parent of the qualifying person if the qualifying person is their child and under age 13.

2. Joint Return Test. The filing status may be single, head of household, or qualifying widow(er) with dependent child. If the taxpayer is married, he or she must file a joint return, unless an exception applies.
3. Provider Identification Test. Taxpayers must identify the care provider on their tax return.
4. If a taxpayer excludes or deducts dependent care benefits provided by a dependent care benefit plan, the total amount excluded or deducted must be less than the dollar limit for qualifying expenses (for 2021 it is $8,000 if one qualifying person was cared for or $16,000 if two or more qualifying persons were cared for).

Who Is a Qualifying Person?

Child and dependent care expenses must be for the care of one or more qualifying persons.

A qualifying person is:

- The qualifying child who is the dependent and who was under age 13 when the care was provided;
- The spouse who wasn't physically or mentally able to care for himself or herself and lived with the taxpayer for more than half the year; or
- A person who wasn't physically or mentally able to care for himself or herself, lived with the taxpayer for more than half the year, and either:
- Was the dependent, or
- Would have been the dependent except that:
- He or she received gross income of $4,300 or more,
- He or she filed a joint return, or
- The taxpayer, or his or her spouse if filing jointly, could be claimed as a dependent on someone else's 2021 return.

To claim the credit, the taxpayer (and his or her spouse if filing jointly) must have earned income during the year.

Earned Income

Earned income includes wages, salaries, tips, other taxable employee compensation, and net earnings from self-employment. A net loss from self-employment reduces earned income. Earned income also includes strike benefits and any disability pay reported as wages.

Generally, only taxable compensation is included. For example, foreign earned income the taxpayer excludes from income isn't included. However, the taxpayer can elect to include nontaxable combat pay in earned income. If the taxpayer is filing a joint return and both the taxpayer and the spouse received nontaxable combat pay, the taxpayers can each make their own election. (In other words, if one of them makes the election, the other one can also make it but doesn't have to.) Including this income will give the individual a larger credit only if the taxpayer's (or his or her spouse's) other earned income is less than the amount entered on line 3 of Form 2441. Figure out the credit both ways and make the election that brings a greater tax benefit.

THE CHILD TAX CREDIT & ADDITIONAL CHILD TAX CREDIT

For tax year 2021, the Child Tax Credit increased from $2,000 per qualifying child to:

- $3,600 for children ages 5 and under at the end of 2021; and
- $3,000 for children ages 6 through 17 at the end of 2021.

Note: The $500 nonrefundable Credit for Other Dependents amount has not changed.

This amount will depend on the following:

If the taxpayer received advance Child Tax Credit payments for a qualifying child. Taxpayers may have received a portion of their Child Tax Credit through advance Child Tax Credit payments during 2021. Generally, the total amount of advance payments for each of their qualifying children equaled 50 percent of the amount of the credit that the IRS estimated you would be eligible to claim on your 2021 tax return for those children.

Reduced amounts

If the taxpayer's 2021 income is high enough, the amount of Child Tax Credit they can claim will be reduced. The amount of your Child Tax Credit will not be reduced if their 2021 modified adjusted gross income (AGI) is at or below:

- $150,000 if married and filing a joint return, or if filing as a qualifying widow or widower;
- $112,500 if filing as a head of household; or
- $75,000 if a single filer or are married and filing a separate return.

Next phaseout amounts

The Child Tax Credit won't begin to be reduced below $2,000 per child until the taxpayer's modified AGI in 2021 exceeds:

- $400,000 if married and filing a joint return; or
- $200,000 for all other filing statuses.

The second phaseout reduces the Child Tax Credit by $50 for each $1,000 (or fraction thereof) by which the taxpayer's modified AGI exceeds the income threshold described above.

Publication 972 contains a worksheet to help taxpayers figure their child tax credit if they have 3 or more children; have foreign earned income; meet a specific income requirement; or claim certain adoption or mortgage tax credit.

The purpose of this publication is:

- To figure the child tax credit claimed on Form 1040, Form 1040A, or Form 1040NR; and
- To figure the amount of earned income entered on Schedule 8812 (Form 1040A or 1040), Child Tax Credit.

A child qualifies a taxpayer for the CTC if the child meets all of the following conditions.

- The child is the son, daughter, stepchild, eligible foster child, brother, sister, stepbrother, stepsister, half-brother, half-sister, or a descendant of any of them (for example, the grandchild, niece, or nephew).
- The child was under age 18 at the end of 2021.
- The child did not provide over half of his or her own support for 2021.
- The child lived with the taxpayer for more than half of 2021
- The child is claimed as a dependent on the return.
- The child does not file a joint return for the year (or files it only to claim a refund of withheld income tax or estimated tax paid).
- The child was a U.S. citizen, U.S. national, or U.S. resident alien.

Example:

Maya's son turned 18 on December 30, 2021. He is a citizen of the United States and she claimed him as a dependent on her return. She cannot use him to claim the CTC because he was not under age 18 at the end of 2021.

Advance Child Tax Credit Payments - Repayment Protection

Taxpayers who received advance payments of their expected 2021 Child Tax Credit will need to reconcile the advance payment amounts on their 2021 tax return. In January, 2021 taxpayers will receive IRS Letter 6419 to provide the total amount of advance Child Tax Credit payments that were disbursed to them.

If the taxpayer received advance child tax credit payments in excess of their 2021 calculated child tax credit amount, they may have to repay some or all of the excess amount.

Full Repayment Relief - Taxpayers will not be required to pay back any excess child tax credit amounts if their AGI is at or below:

- $60,000 for Married Filing Jointly or qualifying widow(er) filing status
- $50,000 for Head of Household filing status
- $40,000 for Single or Married Filing Separately filing status

Partial Repayment Relief - Taxpayers will be required to pay back part of the excess child tax credit amounts if their AGI is between:

- $60,001 to $119,999 for Married Filing Jointly or qualifying widow(er) filing status
- $50,001 to $99,999 for Head of Household filing status
- $40,001 to $79,999 for Single or Married Filing Separately filing status

No Repayment Relief - Taxpayers will be required to pay back all of the excess child tax credit amounts if their AGI is at or over:

- $120,000 for Married Filing Jointly or qualifying widow(er) filing status
- $100,000 for Head of Household filing status
- $80,000 for Single or Married Filing Separately filing status

The repayment calculation takes place on Schedule 8812, page 3, Part III.

Credit for Other Dependents (ODC)

This credit is for individuals with a dependent who meets additional conditions (described later). This credit is in addition to the credit for child and dependent care expenses (on Schedule 3 (Form 1040 or 1040-SR), line 2, or Form 1040-NR, line 47) and the earned income credit (on Form 1040 or 1040-SR, line 18a).

The maximum amount that can be claimed for the credit is $500 for each dependent who qualifies for the ODC. But, see Limits on the CTC and ODC, later.

A person qualifies a taxpayer for the ODC if the person meets all of the following conditions.

1. The person is claimed as a dependent on the return. See Pub. 501 for more information about claiming someone as a dependent.
2. The person cannot be used by the taxpayer to claim the CTC or ACTC. See Child Tax Credit (CTC), earlier
3. The person was a U.S. citizen, U.S. national, or U.S. resident alien. For more information, see Pub. 519. If the person is the adopted child, see Adopted child, earlier.

Example.

Jordan's 10-year-old nephew lives in Mexico and qualifies as his dependent. He is not a U.S. citizen, U.S. national, or U.S. resident alien. Jordan cannot use him to claim ODC. He cannot use the same child to claim both the CTC (or ACTC) and ODC.

Claiming the CTC and ODC

To claim the CTC or ODC, the taxpayer needs to meet the following requirements.

- The taxpayer must file Form 1040, Form 1040-SR, or Form 1040-NR and include the name and TIN of each dependent for whom the taxpayer is claiming the CTC or ODC.
- The taxpayer must file Form 8862 if applicable. See Improper Claims, earlier.

- The taxpayer must enter a timely issued TIN on the tax return for himself and the spouse (if filing jointly). See Taxpayer Identification Number Requirements, earlier.
- For each qualifying child under 17 for whom the taxpayer is claiming the CTC, he must enter the required SSN for the child in column (2) of the Dependents section of the tax return and check the Child tax credit box in column (4). See Child Tax Credit (CTC), earlier.
- For each dependent for whom the taxpayer is claiming the ODC, he must enter the timely issued TIN for the dependent in column (2) of the Dependents section of the tax return and check the Credit for other dependents box in column (4).
- Do not check both the Child tax credit box and the Credit for other dependents box for the same person.

ADDITIONAL CHILD TAX CREDIT (ACTC)

This credit is for certain individuals who get less than the full amount of the CTC. The ACTC may give individuals a refund even if they do not owe any tax.

The ODC cannot be used to figure the ACTC. Only the CTC can be used to figure the ACTC. If the individuals are claiming the ODC but not the CTC, they cannot claim the ACTC.

CREDIT FOR OTHER DEPENDENTS

Dependents who can't be claimed for the Child Tax Credit may still qualify certain individuals for the Credit for Other Dependents. This is a non-refundable tax credit of up to $500 per qualifying person. The qualifying dependent must be a U.S. citizen, U.S. national, or U.S. resident alien.

More families may be eligible for the Child Tax Credit or the Credit for Other Dependents. Both credits begin to phase out at $200,000 of modified adjusted gross income ($400,000 for married couples filing jointly).

Use the IRS's Interactive Tax Assistant beginning in January to check if the taxpayer is eligible to claim the Child Tax Credit or Credit for Other Dependents.

ADOPTION CREDIT

Tax benefits for adoption include both a tax credit for qualified adoption expenses paid to adopt an eligible child and an exclusion from income for employer-provided adoption assistance. The credit is nonrefundable, which means it's limited to the tax liability for the year. However, any credit in excess of the tax liability may be carried forward for up to five years. The maximum amount (dollar limit) for 2021 is $14,440 per child.

Qualified Adoption Expenses

For both the credit and the exclusion, qualified adoption expenses, defined in section 23(d)(1) of the Code, include:

1. Reasonable and necessary adoption fees,
2. Court costs and attorney fees,
3. Traveling expenses (including amounts spent for meals and lodging while away from home), and
4. Other expenses that are directly related to and for the principal purpose of the legal adoption of an eligible child.

An expense may be a qualified adoption expense even if the expense is paid before an eligible child has been identified. For example, prospective adoptive parents who pay for a home study at the outset of an adoption effort may treat the fees as qualified adoption expenses. An eligible child is an individual who is under the age of 18 or is physically or mentally incapable of self-care.

Qualified adoption expenses don't include expenses that a taxpayer pays to adopt the child of the taxpayer's spouse Qualified adoption expenses include expenses paid by a registered domestic partner who lives in a state that allows same-sex second parent or co-parent to adopt his or her partner's child, as long as those expenses otherwise qualify for the credit.

Income and Dollar Limitations

The credit and exclusion are each subject to an income limitation and a dollar limitation. The income limit on the adoption credit or exclusion is based on the modified adjusted gross income (MAGI). If the MAGI amount for 2021 falls between certain dollar limits, the credit or exclusion is subject to a phaseout (is reduced or eliminated). For tax year 2021, the MAGI phaseout begins at $216,660 and ends at $256,660. Thus, if the MAGI amount is below $216,660 for 2021, the credit or exclusion won't be affected by the MAGI phaseout.

Individuals must reduce the dollar limit for a particular year by the amount of qualified adoption expenses paid and claimed in previous years for the same adoption effort.

For example, if an individual claimed a $3,000 credit in connection with a domestic adoption in 2021 and paid an additional $14,300 of qualified adoption expenses in 2021 (when the adoption became final), the maximum credit that he can claim in 2021 is $11,440 ($14,440 dollar limit less $3,000 of qualified adoption expenses claimed in 2021).

The tax year for which a taxpayer can claim the credit depends on the following

- When the expenses are paid;
- Whether it's a domestic adoption or a foreign adoption; and
- When, if ever, the adoption was finalized.

Generally, the credit is allowable whether the adoption is domestic or foreign. However, the timing rules for claiming the credit for qualified adoption expenses differ, depending on the type of adoption. A domestic adoption is the adoption of a U.S. child (an eligible child who is a citizen or resident of the

U.S. or its possessions before the adoption effort begins). Qualified adoption expenses paid before the year the adoption becomes final are allowable as a credit for the tax year following the year of payment (even if the adoption is never finalized and even if an eligible child was never identified).

A foreign adoption is the adoption of an eligible child who isn't yet a citizen or resident of the U.S. or its possessions before the adoption effort begins. Qualified adoption expenses paid before and during the year are allowable as a credit for the year when it becomes final.

Once an adoption becomes final, and subject to the dollar limitation, qualified adoption expenses paid during or after the year of finality are allowable as a credit for the year of payment, whether the adoption is foreign or domestic.

As a result of the timing rules, qualified adoption expenses allowable in the current year may include expenses paid in a former year or years. Example 4 illustrates the difference between the domestic and the foreign timing rules.

Example

An adoptive parent pays qualified adoption expenses of $3,000 in 2018, $4,000 in 2019, and $5,000 in 2020. In 2020, the adoption becomes final.

If individuals filed their return using the married filing separately filing status in the year particular qualified adoption expenses are first allowable, they generally can't claim the credit or exclusion for those particular expenses. They may need to file an amended return to change to a qualifying filing status within the period of limitations. However, see Married Persons Not Filing Jointly in the Instructions for Form 8839 (PDF), which describes an exception for certain taxpayers living apart from their spouse and meeting other requirements.

EDUCATION CREDITS

Use Form 8863 to figure and claim the education credits, which are based on qualified education expenses paid to an eligible postsecondary educational institution. There are two education credits.

- The American Opportunity Credit, part of which may be refundable.
- The Lifetime Learning Credit, which is nonrefundable.

AMERICAN OPPORTUNITY TAX CREDIT (AOTC)

The American opportunity tax credit (AOTC) is a credit for qualified education expenses paid for an eligible student for the first four years of higher education. Individuals can get a maximum annual credit of $2,500 per eligible student. If the credit brings the amount of tax owed to zero, individuals can have 40 percent of any remaining amount of the credit (up to $1,000) refunded to the individual.

The amount of the credit is 100 percent of the first $2,000 of qualified education expenses paid for each eligible student and 25 percent of the next $2,000 of qualified education expenses paid for that student. But, if the credit pays the tax down to zero, individuals can have 40 percent of the remaining amount of the credit (up to $1,000) refunded to them.

To be eligible for AOTC, the student must

- Be pursuing a degree or other recognized education credential
- Be enrolled at least half time for at least one academic period beginning in the tax year
- Not have finished the first four years of higher education at the beginning of the tax year
- Not have claimed the AOTC or the former Hope credit for more than four tax years
- Not have a felony drug conviction at the end of the tax year
- Academic Period can be semesters, trimesters, quarters, or any other period of study such as a summer school session. The schools determine the academic periods. For schools that use clock or credit hours and do not have academic terms, the payment period may be treated as an academic period.

To be eligible to claim the AOTC or the lifetime learning credit (LLC), the law requires a taxpayer (or a dependent) to have received Form 1098-T, Tuition Statement, from an eligible educational institution, whether domestic or foreign.

Generally, students receive a Form 1098-T Tuition Statement, from their school by January 31. This statement helps taxpayers figure the credit. The form will have an amount in box 1 to show the amounts received during the year. But, this amount may not be the amount that can be claimed.
Check the Form 1098-T to make sure it is correct. If it isn't correct or if the taxpayer did not receive the form, contact the school.

To claim AOTC, the taxpayer must complete the Form 8863 and attach the completed form to the tax return.

Make sure the taxpayer is qualified before claiming the credit. And, make sure the taxpayer keeps copies of all the documents used to find out if the taxpayer qualifies and determines the amount of the credit. If the IRS audits the return and finds the AOTC claim is incorrect and the taxpayer does not have the documents to show he qualified, he must pay back the amount of the AOTC received in error with interest. The IRS may also charge the taxpayer with an accuracy or a fraud penalty. Or, he can be banned from claiming the AOTC for two to ten years.

Taxpayers may not claim the AOTC unless they, or their spouse (if they are filing a joint return) and the qualifying student have a valid taxpayer identification number (TIN) issued or applied for on or before the due date of the return (including extensions). A TIN is a Social Security number, an individual taxpayer identification number (ITIN) or an adoption taxpayer identification number (ATIN).

Taxpayers may not claim the AOTC on a later original return or an amended return if the TIN is issued on or applied for after the due date of the return (including extensions).
To ensure that the taxpayer receives the benefit of the AOTC if he qualifies for it, he should timely obtain the required TIN.

What are the income limits for AOTC?

Individuals can claim the full credit, the MAGI, modified adjusted gross income must be $80,000 or less ($160,000 or less for married filing jointly).

Individuals can receive a reduced amount of the credit if their MAGI is over $80,000 but less than $90,000 (over $160,000 but less than $180,000 for married filing jointly).

Individuals cannot claim the credit if their MAGI is over $90,000 ($180,000 for joint filers).

MAGI for most people is the amount of AGI, adjusted gross income, shown on the tax return. If an individual files Form 1040, he can add the following amounts to AGI (line 7):

If he files Form 1040, he can add the following amounts to AGI:

- Foreign earned income exclusion,
- Foreign housing exclusion,
- Foreign housing deduction,
- Exclusion of income by bona fide residents of American Samoa, or of Puerto Rico.

If the individual needs to adjust the AGI to find the MAGI, there are worksheets in Publication 970 to help.

LIFETIME LEARNING CREDIT

The lifetime learning credit (LLC) is for qualified tuition and related expenses paid for eligible students enrolled in an eligible educational institution. This credit can help pay for undergraduate, graduate and professional degree courses — including courses to acquire or improve job skills. There is no limit on the number of years an individual can claim the credit. It is worth up to $2,000 per tax return.

To claim a LLC, taxpayers must meet all three of the following:

- The taxpayer, the dependent or a third party needs to pay qualified education expenses for higher education.
- The taxpayer, the dependent or a third party needs to pay the education expenses for an eligible student enrolled at an eligible educational institution
- The eligible student is the taxpayer, his or her spouse or a dependent listed on the tax return.

Use the interactive app, Am I Eligible to Claim an Education Credit?, to find out if the taxpayer can claim an education credit.

To be eligible for LLC, the student must:

- Be enrolled or taking courses at an eligible educational institution.
- Be taking higher education courses or courses to get a degree or other recognized education credential or to get or improve job skills.
- Be enrolled for at least one academic period* beginning in the tax year.

Academic Period can be semesters, trimesters, quarters or any other period of study such as a summer school session. Academic periods are determined by the school. For schools that use clock or credit hours and do not have academic terms, the payment period may be treated as an academic period.

Important Differences between LLC and AOTC

What are the income limits for LLC?

- For TY2021, the amount of the LLC is gradually reduced (phased out) if the MAGI is between $80,000 and $90,000 ($160,000 and $180,000 if the taxpayer files a joint return).
- Taxpayers can't claim the credit if the MAGI is $90,000 or more ($180,000 or more if the taxpayer files a joint return).
- To be eligible to claim the AOTC or LLC, the law requires a taxpayer (or a dependent) to have received Form 1098-T, Tuition Statement (PDF), from an eligible educational institution, whether domestic or foreign. Generally, students receive a Form 1098-T, Tuition Statement, from their school by January 31. This statement helps taxpayers figure their credit. The form will have an amount in box 1 to show the amounts received during the year. But

this amount may not be the amount they can claim. See qualified education expenses for more information on what amount to claim.

- Check the Form 1098-T to make sure it is correct. If it isn't correct or the taxpayer does not receive the form, contact the school.
- To claim the LLC, the taxpayer must complete the Form 8863 (PDF). Attach the completed form to the Form 1040 or Form 1040-SR.

What is the LLC worth?

The amount of the credit is 20 percent of the first $10,000 of qualified education expenses or a maximum of $2,000 per return. The LLC is not refundable. So, the taxpayer can use the credit to pay any tax owed but he won't receive any of the credit back as a refund.

EARNED INCOME TAX CREDIT (EITC)

The Earned Income Tax Credit, EITC or EIC, is a benefit for working people with low to moderate income. To qualify, individuals must meet certain requirements and file a tax return, even if they do not owe any tax or are not required to file. EITC reduces the amount of tax owed and may give a refund.

If taxpayers claim the earned income tax credit (EITC) or the additional child tax credit (ACTC) on the tax return, by law the IRS, can't issue the refund before mid-February. Find out more on when to expect your refund.

To qualify for EITC taxpayers must have earned income from working for someone or from running or owning a business or farm and meet basic rules. And, they must either meet additional rules for workers without a qualifying child or have a child that meets all the qualifying child rules.

Individuals can't get EITC, unless they file a Federal tax return and claim it. If they have a qualifying child, they must file the Schedule EIC listing the children with the Form 1040, US Individual Income Tax Return (PDF) or Form 1040 SR, U.S. Tax Return for Seniors (PDF).

Note: If individuals claim the earned income tax credit (EITC) or the additional child tax credit (ACTC) on the tax return, by law, the IRS can't issue the refund before mid-February — even the portion of the refund not associated with EITC or ACTC.

Gather the Following Documents Before Start Working on a Tax Return

- If taxpayers have someone prepare the tax return, they need to bring the documents to the preparer to make sure the tax return is prepared correctly.
- Social Security cards, a Social Security number verification letter, or other U.S. government document verification for all persons that may be listed on the return.
- Birth dates for all persons that may be listed on return.
- Copies of last year's federal and state returns.

- All income statements: Forms W-2 and 1099, Social Security, unemployment, and other statements, such as pensions, stocks, interest and any documents showing taxes withheld. If the taxpayer owns or runs a business or farm, he or she needs to collect records of all income.
- All records of expenses, such as tuition, mortgage interest, or real estate taxes. If the taxpayer owns or runs a business or farm, he or she needs to collect records of all expenses.

QUALIFYING CHILDREN FOR EITC PURPOSES

All information reporting forms such as the 1095-A, 1095-B or 1095-C. Bank routing numbers and account numbers to direct deposit any refund.

- Dependent child care information: name and address of paid caretakers and either their Social Security number or other tax identification number.

Number of Qualifying Children	For Single/Head of Household or Qualifying Widow(er), Income Must be Less Than	For Married Filing Jointly, Income Must be Less Than	Range of EITC
No Child	$21,430	$27,380	up to $1502
One Child	$42,158	$48,108	up to $3618
Two Children	$47,915	$53,865	up to $5,980
Three or More Children	$51,464	$57,414	up to $6,728

Certain Rules for Income Earned During 2021

- The tax year investment income must be $10,000 or less for the year.
- Must not file Form 2555, Foreign Earned Income or Form 2555-EZ, Foreign Earned Income Exclusion.

- The total earned income must be at least $1.

With a Qualifying Child

If a taxpayer (and his or her spouse if filing a joint return) meets the criteria above and that taxpayer has a child who lives with him, he may be eligible for the EITC. Each claimed child must pass the relationship, age, residency, and joint return tests to be the qualifying child. See the Qualifying Child Rules for guidance.

Without a Qualifying Child

If a taxpayer (and his or her spouse if filing a joint return) meets the basic EITC rules for everyone, he qualifies for the EITC:

- The taxpayer (and his or her spouse if filing a joint return) has the main home in the United States for more than half of the tax year; AND
- The taxpayer (and his or her spouse if filing a joint return) cannot be claimed as a dependent or qualifying child on anyone else's return; AND
- The taxpayer (and his or her spouse if filing a joint return) must have been at least 25 but under 65 years old at the end of the tax year.
- The child must have the required Social Security number that was issued on or before the due date of the tax return (including extensions) and must pass all of the following tests to be the qualifying child for the EITC:

Qualifying Children for EITC Purposes

Relationship

- The son, daughter, adopted child1, stepchild, foster child or a descendent of any of them, such as the grandchild
- Brother, sister, half-brother, half-sister, step brother, step sister or a descendant of any of them, such as a niece or a nephew

Age

- At the end of the filing year, the child was younger than the individual (or the spouse if filing a joint return) and younger than 19
- At the end of the filing year, the child was younger than the individual (or the spouse if filing a joint return), younger than 24, and a full-time student
- At the end of the filing year, the child was any age and permanently and totally disabled
- The child must have the same main home as the individual (or the spouse if filing a joint return) in the United States for more than half of the tax year

Joint Return

The child cannot file a joint return for the tax year unless neither the child nor the child's spouse would have had a separate filing requirement and they filed the joint return only to claim a refund of withheld or estimated taxes.

IMPORTANT: Generally, only one person may claim a child as a qualifying child for the child-related tax benefits. If a child is a qualifying child of more than one person and one of the persons is a parent, a non-parent can claim the child if no parent claims the child and the non-parent's AGI is higher than the AGI of any parent who may claim the child. If a child is the qualifying child of more than one person, the IRS applies tiebreaker rules.

EARNED INCOME AND AGI LIMITS

The adjusted gross income (AGI) must be less than:

- $51,464 ($57,414 for married filing jointly) if the taxpayer has three or more qualifying children,
- $47,915 ($53,865 for married filing jointly) if the taxpayer has two qualifying children,
- $42,158 ($48,108 for married filing jointly) if the taxpayer has one qualifying child, or
- $21,430 ($27,380 for married filing jointly) if the taxpayer doesn't have a qualifying child.

Adjusted Gross Income (AGI)

AGI is the amount on line 11 Form 1040.. If the AGI is equal to or more than the applicable limit listed above, the taxpayer can't claim the EIC.

Example:

Taxpayer A AGI is more than the limit. The AGI is $43,485, he is single, and he has one qualifying child. He can't claim the EIC because his AGI isn't less than $42,158. However, if his filing status was married filing jointly, he might be able to claim the EIC because his AGI is less than $48,108..

Community Property

If a taxpayer is married but qualifies to file as head of household under special rules for married taxpayers living apart and living in a state that has community property laws, the AGI includes that portion of both the and the spouse's wages that the taxpayer is required to include in gross income. This is different from the community property rules that apply under Rule 7.

RETIREMENT SAVINGS CONTRIBUTIONS CREDIT (SAVER'S CREDIT)

Individuals may be able to take a tax credit for making eligible contributions to the IRA or employer-sponsored retirement plan. And, beginning in 2018, if an individual is the designated beneficiary he or she may be eligible for a credit for contributions to the Achieving a Better Life Experience (ABLE) account.
An individual is eligible for the credit if he or she is:

- Age 18 or older;
- Not a full-time student; and
- Not claimed as a dependent on another person's return.

Amount of the Credit

The amount of the credit is 50%, 20% or 10% of the retirement plan or IRA or ABLE account contributions depending on the adjusted gross income (reported on the Form 1040 series return). The maximum contribution amount that may qualify for the credit is $2,000 ($4,000 if married filing jointly), making the maximum credit $1,000 ($2,000 if married filing jointly).

2021 Savers Credit

Credit Rate	Married Filing Jointly	Head of Household	All Other Filers*
50% of the contribution	AGI not more than $39,500	AGI not more than $29,625	AGI not more than $19,750
20% of the contribution	$39,501 - $43,000	$29,626 - $32,250	$19,751 - $21,500
10% of the contribution	$43,001 - $66,000	$32,251 - $49,500	$21,501 - $33,000
0% of the contribution	more than $66,000	more than $49,500	more than $33,000

ABLE Contributions Eligible for the Credit

The Saver's Credit can be taken for the contributions to an ABLE account if an individual is the designated beneficiary.

Rollover contributions (money that moved from another ABLE account or from a Qualified Tuition Plan (QTP) account do not qualify for the credit. Also, the eligible contributions may be reduced by any recent distributions received from the ABLE account.

Retirement Savings Eligible for the Credit

The Saver's Credit can be taken for the contributions to a traditional or Roth IRA; the 401(k), SIMPLE IRA, SARSEP, 403(b), 501(c)(18) or governmental 457(b) plan; and the voluntary after-tax employee contributions to the qualified retirement and 403(b) plans.

Rollover contributions (money that moved from another retirement plan or IRA) aren't eligible for the Saver's Credit. Also, the eligible contributions may be reduced by any recent distributions received from a retirement plan or IRA.

Jill, who works at a retail store, is married and earned $41,000 in 2021. Jill's spouse was unemployed in 2021 and didn't have any earnings. Jill contributed $2,000 to her IRA for 2021. After deducting her IRA contribution, the adjusted gross income shown on her joint return is $39,000. Jill may claim a 50% credit of $1,000 for her $2,000 IRA contribution on her 2021 tax return.

CREDIT FOR EXCESS SOCIAL SECURITY AND RRTA TAX WITHHELD

Most employers must withhold social security tax from the wages. Certain government employers (some federal, state and local governments) don't have to withhold social security tax.

If a taxpayer works for a railroad employer, the employer must withhold Tier 1 Railroad Retirement Tax Act (RRTA) tax and Tier 2 RRTA tax. Tier 1 RRTA provides social security and Medicare equivalent benefits, and Tier 2 RRTA provides a private pension benefit.

Employer's error - If any one employer withheld too much social security, Tier 1 RRTA tax, or Tier 2 RRTA tax, the taxpayer can't claim the excess as a credit against the income tax. The employer should adjust the excess. If the employer doesn't adjust the overcollection, the taxpayer can use Form 843, Claim for Refund and Request for Abatement to claim a refund.

Two or more employers - If a taxpayer had more than one employer during the taxable year and the total wages and compensation were over the wage base limit for the year, the total social security tax or social security equivalent Tier 1 RRTA tax withheld may have exceeded the maximum amount due for the tax year. If the taxpayer had more than one railroad employer, and the total compensation was over the maximum amount of wages subject to Tier 2 RRTA, the total Tier 2 RRTA tax withheld may have exceeded the maximum due for the tax year.

If a taxpayer had more than one employer and too much social security tax or Tier 1 RRTA tax withheld, the taxpayer may be able to claim the excess as a credit against the income tax on the income tax return.

If a taxpayer had more than one employer and too much Tier 2 RRTA tax withheld, the taxpayer may request a refund of the excess Tier 2 RRTA tax using Form 843 (PDF).

Joint returns - If the taxpayer is filing a joint return, together with his or her spouse he must figure any excess social security tax or Tier 1 RRTA tax separately.

POP QUIZ & ANSWER SHEET

INDIVIDUAL TAX CREDITS

POP QUIZ

Test your knowledge on *Individual Tax Credits* by answering the questions below. The answer sheet may be found at the end of the Pop Quiz.

Q1: All of the following are non-refundable tax credits, except:
A. Alternative Motor Vehicle Credit
B. Additional Child Tax Credit
C. Foreign Tax Credit
D. Adoption Credit

Q2: For purposes of the child and dependent care credit a "qualifying person" is all of the following, except:
A. A child under the age of 13
B. A cousin who lives with the taxpayer for the year
C. A spouse who is physically or mentally disabled
D. Any other disabled person who is unable to care for himself and that the taxpayer either claims as a dependent

Q3: Taxpayers must meet all the following tests to be able to claim the credit for child and dependent care expenses, except:
A. Earned Income Test
B. Personal Identification Test
C. Work Related Expense Test
D. Qualifying Person Test

Q4: Taxpayer A was examined, and the IRS determined that Taxpayer A with reckless disregard of EITC rules erroneously claimed the Earned Income Tax Credit. How many years is Taxpayer A prohibited from claiming EITC?
A. Ten Years
B. Three Years
C. Two Years
D. One Year

Q5: Taxpayer A has three children ages Nine, Twelve, and Eighteen. How much of the non-refundable child tax credit does Taxpayer A qualify for if all other tests are met?
A. $6,000

B. $4,000
C. $8,000
D. $2,000

Q6: Which is an example of Other Dependents Credit (ODC)?
A. Taxpayers 18 year old nephew lives in Mexico and is a US Citizen. He has been providing more than half of his own support for more than a year.
B. Taxpayers 23 year old cousin is on a vacation in Mexico and qualifies as their dependent because he lives with the taxpayer all year and is supported by the taxpayer.
C. Taxpayers 8 year old niece lives in Canada and qualifies as their dependent. She is not a US citizen, US national or a US resident alien.
D. Taxpayers 15 year old son is living with the taxpayer all year long and qualifies as their dependent taxpayer also used him to claim CTC.

Q7: Can one claim the Child tax credit and the credit for other dependents for the same person?
A. No, you cannot file both for the same dependent.
B. No, you cannot file both, you must use form 1040-ES.
C. Yes, as long as you enter the timely issued TIN for the dependent.
D. Yes, as long as the dependent is under 17.

Q8: What do you call the credit for certain individuals who get less than the full amount of the Child Tax Credit?
A. ODC
B. ACTC
C. ITIN
D. ATIN

Q9: All are qualified adoption expenses, except:
A. Court Costs & Attorney Fees
B. Traveling Expenses (including amounts spent for meals and lodging while away from home)
C. Expenses that Taxpayers Pay to Adopt the Child of the Taxpayer's Spouse
D. Other Expenses that are Directly Related to and for the Principal Purpose of the Legal Adoption of an Eligible Child

Q10: The two education credits are:
A. The American Opportunity Credit, part of which is refundable. The Lifetime Learning Credit, part of which is refundable.
B. The American Opportunity Credit, part of which may be refundable. The Lifetime Learning Credit, which is nonrefundable.
C. The American Opportunity Credit, which is nonrefundable. The Lifetime Learning Credit, which is nonrefundable.
D. The American Opportunity Credit, which is nonrefundable. The Lifetime Learning Credit, part of which is refundable.

ANSWER SHEET

1. Answer is B – Additional Child Tax Credit

2. Answer is B – A cousin who lives with the taxpayer for the year

3. Answer is B – Personal Identification Test

4. Answer is C – Two Years

5. Answer is B – $4,000

6. Answer is B – Taxpayers 23-year-old cousin is on a vacation in Mexico and qualifies as their dependent because he lives with the taxpayer all year and is supported by the taxpayer.

7. Answer is A – No, you cannot file both for the same dependent.

8. Answer is B – ACTC

9. Answer is C – Expenses that Taxpayers Pay to Adopt the Child of the Taxpayer's Spouse.

10. Answer is B – The American Opportunity Credit, part of which may be refundable. The Lifetime Learning Credit, which is nonrefundable.

STANDARD DEDUCTIONS & ITEMIZED DEDUCTIONS

THE STANDARD DEDUCTION

The standard deduction is a specific dollar amount that reduces the amount of income on which taxpayers are taxed. The standard deduction consists of the sum of the basic standard deduction and any additional standard deduction amounts for age and/or blindness.

In general, the standard deduction is adjusted each year for inflation and varies according to the filing status, whether the individual is 65 or older and/or blind, and whether another taxpayer can claim an individual as a dependent.
The standard deduction isn't available to certain taxpayers. Individuals can't take the standard deduction if they itemize the deductions.

Not Eligible for the Standard Deduction

Certain taxpayers aren't entitled to the standard deduction:

- A married individual filing as married filing separately whose spouse itemizes deductions
- An individual who was a nonresident alien or dual status alien during the year (with certain exceptions)
- An individual who files a return for a period of less than 12 months due to a change in his or her annual accounting period
- An estate or trust, common trust fund, or partnership

However, certain individuals who were nonresident aliens or dual status aliens during the year may take the standard deduction in the following cases:

- A nonresident alien who is married to a U.S. citizen or resident alien at the end of the tax year and makes a joint election with his or her spouse to be treated as a U.S. resident for the entire tax year;
- A nonresident alien at the beginning of the tax year who is a U.S. citizen or resident by the end of the tax year, is married to a U.S. citizen or resident at the end of such tax year, and makes a joint election with his or her spouse to be treated as a U.S. resident for the entire tax year; and
- Students and business apprentices who are residents of India and are eligible for benefits under paragraph 2 of Article 21 (Payments Received by Students and Apprentices) of the United States- India Income Tax Treaty

ADDITIONAL STANDARD DEDUCTION

Individuals are allowed an additional deduction if they are age 65 or older at the end of the tax year. Individuals are considered to be 65 on the day before their 65th birthday.

Individuals are allowed an additional deduction for blindness if they are blind on the last day of the tax year.
For example, a single taxpayer who is age 65 and blind would be entitled to a basic standard deduction and an additional standard deduction equal to the sum of the additional amounts for both age and blindness.

- For example, a single taxpayer who is age 65 and blind would be entitled to a basic standard deduction and an additional standard deduction equal to the sum of the additional amounts for both age and blindness.
- Single, HOH: $1700 additional amount
- MFS, MFJ, QW: $1350 additional amount

Example:

- Taxpayer A is 57 and legally blind. The standard deduction for this taxpayer is $14,650 ($12,950 standard deduction + $1700 additional standard deduction for blindness)
- Taxpayer A is 67 and legally blind. The standard deduction for this taxpayer is $16,350 ($12,950 standard deduction + $1700 additional for over 65 + $1700 additional for blindness.

STANDARD DEDUCTION FOR CERTAIN DEPENDENTS

If a taxpayer can be claimed as a dependent by another taxpayer, the standard deduction for 2021 is limited to the greater of: (1) $1,100, or (2) the earned income plus $350 (but the total can't be more than the basic standard deduction for the filing status).
Example:

- Dependent earns $8500. Their standard deduction will be $8850 ($8500 + $350)
- Dependent earns $800. Their standard deduction will be $1100
- Dependent earns $13,540. Their standard deduction will be $12,400 which is the regular standard deduction

ITEMIZED DEDUCTIONS

Taxpayers may need to itemize deductions because they can't use the standard deduction. They may also itemize deductions when this amount is greater than their standard deduction. Taxpayers who itemize file Schedule A, Form 1040, Itemized Deductions or Form 1040-SR, U.S. Tax Return for Seniors.

A taxpayer may benefit by itemizing deductions for things that include:

- State and local income or sales taxes
- Real estate and personal property taxes
- Mortgage interest
- Mortgage insurance premiums
- Personal casualty and theft losses from a federally declared disaster
- Donations to a qualified charity
- Unreimbursed medical and dental expenses that exceed 7.5% of adjusted gross income

Individual itemized deductions may be limited. Schedule A, Form 1040 Instructions can help determine what limitations may apply.

When to itemize?

Individuals may benefit from itemizing their deductions on Schedule A (Form 1040 or 1040-SR) if they:

- Don't qualify for the standard deduction,
- Had large uninsured medical and dental expenses during the year,
- Paid interest and taxes on their home,
- Had large uninsured casualty or theft losses,
- Made large contributions to qualified charities, or
- Have total itemized deductions that are more than the standard deduction to which they otherwise are entitled.

MEDICAL AND DENTAL EXPENSES

If a taxpayer itemizes deductions for a taxable year on Schedule A (Form 1040 or 1040-SR), Itemized Deductions, he or she may be able to deduct expenses paid that year for medical and dental care for themselves, their spouse, and their dependents. Individuals may deduct only the amount of the total medical expenses that exceed 7.5% of the adjusted gross income. The amount allowed to be deducted is on Schedule A (Form 1040 or 1040-SR).

Medical care expenses include payments for the diagnosis, cure, mitigation, treatment, or prevention of disease, or payments for treatments affecting any structure or function of the body.

Deductible medical expenses may include but aren't limited to the following:

- **Payments of fees to doctors**, dentists, surgeons, chiropractors, psychiatrists, psychologists, and nontraditional medical practitioners.
- **Payments for inpatient hospital** care or residential nursing home care, if the availability of medical care is the principal reason for being in the nursing home, including the cost of meals and lodging charged by the hospital or nursing home. If the availability of medical care isn't the principal reason for residence in the nursing home, the deduction is limited to that part of the cost that's for medical care.

- **Payments for acupuncture** treatments or inpatient treatments at a center for alcohol or drug addiction; or for participation in a smoking-cessation program and for drugs to alleviate nicotine withdrawal that require a prescription.
- **Payments to participate** in a weight-loss program for a specific disease or diseases diagnosed by a physician, including obesity, but not ordinarily payments for diet food items or the payment of health club dues.
- **Payments for insulin** and for drugs that require a prescription for its use by an individual.
- **Payments made for admission and transportation** to a medical conference relating to a chronic illness of a taxpayer, his or her spouse, or his or her dependent (if the costs are primarily for and essential to necessary medical care). However, individuals may not deduct the costs for meals and lodging while attending the medical conference.
- **Payments for false teeth**, reading or prescription eyeglasses, contact lenses, hearing aids, crutches, wheelchairs, and for a guide dog or other service animal to assist a visually impaired or hearing disabled person, or a person with other physical disabilities.
- **Payments for transportation** primarily for and essential to medical care that qualify as medical expenses, such as payments of the actual fare for a taxi, bus, train, ambulance, or for transportation by personal car; the amount of the actual out-of-pocket expenses such as for gas and oil; or the amount of the standard mileage rate for medical expenses, plus the cost of tolls and parking.
- **Payments for insurance premiums** paid for policies that cover medical care or for a qualified long-term care insurance policy covering qualified long-term care services. However, if the taxpayer is an employee, don't include in medical expenses the portion of the premiums treated as paid by the employer. Employer-sponsored premiums paid under a premium conversion plan, cafeteria plan, or any other medical and dental expenses paid by the plan aren't deductible unless the premiums are included in box 1 of the Form W-2, Wage and Tax Statement (PDF). For example, if the taxpayer is a federal employee participating in the premium conversion plan of the Federal Employee Health Benefits (FEHB) program, the premiums paid for the policy as a medical expense may not be included.

STATE AND LOCAL INCOME TAXES

State and local income taxes withheld from the wages during the year appear on the Form W-2, Wage and Tax Statement. Taxpayers can elect to deduct state and local general sales taxes instead of state and local income taxes, but they can't deduct both. If they elect to deduct state and local general sales taxes, they can use either the actual expenses or the optional sales tax tables. The following amounts are also deductible:

- Any estimated taxes paid to state or local governments during the year, and Any
- Prior year's state or local income tax paid during the year.

Generally, taxpayers can take either a deduction or a tax credit for foreign income taxes imposed on them by a foreign country or a United States possession.

The law limits the deduction of state and local income, sales, and property taxes to a combined, total deduction of $10,000. The amount is $5,000 for married taxpayers filing separate returns. Taxpayers cannot deduct any state and local taxes paid above this amount.

TYPES OF DEDUCTIBLE INTEREST

Types of interest deductible as itemized deductions include:

- Investment interest (limited to the net investment income) and
- Qualified mortgage interest including points (if the buyer)

Types of interest deductible elsewhere on the return include:

- A Student loan interest as an adjustment to income on Form 1040, U.S. Individual Income Tax Return or Form 1040-SR, U.S. Tax Return for Seniors.
- Non-farm business interest. Farm business interest.
- Interest incurred to produce rents or royalties (this may be limited).

Qualified mortgage interest and points are generally reported on Form 1098, Mortgage Interest Statement (PDF) by the mortgage holder to which the payments are made. Taxpayers can deduct interest for the following types of mortgages:

- A mortgage taken out on or before October 13, 1987 (grandfathered debt)
- A mortgage taken out after October 13, 1987, to buy, build, or improve the home (called home acquisition debt) but only if throughout the year these mortgages plus any grandfathered debt totaled $1 million or less. The limit is $500,000 if the taxpayer is married filing separately. For homes acquired after December 15, 2017, the debt limitation is $750,000, or $375,000 if the taxpayer is married filing separately.

HOME MORTGAGE INTEREST

Home mortgage interest is any interest taxpayers pay on a loan secured by their home (main home or a second home). The loan may be a mortgage to buy the home, or a second mortgage. Taxpayers can deduct home mortgage interest if all the following conditions are met. They file Form 1040 or 1040-SR and itemize deductions on Schedule A (Form 1040 or 1040-SR). The mortgage is a secured debt on a qualified home in which they have an ownership interest.

MORTGAGE DEDUCTION LIMITS

The home mortgage interest deduction is limited to the interest on the part of the home mortgage debt that isn't more than the qualified loan limit. This is the part of the home mortgage debt that is grandfathered debt or that isn't more than the limits for home acquisition debt.

POINTS AND PREPAID MORTGAGE INTEREST

The term "points" is often used to describe some of the charges paid, or treated as paid, by a borrower to take out a loan or a mortgage. These charges are also called loan origination fees, maximum loan charges, or premium charges. Any of these charges (points) that are solely for the use of money are interest. Because points are prepaid interest, taxpayers generally can't deduct the full amount in the year paid, but must deduct the interest over the term of the loan.

The method used to figure the amount of points that can be deducted each year follows the original issue discount (OID) rules. In this case, points are equivalent to OID, which is the difference between:

- The amount borrowed (redemption price at maturity, or principal); and
- The proceeds (issue price).

If the taxpayer pays interest in advance for a period that goes beyond the end of the tax year, he or she must spread this interest over the tax years to which it applies. The taxpayer can deduct in each year only the interest that qualifies as home mortgage interest for that year.

INVESTMENT INTEREST EXPENSE

If taxpayers borrow money to buy property held for investment, the interest paid is investment interest. They can deduct investment interest subject to the limit discussed later. However, they cannot deduct interest incurred to produce tax-exempt income.

Investment interest does not include any qualified home mortgage interest, or any interest taken into account in computing income or loss from a passive activity.

An investment interest expense is any amount of interest that is paid on loan proceeds used to purchase investments or securities. Investment interest expenses include margin interest used to leverage securities in a brokerage account and interest on a loan used to buy property held for investment. An investment interest expense is deductible in certain circumstances.

CHARITABLE CONTRIBUTIONS

A charitable contribution is a donation or gift to, or for the use of, a qualified organization. It is voluntary and is made without getting, or expecting to get, anything of equal value.

QUALIFIED ORGANIZATIONS

Taxpayers may deduct a charitable contribution made to, or for the use of, any of the following organizations that otherwise are qualified under section 170(c) of the Internal Revenue Code:

- A state or United States possession (or political subdivision thereof), or the United States or the District of Columbia, if made exclusively for public purposes;
- A community chest, corporation, trust, fund, or foundation, organized or created in the United States or its possessions, or under the laws of the United States, any state, the District of Columbia or any possession of the United States, and organized and operated exclusively for charitable, religious, educational, scientific, or literary purposes, or for the prevention of cruelty to children or animals;
- A church, synagogue, or other religious organization;
- A war veterans' organization or its post, auxiliary, trust, or foundation organized in the United States or its possessions;
- A nonprofit volunteer fire company;
- A civil defense organization created under federal, state, or local law (this includes unreimbursed expenses of civil defense volunteers that are directly connected with and solely attributable to their volunteer services);
- A domestic fraternal society, operating under the lodge system, but only if the contribution is to be used exclusively for charitable purposes;
- A nonprofit cemetery company if the funds are irrevocably dedicated to the perpetual care of the cemetery as a whole and not a particular lot or mausoleum crypt.

NON-QUALIFYING ORGANIZATIONS

Individuals can't deduct contributions to organizations that aren't qualified to receive tax-deductible contributions, including the following.

1. Certain state bar associations if:
    1. The bar isn't a political subdivision of a state;
    2. The bar has private, as well as public, purposes, such as promoting the professional interests of members; and
    3. The contribution is unrestricted and can be used for private purposes.
2. Chambers of commerce and other business leagues or organizations.
3. Civic leagues and associations.
4. Country clubs and other social clubs.

Foreign organizations other than certain Canadian, Israeli, or Mexican charitable organizations. Also, individuals can't deduct a contribution made to any qualifying organization if the contribution is earmarked to go to a foreign organization. However, certain contributions to a qualified organization for use in a program conducted by a foreign charity may be deductible as long as they aren't earmarked to go to the foreign charity. For the contribution to be deductible, the qualified organization must approve the program as furthering its own exempt purposes and must keep control over the use of the contributed funds. The contribution also is deductible if the foreign charity is only an administrative arm of the qualified organization.

- Homeowners' associations.
- Labor unions.
- Political organizations and candidates.

SUBSTANTIATION REQUIREMENTS OF CHARITABLE GIFTS

Individuals must keep records to prove the amount of the contributions made during the year. The kind of records that must be kept depends on the amount of the contributions and whether they are:

- Cash contributions,
- Non-cash contributions, or
- Out-of-pocket expenses when donating services.

RULES FOR CASH DONATIONS

Cash contributions include payments made by cash, check, electronic funds transfer, online payment service, debit card, credit card, payroll deduction, or a transfer of a gift card redeemable for cash.

Individuals can't deduct a cash contribution, regardless of the amount, unless they keep one of the following.

- A bank record that shows the name of the qualified organization, the date of the contribution, and the amount of the contribution. Bank records may include:
    - A canceled check.
    - A bank or credit union statement. A credit card statement.
    - An electronic fund transfer receipt.
    - A scanned image of both sides of a canceled check obtained from a bank or credit union website.
- A receipt (or a letter or other written communication such as an e-mail) from the qualified organization showing the name of the organization, the date of the contribution, and the amount of the contribution.
- The payroll deduction records described next.

CASH DONATIONS OF $250 OR MORE

Individuals can claim a deduction for a contribution of $250 or more only if they have a contemporaneous written acknowledgment of the contribution from the qualified organization or certain payroll deduction records. If they made more than one contribution of $250 or more, they must have either a separate acknowledgment for each or one acknowledgment that lists each contribution and the date of each contribution and shows the total contributions.

Amount of contribution

In figuring whether the contribution is $250 or more, don't combine separate contributions. For example, if a taxpayer gave his church $25 each week, the weekly payments don't have to be combined. Each payment is a separate contribution.

If contributions are made by payroll deduction, the deduction from each paycheck is treated as a separate contribution.

RULES FOR NON-CASH DONATIONS

Substantiation requirements for contributions not made in cash depend on whether the deduction for the contribution is:

- Less than $250,
- At least $250 but not more than $500, Over $500 but not more than $5,000, or
- Over $5,000.

The substantiation requirements for non-cash contributions of more than $500 also apply to any return filed for any carryover year.

Amount of Deduction

In figuring whether the deduction is $500 or more, combine the claimed deductions for all similar items of property donated to any charitable organization during the year.

- Total deduction over $500.
- If the total deduction for all noncash contributions for the year is over $500, taxpayers must complete Form 8283 and attach it to the Form 1040 or 1040-SR. Use Section A of Form 8283 to report noncash contributions for which a deduction of $5,000 or less per item is claimed(or group of similar items). Also use Section A to report contributions of publicly traded securities. See Deduction over $5,000 next, for the items that must be reported on Section B.
- The IRS may disallow the deduction for noncash charitable contributions if it is more than $500 and if Form 8283 is submitted with the return.
- Deduction over $5,000. Taxpayers must complete Section B of Form 8283 for each item or group of similar items for which claimed deduction of over $5,000. (However, if you contributed publicly traded securities, complete Section A instead.) In figuring whether the deduction for a group of similar items was more than $5,000, consider all items in the group, even if items in the group were donated to more than one organization. However, a separate

Form 8283 must be filed, Section B, for each organization. The organization that received the property must complete and sign Part IV of Section B.

SPECIAL RULES OF DONATED VEHICLES

A qualified vehicle is:

- A car or any motor vehicle manufactured mainly for use on public streets, roads, and highways; A boat; or
- An airplane.

Deduction more than $500

If individuals donate a qualified vehicle with a claimed fair market value of more than $500, they can deduct the smaller of:

- The gross proceeds from the sale of the vehicle by the organization, or
- The vehicle's fair market value on the date of the contribution. If the vehicle's fair market value was more than the cost or other basis, taxpayers may have to reduce the fair market value to figure the deductible amount.

If a taxpayer donated a car, boat, airplane, or other vehicle, he may have to attach a copy of Form 1098-C

The taxpayer must attach to the return Copy B of the Form 1098-C, Contributions of Motor Vehicles, Boats, and Airplanes (or other statement containing the same information as Form 1098-C) received from the organization. The Form 1098-C (or other statement) will show the gross proceeds from the sale of the vehicle.

If the taxpayer does not attach Form 1098-C (or other statement), he can't deduct the contribution. The taxpayer must get Form 1098-C (or other statement) within 30 days of the sale of the vehicle. But if exception 1 or 2 (described later) applies, get Form 1098-C (or other statement) within 30 days of the donation.

CONTRIBUTION LIMITS

The limit that applies to a contribution depends on the type of property given and which category of qualified organization has given it to. The amount of a contribution that can be deducted generally is limited to a percentage of the adjusted gross income (AGI), but may be further reduced if the contributions made are subject to more than one of the limits discussed in this section.

- The total deduction of charitable contributions can't exceed the AGI. If the contributions are subject to more than one of the limits, include all or part of each contribution in a certain order, carrying over any excess to a subsequent year (if allowed).

CHARITABLE CONTRIBUTIONS CARRYOVERS

Individuals can carry over any contributions that can't be deducted in the current year because they exceed the limits based on the adjusted gross income (AGI). Except for qualified conservation contributions, individuals may be able to deduct the excess in each of the next 5 years until it is used up, but not beyond that time.

A carryover of a qualified conservation contribution can be carried forward for 15 years.

Contributions carried over are subject to the same percentage limits in the year to which they are carried. For example, contributions subject to the 20% limit in the year in which they are made are 20% limit contributions in the year to which they are carried.

SPECIAL RULES FOR CONSERVATION BASEMENTS

"Conservation easement" is the generic term for easements granted for preservation of land areas for outdoor recreation, protection of a relatively natural habitat for fish, wildlife, or plants, or a similar ecosystem, preservation of open space for the scenic enjoyment of the public or pursuant to a Federal, State, or local governmental conservation policy, and preservation of a historically important land area or historic building.

Conservation easements permanently restrict how land or buildings are used. The "deed of conservation easement" describes the conservation purpose, the restrictions and the permissible uses of the property. The deed must be recorded in the public record and must contain legally binding restrictions enforceable by the donee organization.

To be deductible, donated conservation easements must be legally binding, permanent restrictions on the use, modification and development of property such as parks, wetlands, farmland, forest land, scenic areas, historic land or historic structures. The restrictions on the property must be in perpetuity. Current and future owners of the easement and the underlying property must all be bound by the terms of the conservation easement deed.

The general rule is that no charitable contribution deduction is allowed for a transfer of property of less than the taxpayer's entire interest in the property. I.R.C. § 170(f)(3). Section 170(f)(3) (B)(iii) provides an exception to the partial interest rule for contributions of qualified conservation easements.

PERSONAL CASUALTY AND THEFT LOSSES

Personal casualty and theft losses of an individual, sustained in a tax year beginning after 2017, are deductible only to the extent that the losses are attributable to a federally declared disaster. Personal casualty and theft losses attributable to a federally declared disaster are subject to the $500 per casualty.

An exception to the rule above, limiting the personal casualty and theft loss deduction to losses attributable to a federally declared disaster, applies if the individual has personal casualty gains for the tax year. In this case, he or she will reduce the personal casualty gains by any casualty losses not attributable to a federally declared disaster. Any excess gain is used to reduce losses from a federally declared disaster.

MISCELLANEOUS ITEMIZED DEDUCTIONS

- Amortizable premium on taxable bonds.
- Casualty and theft losses from income-producing property.
- Excess deductions (including administrative expenses) allowed a beneficiary on termination of an estate or trust.
- Federal estate tax on income in respect of a decedent.
- Fines or penalties.
- Gambling losses up to the amount of gambling winnings.
- Impairment-related work expenses of persons with disabilities.
- Losses from Ponzi-type investment schemes.
- Repayments of more than $3,000 under a claim of right.
- Unlawful discrimination claims.
- Unrecovered investment in an annuity.
- An ordinary loss attributable to a contingent payment debt instrument or an inflation-indexed debt instrument (for example, a Treasury Inflation-Protected Security).

DEDUCTIONS FOR NON-RESIDENT ALIENS

If a taxpayer is a nonresident alien, he or she cannot claim the standard deduction.

The taxpayer can claim deductions to figure the effectively connected taxable income (shown on page 1 of Form 1040NR). Taxpayers generally cannot claim deductions related to income that is not connected with the U.S. business activities (shown on page 4 of Form 1040NR). Except for certain itemized deductions, that can be claimed as deductions only to the extent they are connected with the effectively connected income.

Nonresident aliens can deduct certain itemized deductions if they receive income effectively connected with their U.S. trade or business. These deductions include:

- State and local income taxes,
- Charitable contributions to U.S. non-profit organizations, Casualty and theft losses, from a federally declared disaster, and Other

- itemized deductions.

Use Schedule A of Form 1040NR to claim itemized deductions. If a taxpayer is filing Form 1040NR-EZ, he or she can only claim a deduction for state or local income taxes. If the taxpayer is claiming any other deduction, he or she must file Form 1040NR. Exemptions. For tax years beginning after December 31, 2017, nonresident aliens cannot claim a personal exemption deduction for themselves, their spouses, or their dependents.

NON-DEDUCTIBLE EXPENSES

- Adoption expenses (may be able to claim adoption credit)
- Broker's commissions.
- Burial or funeral expenses, including the cost of a cemetery lot.
- Campaign expenses.
- Capital expenses.
- Check-writing fees.
- Club dues.
- Commuting expenses.
- Fees and licenses, such as car licenses, marriage licenses, and dog tags.
- Fines or penalties.
- Health spa expenses.
- Hobby losses
- Home repairs, insurance, and rent.
- Home security system.
- Illegal bribes and kickbacks
- Investment-related seminars.
- Life insurance premiums paid by the insured.
- Lobbying expenses.
- Losses from the sale of your home, furniture, personal car, etc.
- Lost or misplaced cash or property.
- Lunch with coworkers.
- Meals while working late.
- Medical expenses as business expenses other than medical examinations required by your employer.
- Personal disability insurance premiums.
- Personal legal expenses.
- Personal, living, or family expenses.
- Political contributions.
- Professional accreditation fees.
- Professional reputation improvement expenses.
- Relief fund contributions.
- Residential telephone line.
- Stockholders' meeting attendance expenses.
- Tax-exempt income earning/collecting expenses.
- The value of wages never received or lost vacation time.

- Travel expenses for another individual.
- Voluntary unemployment benefit fund contributions.
- Wristwatches

POP QUIZ & ANSWER SHEET

STANDARD DEDUCTIONS & ITEMIZED DEDUCTIONS

POP QUIZ

Test your knowledge on *Standard Deductions & Itemized Deductions* by answering the questions below. The answer sheet may be found at the end of the Pop Quiz.

Q1: Who is eligible for the standard deduction?

A. An individual who was a nonresident alien or dual status alien during the year.

B. An individual who files a return for a period of less than 12 months due to a change in his or her annual accounting period.

C. An estate or trust, common trust fund, or partnership.

D. A nonresident alien who is married to a U.S. citizen or resident alien at the end of the tax year and makes a joint election with his or her spouse to be treated as a U.S. resident for the entire tax year.

Q2: A taxpayer may benefit by itemizing deductions for things that include:

A. Real estate and personal property taxes

B. Mortgage insurance premiums

C. Donations to a qualified charity

D. All of the Above

Q3: All of the following are benefits from itemizing deductions on Schedule A, except:

A. Itemized deductions are less than 7.5% of Adjusted Gross Income.

B. Had large uninsured medical and dental expenses during the year.

C. Paid interest and taxes on your home.

D. Made large contributions to qualified charities.

Q4: Which of the following medical expenses do not qualify for deductions?

A. Payments of fees to doctors, dentists, surgeons, chiropractors, psychiatrists, psychologists, and nontraditional medical practitioners.

B. Costs for meals and lodging while attending a medical conference.

C. Payments to participate in a weight-loss program for a specific disease or diseases diagnosed by a physician, including obesity, but not ordinarily payments for diet food items or the payment of health club dues.

D. Payments for insurance premiums you paid for policies that cover medical care or for a qualified long-term care insurance policy covering qualified long-term care services.

Q5: What is the total combined limit for the deduction of state and local income, sales or property taxes?

A. $5,000
B. $7,500
C. $10,000
D. $15,000

Q6: All of the following are items that a taxpayer can use to substantiate a cash contribution of $250 or less, except:

A. A bank record that shows the name of the qualified organization, the date of the contribution, and the amount of the contribution.
B. A receipt (or a letter or other written communication such as an e-mail) from the qualified organization showing the name of the organization, the date of the contribution, and the amount of the contribution.
C. No docs are needed for cash donations less than $250.
D. Canceled check or bank statement showing the name of the qualified organization, the date and amount.

Q7: What form should be filed to qualify a deduction for a donated vehicle of more than $500 deduction?

A. Form 1098-C
B. Form 8962
C. Form 1095-A
D. Form 8283

Q8: How long can a carryover of a qualified conservation contribution be carried?

A. 5 years
B. 10 years
C. 15 years
D. 20 years

Q9: If you make a qualified contribution for relief efforts in a qualified disaster area, how much deduction would be for the qualified contribution?

A. 25% of your adjusted gross income minus your deduction for all other contributions.
B. 50% of your adjusted gross income minus your deduction for all other contributions.
C. 75% of your adjusted gross income minus your deduction for all other contributions.
D. 100% of your adjusted gross income minus your deduction for all other contributions.

Q10: Non-Resident Aliens can take the following itemized deductions if they are connected with income related to their US trade or business, except:

A. State and local income taxes
B. Qualifying charitable contributions to US nonprofit organizations
C. Casualty and theft losses in a presidentially declared disaster area
D. Medical expenses from a US car accident

ANSWER SHEET

1. Answer is D – A nonresident alien who is married to a U.S. citizen or resident alien at the end of the tax year and makes a joint election with his or her spouse to be treated as a U.S. resident for the entire tax year.

2. Answer is D – All of the Above

3. Answer is A – Itemized deductions are less than 7.5% of Adjusted Gross Income.

4. Answer is B – Costs for meals and lodging while attending a medical conference.

5. Answer is C – $10,000

6. Answer is C – No docs are needed for cash donations less than $250.

7. Answer is A – Form 1098-C

8. Answer is C – 15 years

9. Answer is D – 100% of your adjusted gross income minus your deduction for all other contributions.

10. Answer is D – Medical expenses from a US car accident.

THE AFFORDABLE CARE ACT

OVERVIEW

- Taxpayers who choose the advance premium tax credit payment must file a tax return
- The reconciliation is calculated on form 8962, Premium tax credit
- If at the end of the year the taxpayer has taken more premium tax credit in advance than they are due based on their final income the taxpayer will have to pay back the excess when they file their taxes.
- The American rescue plan act passed on March 11, 2021 retroactively waived the payback for the advanced premium tax credit. In 2020 no repayment is required for taxpayers receiving excess advance PTCs
- The premium tax credit is a refundable credit. If the amount of the credit is more than the amount of the tax liability the taxpayer may receive the difference as a refund.

Dependency Relationships

The Affordable Care Act includes the individual shared responsibility provision and the premium tax credit that may affect the tax return.

The individual shared responsibility provision requires taxpayers, their spouses, and their dependents to have qualifying health insurance for the entire year. In addition, taxpayers may be eligible for the premium tax credit if they purchased health coverage through the Health Insurance Marketplace.

Health Coverage for Older Children

Health coverage for an employee's children under 26 years of age is generally tax free to the employee.

This health care tax benefit applies to various workplace and retiree health plans. As a result, employers with cafeteria plans – plans that allow employees to choose from a menu of tax-free benefit options and cash or taxable benefits – are allowed to permit employees to begin making pre-tax contributions to pay for this expanded benefit. Tax-free treatment for employer-provided health care to an employee's child has been extended until the end of the year in which the child turns age 26.

The costs and reimbursements under employer health plans for coverage for an employee's eligible children are free of income, FICA and FUTA taxes, without regard to the IRS's dependency tests.

This tax benefit also applies to self-employed individuals who qualify for the self-employed health insurance deduction on their federal income tax return

Additional Medicare Tax

A 0.9 percent Additional Medicare Tax applies to an individual's wages, Railroad Retirement Tax Act compensation, and self-employment income that exceed a threshold amount based on the individual's filing status.

- $250,000 for married filing jointly;
- $125,000 for married filing separately; and
- $200,000 for all other taxpayers.

If individuals receive both Medicare wages and self-employment income, calculate the Additional Medicare Tax by:

- Calculating the Additional Medicare Tax on any Medicare wages in excess of the applicable threshold for the taxpayer's filing status, without regard to whether any tax was withheld;
- Reducing the applicable threshold for the filing status by the total amount of Medicare wages received (but not below zero); and
- Calculating the Additional Medicare Tax on any self-employment income in excess of the reduced threshold.

Don't consider a self-employment loss for purposes of this tax. Compare Railroad retirement (RRTA) compensation separately to the threshold.

All Medicare wages, railroad retirement (RRTA) compensation, and self-employment income subject to Medicare Tax are subject to Additional Medicare Tax, if paid in excess of the applicable threshold for the taxpayer's filing status.\

An employer is responsible for withholding the Additional Medicare Tax from wages or compensation it pays to an employee in excess of $200,000 in a calendar year.

PREMIUM TAX CREDIT

The premium tax credit – also known as PTC – is a refundable credit that helps eligible individuals and families cover the premiums for their health insurance purchased through the Health Insurance Marketplace. To get this credit, individuals must meet certain requirements and file a tax return with Form 8962, Premium Tax Credit.

Who Qualifies?

Individuals are eligible for the premium tax credit if they meet all of the following requirements:

- Have household income that falls within a certain range.

- Do not file a tax return using the filing status of Married Filing Separately
    - There is an exception to this rule that allows certain victims of domestic abuse and spousal abandonment to claim the credit using Married Filing Separately.
- Cannot be claimed as a dependent by another person.

Individuals need to meet these additional requirements: In the same month, they or a family member:

- Have health insurance coverage through a Health Insurance Marketplace.
- Are not able to get affordable coverage through an eligible employer-sponsored plan that provides minimum value.
- Are not eligible for coverage through a government program, like Medicaid, Medicare, CHIP or TRICARE.
- Pay the share of premiums not covered by advance credit payments.

When individuals enroll, the Marketplace will determine if they are eligible for advance payments of the premium tax credit, also called advance credit payments. Advance credit payments are amounts paid to the insurance company on the behalf to lower the out- of-pocket cost for the health insurance premiums.

Change in Circumstances

If an individual benefits from advance payments of the premium tax credit, it is important to report life changes to the Marketplace as they happen throughout the year.

Certain changes to the household, income or family size may affect the amount of the premium tax credit.

These changes can alter the tax refund, or cause the individual to owe tax. Reporting these changes promptly will help get the proper type and amount of financial assistance.

Claiming and Reconciling the Credit

If taxpayers get the benefit of advance credit payments in any amount – or if they plan to claim the premium tax credit – they must file a federal income tax return and attach Form 8962, Premium Tax Credit, to the return. Taxpayers can claim the premium tax credit and reconcile the credit with the amount of the advance credit payments for the year on Form 8962.

Taxpayers must file a return even if they are usually not required to do so. Filing the return without reconciling the advance payments will delay the refund and may affect future advance credit payments. For more information on filing a return to claim and reconcile the credit see Premium Tax Credit: Claiming the Credit and Reconciling Advance Credit Payments.

Filing electronically is the easiest way to file a complete and accurate tax return. Electronic filing options include free volunteer assistance, IRS Free File, commercial software and professional assistance.

Key Documents and Forms

1. Form 1095-A, Health Insurance Marketplace Statement

The Marketplace will provide Form 1095-A if a taxpayer or one of his dependents had coverage through a Marketplace. For more information, visit our Health Insurance Marketplace Statement page.

If the taxpayer also receives Form 1095-B or Form 1095-C, which are unrelated to the Marketplace, see our questions and answers for information about how these forms affect the tax return.

2. Form 8962, Premium Tax Credit

Use the information on Form 1095-A to claim the credit or reconcile advance credit payments on Form 8962, Premium Tax Credit.

3. Form 1040

File Form 8962 with the 1040 or 1040-NR.

4. Pub. 974, Premium Tax Credit

PREMIUM TAX CREDIT ELIGIBILITY

Taxpayers may be allowed a premium tax credit if:

- The taxpayer or a tax family member enrolled in health insurance coverage through the Marketplace for at least one month of a calendar year in which he or she was not eligible for affordable coverage through an eligible employer-sponsored plan that provides minimum value or eligible to enroll in government health coverage – like Medicare, Medicaid, or TRICARE.
- The health insurance premiums for at least one of those same months are paid by the original due date of the return. They can be paid either through advance credit payments, by the taxpayers, or by someone else
- The taxpayer is within certain income limits
- Taxpayers do not file a married filing separately tax return
    - There are exceptions for certain victims of domestic abuse and spousal abandonment. For more information about these exceptions, see the Premium Tax Credit questions and answers
- Taxpayers cannot be claimed as a dependent by another person

They are not eligible for the premium tax credit for coverage purchased outside the Marketplace. Answer the yes-or-no questions in the eligibility chart or use the "Am I Eligible to Claim the Premium Tax Credit" interview tool to see if the taxpayer may qualify for the premium tax credit.

Income Criteria

To be eligible for the premium tax credit, the household income must be at least 100 – but no more than 400 – percent of the federal poverty line for the family size, although there are two exceptions for individuals with household income below 100 percent of the applicable federal poverty line.

Remember that simply meeting the income requirements does not mean the taxpayer is eligible for the premium tax credit. He or she must also meet the other eligibility criteria

For information about the two exceptions for individuals with household income below 100 percent of the federal poverty line, see the instructions to Form 8962.

Here are four things to remember about how the income affects the premium tax credit:

- The amount of the premium tax credit is based on a sliding scale, with greater credit amounts available to those with lower incomes.
- If the advance credit payments made on the behalf are more than the allowed premium tax credit, the taxpayer will have to repay some or all the excess. If the household income is 400 percent or more of the federal poverty line for the family size, the taxpayer will have to repay all of the excess advance credit payments.
- If the projected household income is close to the 400 percent upper limit, be sure to carefully consider the amount of advance credit payments the taxpayer chooses to have paid on his behalf.
- If the household income on the tax return is more than 400 percent of the federal poverty line for the family size, the taxpayer is not allowed a premium tax credit and will have to repay all of the advance credit payments made on behalf of the taxpayer and his or her tax family members.

Other Criteria

Aside from the income, there are other factors that affect the credit amount, including:

- Cost of available insurance coverage
- Where the individual lives
- The address
- The family size

Married Filing Separately

If the taxpayer is married and he or she files the tax return using the filing status married filing separately, the taxpayer will not be eligible for the premium tax credit unless he or she is a victim of domestic abuse and spousal abandonment and can meet certain criteria. Details regarding this relief are in the instructions for Form 8962 and Publication 974.

Generally, a taxpayer who lives apart from his or her spouse for the last six months of the tax year is considered unmarried if the taxpayer files a separate return, maintains a household that is also the main home of the taxpayer's dependent child for more than half the year, and furnishes more than half the cost of the household during the tax year.

For help in finding out if the taxpayer is eligible for the premium tax credit, check out the Premium Tax Credit Flow Chart or through the accessible text Answering a few yes-or-no questions can help determine if the individual might be eligible for the credit.

ADVANCE PREMIUM TAX CREDIT REPAYMENTS

When a taxpayer enrolls in coverage and requests financial assistance, the Marketplace will estimate the amount of the premium tax credit will be allowed for the year of coverage.

To make this estimate, the Marketplace uses the information provided, including information about:

- The family composition
- The household income
- Whether those enrolling are eligible for other non-Marketplace coverage

Based on the estimate from the Marketplace, taxpayers can choose to have all, some, or none of the estimated credit paid in advance directly to the insurance company on their behalf.

These payments – which are called advance payments of the premium tax credit or advance credit payments – lower what is paid out-of-pocket for the monthly premiums.

If the taxpayers do not get advance credit payments, they will be responsible for paying the full monthly premium.

Filing a federal tax return to claim and reconcile the Credit

If the taxpayer or someone in his or her family receives advance payments of the premium tax credit through the Health Insurance Marketplace, the taxpayer must complete Form 8962, Premium Tax Credit.

The taxpayer will receive Form 1095-A, Health Insurance Marketplace Statement, which provides information about the health care coverage.

Use the information from Form 1095-A to complete Form 8962 to reconcile advance payments of the premium tax credit on the tax return.

Filing the return without reconciling the advance payments will delay the refund. Taxpayers must file an income tax return for this purpose even if they are not otherwise required to do so.

If the taxpayer chooses not to get advance credit payments, he or she can claim the full amount of the premium tax credit allowed when filing the tax return. This will increase the refund or lower the amount of tax owed.

Taxpayers must file if:

- They are claiming the premium tax credit.
- Advance credit payments were paid to the health insurer for themselves or someone else in their tax family. For purposes of the premium tax credit, the tax family is every individual claimed on the tax return – the taxpayer, his or her spouse if filing jointly, and the dependents.
- Taxpayers told the Marketplace that they would claim an exemption for someone on the tax return who was benefiting from advance credit payments, however, no one ended up claiming that individual.

Failing to file the tax return may prevent future advance credit payments

If advance credit payments are made for a taxpayer or an individual in his or her tax family, and the taxpayer does not file a tax return, he or she will not be eligible for advance credit payments in future years. This means the taxpayer will be responsible for the full cost of the monthly premiums.

In addition, the taxpayer may have to pay back some or all of the advance credit payments that are made on behalf of the taxpayer or an individual in the tax family.

Advance payments of the premium tax credit are reviewed in the fall by the Health Insurance Marketplace for the next calendar year as part of their annual enrollment process.

Reporting changes in circumstances

If the household income goes up or the size of the household is smaller than the taxpayer reported to the Marketplace - for example, because a son or daughter the taxpayer thought would be his or her dependent will not be the dependent for the year of coverage - the advance credit payments may be more than the premium tax credit allowed for the year.

If taxpayers report the change, the Marketplace can lower the amount of the advance credit payments. If the household income goes down or the taxpayer gains a household member, he or she could qualify for more advance credit payments than are now being paid. This could lower what needs to be paid in monthly premiums.

Changes in circumstances that can affect the amount of the actual premium tax credit include:

- Increases or decreases in household income. Events that could result in a significant increase to household income include:
    - Lump sum payments of Social Security benefits, including Social Security Disability Insurance
    - Lump sum taxable distributions from an individual retirement account or other retirement arrangement
    - Debt forgiveness or cancellation, such as the cancellation of credit card debt
- Marriage or divorce
- Birth or adoption of a child
- Other changes affecting the composition of the tax family which includes the taxpayer, the spouse if filing jointly, and the dependents
- Gaining or losing eligibility for government sponsored or employer sponsored health care coverage
- Moving to a different address

Repaying excess advance credit payments

The amount of the excess advance credit payments that increases the tax liability may be limited if the household income is less than 400 percent of the applicable federal poverty line.

On the other hand, if the household income is 400 percent or more of the applicable federal poverty line, the taxpayer will have to repay all of the excess advance credit payments.

If the filing status is Married Filing Separately, the repayment limitation above applies to both spouses separately based on the household income reported on each return.

The Marketplace will send the taxpayer a Health Insurance Marketplace statement, Form 1095-A, by January 31 of the year following the year of coverage. This form shows the amount of the premiums for the taxpayer's and the family's health care plans. This form also includes other information – such as advance credit payments made on the taxpayer's behalf – that need to compute the premium tax credit. For more information about Form 1095-A see Health Insurance Marketplace Statements.

If the taxpayer also receives Form 1095-B or 1095-C, which are unrelated to the Marketplace, see our questions and answers for information about how these forms affect the tax return.

How advance credit payments affect the refund

If the premium tax credit computed on the return is more than the advance credit payments made on the taxpayer's behalf during the year, the difference will increase the refund or lower the amount of tax owed. This will be reported on Form 1040, Schedule 3.

If the advance credit payments are more than the amount of the premium tax credit the taxpayer is allowed, called excess advance credit payments, the taxpayer will add all – or a portion of – the excess advance credit payments to the tax liability will be entered on Form 1040, Schedule 2. This will result in either a smaller refund or a larger balance due.

NET INVESTMENT INCOME TAX (NIIT)

Premium Tax Credit
If an individual has income from investments, the individual may be subject to net investment income tax. Individual taxpayers are liable for a 3.8% Net Investment Income Tax on the lesser of their net investment income, or the amount by which their modified adjusted gross income exceeds the statutory threshold amount based on their filing status.

The statutory threshold amounts are:

- Married filing jointly — $250,000,
- Married filing separately — $125,000,
- Single or head of household — $200,000, or
- Qualifying widow(er) with a child — $250,000.

Who Qualifies

In general, net investment income includes, but is not limited to: interest, dividends, capital gains, rental and royalty income, and non-qualified annuities.

Net investment income generally does not include wages, unemployment compensation, Social Security Benefits, alimony, and most self-employment income.

Additionally, net investment income does not include any gain on the sale of a personal residence that is excluded from gross income for regular income tax purposes. To the extent the gain is excluded from gross income for regular income tax purposes, it is not subject to the Net Investment Income Tax.

If an individual owes the net investment income tax, the individual must file Form 8960. Form 8960 Instructions provide details on how to figure the amount of investment income subject to the tax.

If an individual has too little withholding or fails to pay enough quarterly estimated taxes to also cover the Net Investment Income Tax, the individual may be subject to an estimated tax penalty.

ADDITIONAL MEDICARE TAX

Nonresident Aliens (NRAs) are not subject to the Net Investment Income Tax. If an NRA is married to a U.S. citizen or resident and has made, or is planning to make, an election under section 6013(g) or 6013(h) to be treated as a resident alien for purposes of filing as Married Filing Jointly, the final regulations provide these couples special rules and a corresponding section 6013(g)/(h) election for the NIIT.

A dual-resident individual, within the meaning of regulation §301.7701(b)-7(a)(1), who determines that he or she is a resident of a foreign country for tax purposes pursuant to an income tax treaty between the United States and that foreign country and claims benefits of the treaty as a nonresident of the United States is considered a NRA for purposes of the NIIT.

A dual-status individual, who is a resident of the United States for part of the year and a NRA for the other part of the year, is subject to the NIIT only with respect to the portion of the year during which the individual is a United States resident. The threshold amount (described in # 3 above) is not reduced or prorated for a dual-status resident.

Claiming and Reconciling the Credit

Estates and trusts are subject to the Net Investment Income Tax if they have undistributed Net Investment Income and also have adjusted gross income over the dollar amount at which the highest tax bracket for an estate or trust begins for such taxable year under section 1(e) (for tax year 2013, this threshold amount is $11,950).

There are special computational rules for certain unique types of trusts, such as Qualified Funeral Trusts, Charitable Remainder Trusts and Electing Small Business Trusts, which can be found in the final regulations (see # 20 below).

The following trusts are not subject to the Net Investment Income Tax:

- Trusts that are exempt from income taxes imposed by Subtitle A of the Internal Revenue Code (e.g., charitable trusts and qualified retirement plan trusts exempt from tax under section 501, and Charitable Remainder Trusts exempt from tax under section 664).
- A trust or decedent's estate in which all of the unexpired interests are devoted to one or more of the purposes described in section 170(c)(2)(B).
- Trusts that are classified as "grantor trusts" under sections 671-679.
- Trusts that are not classified as "trusts" for federal income tax purposes (e.g., Real Estate Investment Trusts and Common Trust Funds).
- Electing Alaska Native Settlement Trusts.
- Perpetual Care (Cemetery) Trusts.

NIIT BASED ON FILING STATUS

Table 5. Repayment Limitation

Individuals will owe the tax if they have Net Investment Income and have modified adjusted gross income over the following thresholds

Filing Status	Threshold Amount
Married filing jointly	$250,000
Married filing separately	$125,000
Single	$200,000
Head of household (with qualifying person)	$200,000
Qualifying widow(er) with dependent child	$250,000

Taxpayers should be aware that these threshold amounts are not indexed for inflation. Individuals who are exempt from Medicare taxes still may be subject to the Net Investment Income Tax if they have Net Investment Income and also have modified adjusted gross income over the applicable thresholds.

Examples of the Calculation of the Net Investment Income Tax

Single taxpayer with income less than the statutory threshold.

Taxpayer, a single filer, has wages of $180,000 and $15,000 of dividends and capital gains. Taxpayer's modified adjusted gross income is $195,000, which is less than the $200,000 statutory threshold. Taxpayers are not subject to the Net Investment Income Tax.

Single taxpayer with income greater than the statutory threshold.

Taxpayer, a single filer, has $180,000 of wages. Taxpayer also received $90,000 from a passive partnership interest, which is considered Net Investment Income. Taxpayer's modified adjusted gross income is $270,000.

Taxpayer's modified adjusted gross income exceeds the threshold of $200,000 for single taxpayers by $70,000. Taxpayer's Net Investment Income is $90,000.

The Net Investment Income Tax is based on the lesser of $70,000 (the amount that Taxpayer's modified adjusted gross income exceeds the $200,000 threshold) or $90,000 (Taxpayer's Net Investment Income). Taxpayer owes NIIT of $2,660 ($70,000 x 3.8%).

Some taxpayers may be required to pay an Additional Medicare Tax if their income exceeds certain limits. Here are some things that individuals should know about this tax:

- **Tax Rate** - The Additional Medicare Tax rate is 0.9 percent.
- **Income Subject to Tax** - The tax applies to the amount of certain income that is more than a threshold amount. The types of income include:
    - Medicare wages,
    - self-employment income and
    - railroad retirement (RRTA) compensation.
- **Threshold Amount** - Taxpayers base the threshold amount on the filing status. If a taxpayer is married and files a joint return, he or she must combine the spouse's wages, compensation, or self-employment income.

Use the combined total to determine if the income exceeds the threshold.
The threshold amounts are:

Filing Status	Threshold Amount
Married filing jointly	$250,000
Married filing separately	$125,000
Single	$200,000
Head of household	$200,000
Qualifying widow(er) with dependent child	$200,000

- **Withholding/Estimated Tax** - Employers must withhold this tax from the wages or compensation when they pay the taxpayer more than $200,000 in a calendar year. If the taxpayer is self-employed, he or she should include this tax when figuring the estimated tax liability.
- **Underpayment of Estimated Tax** - If the taxpayer had too little tax withheld, or did not pay enough estimated tax, he or she may owe an estimated tax penalty. For more on this topic, see Publication 505, Tax Withholding and Estimated Tax.

If the taxpayer owes this tax, file Form 8959, with the tax return. The taxpayer also reports any Additional Medicare Tax withheld by the employer on Form 8959. Visit IRS.gov for more on this topic. The taxpayer can also get forms and publications on IRS.gov/forms anytime.

Each and every taxpayer has a set of fundamental rights they should be aware of when dealing with the IRS. These are the Taxpayer Bill of Rights. Explore the rights and the obligations to protect them on IRS.gov.

ADDITIONAL MEDICARE TAX BASED ON FILING STATUS

All wages that are currently subject to Medicare Tax are subject to Additional Medicare Tax if they are paid in excess of the applicable threshold for an individual's filing status. For more information on what wages are subject to Medicare Tax, see the chart, Special Rules for Various Types of Services and Payments, in section 15 of Publication 15, (Circular E), Employer's Tax Guide.

An individual will owe Additional Medicare Tax on wages, compensation, and self-employment income (and that of the individual's spouse if married filing jointly) that exceed the applicable threshold for the individual's filing status. Medicare wages and self-employment income are combined to determine if income exceeds the threshold. A self-employment loss is not considered for purposes of this tax. RRTA compensation (which does not include non-qualified stock options granted to RR employees) is separately compared to the threshold.
An employer must withhold Additional Medicare Tax from wages it pays to an individual in excess of $200,000 in a calendar year, without regard to the individual's filing status or wages paid by another employer. An individual may owe more than the amount withheld by the employer, depending on the individual's filing status, wages, compensation, and self-employment income. In that case, the individual should make estimated tax payments and/or request additional income tax withholding using Form W-4, Employee's Withholding Certificate.

POP QUIZ & ANSWER SHEET

THE AFFORDABLE CARE ACT

POP QUIZ

Test your knowledge on The Affordable Care Act by answering the questions below. The answer sheet may be found at the end of the Pop Quiz.

Q1: What is the maximum age of the taxpayer's children to qualify as a dependent for insurance?

A. 17 Years Old
B. 20 Years Old
C. 25 Years Old
D. 26 Years Old

Q2: This is a refundable credit that helps eligible individuals and families cover the premiums for their health insurance purchased through the Health Insurance Marketplace.

A. Premium Tax Credit
B. Qualified Health Benefit
C. Fringe Benefit
D. Affordable Care Act

Q3: The following are the requirements needed by an individual to be eligible for the premium tax credit, except:

A. The household income must be at least 100 – but no more than 400 – percent of the federal poverty line for the family size.
B. The individual does not file a tax return using the filing status of Married Filing Separately.
C. The individual is not claimed as a dependent by another person.
D. The premium tax credit is for coverage purchased outside the Marketplace.

Q4: Why is it important for an individual who benefits from the premium tax credit to report life changes to the Marketplace?

A. Certain changes to a taxpayer's household, income or family size may affect the amount of your premium tax credit.
B. These changes can alter the tax refund or cause the individual to owe tax.
C. Both A & B
D. None of the Above

Q5: If an individual received the benefits of an advance credit payments in any amount or plan to claim the premium tax credit, what form is needed to be filed along with its federal income tax return?

A. Form 8962
B. Form 1095-A
C. Form 1040
D. Form 8886

Q6: Aside from the income, which of the following factors will not affect the premium tax credit amount?

A. Cost of Available Insurance Coverage
B. Household Income
C. Family Size
D. Race

Q7: The premium tax credit is only available to taxpayers who purchase their insurance from ___?

A. Blue Cross Blue Shield
B. Medicare
C. Medicaid
D. Federal Exchange (aka the Marketplace)

Q8: If the taxpayer is covered by health insurance the taxpayer will likely receive one of the following forms, except:

A. 1095-D, Health Insurance Issuance Form
B. Form 1095-A, Health Insurance Marketplace Statement
C. Form 1095-B, Health Coverage
D. Form 1095-C, Employer-Provided Health Insurance Offer and Coverage

Q9: Taxpayers that have investment income over the threshold amount will be subject to ___ Net Investment Income Tax (NIIT).

A. 2.20%
B. 3.80%
C. 4.30%
D. 5.80%

Q10: Which of the following is not included as net investment income?

A. Interest
B. Dividend
C. Non-Qualified Annuities
D. Alimony

ANSWER SHEET

1. Answer is D – 26 Years Old

2. Answer is A – Premium Tax Credit

3. Answer is D – The premium tax credit is for coverage purchased outside the Marketplace.

4. Answer is C – Both A & B

5. Answer is A – Form 8962

6. Answer is D – Race

7. Answer is D – Federal Exchange (aka the Marketplace)

8. Answer is A – 1095-D, Health Insurance Issuance Form

9. Answer is B – 3.80%

10. Answer is D – Alimony

ADDITIONAL TAXES & CREDITS

ALTERNATIVE MINIMUM TAX

The AMT is the excess of the tentative minimum tax over the regular tax. Thus, the AMT is owed only if the tentative minimum tax for the year is greater than the regular tax for that year. The tentative minimum tax is figured separately from the regular tax. In general, compute the tentative minimum tax by:

- Computing taxable income eliminating or reducing certain exclusions and deductions, and taking into account differences with respect to when certain items are taken into account in computing regular taxable income and alternative minimum taxable income (AMTI),
- Subtracting the AMT exemption amount,
- Multiplying the amount computed in (2) by the appropriate AMT tax rates, and
- Subtracting the AMT foreign tax credit.

The law sets the AMT exemption amounts and AMT tax rates. Taxpayers can use the special capital gain rates in effect for the regular tax if they're lower than the AMT tax rates that would otherwise apply. In addition, some tax credits that reduce regular tax liability don't reduce AMT tax liability.

AMT PREFERENCE ITEMS

A tax preference item is a type of income, normally received tax-free, that may trigger the alternative minimum tax (AMT) for taxpayers. Tax preference items include interest on private activity municipal-bonds, qualifying exclusions for small business stock, and excess intangible drilling costs for oil and gas - if the amount of these items exceeds 40% of AMT income. Tax preference items are added to the amount of AMT income in the IRS' tax formula.

The tax preference item is income that subjects an individual to the AMT and is treated differently for regular tax and AMT purposes – it is excluded when calculating one's ordinary tax liability but is included when calculating one's liability for the alternative minimum tax. Thus, a tax preference item would be tax-deductible under normal circumstances but is not for purposes of the alternative minimum tax. If the amount of tax preference items exceeds a certain percentage of the taxpayer's income, the taxpayer must add these items back to his or her taxable income to compute the amount of tax owed, thus creating a higher tax bill. To calculate the AMT, then, calculate the taxable income the usual way and then add back preference items for minimum tax purposes.

Tax preference items include:

- Deductions for accelerated depreciation/depletion

- Net income from oil and gas properties
- Excess intangible drilling costs
- Interest on special private activity bonds reduced by any deduction (not allowable in computing the regular tax) which would have been allowable if such interest were included in gross income
- Qualifying exclusion for small business stock
- Capital gains from exercise of stock options
- Investment tax credits

Like the AMT itself, tax preference items are designed to prevent high-income taxpayers from avoiding too much income tax through participating in certain activities. For example, investors who own private-activity bonds (PAB) issued after August 1986 must declare all income received from these bonds, minus investment expenses. This rule, thereby, prevents taxpayers from shielding all of their investment income in this type of bond issue.

CREDIT FOR PRIOR YEAR MINIMUM TAX

For a given tax year, if a taxpayer is not required to pay alternative minimum tax (AMT) but did pay AMT in a previous year, they may be able to claim a minimum tax credit against their current year taxes. This credit may be both refundable and nonrefundable, that is, if the taxpayer qualifies, the credit can not only reduce their tax liability but also increase their refund. A taxpayer cannot claim this credit if they are required to pay AMT in the same year.

AMT is caused by two types of adjustments and preferences—deferral items and exclusion items. Deferral items generally don't cause a permanent difference in taxable income over time. One example is depreciation.

Exclusion items cause a permanent difference in taxable income. Examples are:

- Itemized deductions (including investment interest expense reported on Schedule E)
- Certain tax-exempt interest
- Depletion
- Section 1202 exclusion
- Adjustments related to exclusion items

The minimum tax credit is only allowed for AMT caused by deferral items.

The credit is figured on Form 8801. Even if the taxpayer cannot claim the credit, filing Form 8801 allows them to carry the credit forward

KIDDIE TAX ON INVESTMENT

The following two situations may affect the tax and reporting of the unearned income of certain children.

- If a child's interest, dividends, and other unearned income total more than $2,300, it may be subject to tax. The unearned income of certain children is taxed using the tax brackets and rates for estates and trusts unless an election is made to calculate the child's tax based on the parent's tax rate.
- If a child's only income is interest and dividend income (including capital gain distributions) and totals less than $11,000, the taxpayer may be able to elect to include that income on the return rather than file a return for the child.

Tax for Certain Children Who Have Unearned Income. Use Form 8615, Tax for Certain Children Who Have Unearned Income to figure the tax on unearned income over $2,200 if the taxpayer is under age 18, and in certain situations older. Attach Form 8615 to the tax return if all of the following conditions are met.

1. The unearned income was more than $2,300.
2. The taxpayer meets one of the following age requirements:
    - The taxpayer is under age 18 at the end of the tax year,
    - The taxpayer is age 18 at the end of the tax year and he or she didn't have earned income that was more than half of the support, or
    - The taxpayer is a full-time student at least age 19 and under age 24 at the end of the tax year and he or she didn't have earned income that was more than half of the support.
2. At least one of the parents was alive at the end of the tax year.
3. The taxpayer is required to file a tax return for the tax year.
4. The taxpayer doesn't file a joint return for the tax year.

If the taxpayer is required to file Form 8615, he or she may be subject to the Net Investment Income Tax (NIIT). NIIT is a 3.8% tax on the lesser of net investment income or the excess of the modified adjusted gross income (MAGI) over a threshold amount. Use Form 8960, Net Investment Income Tax to figure this tax.

FIRST TIME HOMEBUYER CREDIT REPAYMENT

General repayment rules for 2008 purchases. If a taxpayer was allowed the first-time homebuyer credit for a qualifying home purchase made between April 9, 2008, and December 31, 2008, he or she generally must repay the credit over 15 years. To repay the credit, the taxpayer must increase the federal income taxes by 6⅔% (or 1/15) of the amount of the credit for each taxable year in the 15-year repayment period. The repayment period begins with the second taxable year following the year of qualifying home

Example:

A taxpayer was allowed a $7,500 first-time homebuyer credit for 2008. He must repay the credit. His 15-year repayment period started with 2010, the second taxable year from 2008. To repay the credit, he must add $500 (which is 6⅔% of $7,500) to his federal income tax for each taxable year in the repayment period.

General repayment rules for post-2008 purchases. For qualifying purchases made after 2008, the repayment requirement of the first-time homebuyer credit is generally waived.

Acceleration of repayment. In general, in the case of a home purchased in 2008 for which a taxpayer received the first-time homebuyer credit, if he or she dispose of it, or if the taxpayer (and the spouse if married) stop using it as a principal residence in any taxable year during a 15-year repayment period, the credit repayment is accelerated. Similarly, in the case of a home purchased after 2008 for which the taxpayer received the credit, if he or she disposes of it or if the taxpayer (and the spouse if married) stop using it as a principal residence within 36 months from the purchase date, the credit repayment is accelerated.

If the taxpayer is subject to an accelerated credit repayment, he or she must increase the federal income tax for the year of disposition or cessation of use by the amount of any excess of the credit allowed over the sum of the additional taxes paid under the credit repayment requirement. However, there are exceptions.

1. In the case of a sale of the home to an unrelated person, the increase in tax due to accelerated repayment is limited to the amount of gain (if any) from the sale. To determine the gain for this purpose, you must reduce the adjusted basis in the home by the amount of the first-time homebuyer credit that hasn't been repaid.
2. In the case of an involuntary conversion of the home, the accelerated repayment requirement doesn't apply if the taxpayer acquires a new principal residence within two years from the date when the disposition or the cessation of use occurs. The general repayment rules apply to the new principal residence as if it were the converted home.
3. If a person who claimed the credit dies, repayment of the remaining balance of the credit isn't required unless the credit was claimed on a joint return. If the credit was claimed on a joint return, then the surviving spouse is required to continue repaying his or her half of the credit (regardless of whether he or she was the purchaser) if none of the other exceptions apply.

NANNY TAX (TAX ON HOUSEHOLD EMPLOYEES)

Social Security and Medicare Taxes (Federal Insurance Contributions Act – FICA). The social security and Medicare taxes, also commonly referred as FICA tax, applies to both employees and employers, each paying 7.65 percent of wages.

An employer is generally required to withhold the employee's share of FICA tax from wages. If the taxpayer pays cash wages of $2,300 or more for 2021 (this threshold can change from year to year) to any one household employee, the taxpayer generally must withhold 6.2% of social security and 1.45% of Medicare taxes (for a total of 7.65%) from all cash wages paid to that employee, unless the taxpayer prefer to pay the employee's share of social security and Medicare taxes from the own funds.

The taxpayer must also pay the share of social security and Medicare taxes, which is also 7.65% of cash wages (cash wages include wages paid by check, money order, etc.).

Additional Medicare Tax

Additional Medicare Tax applies to an individual's Medicare wages that exceed a threshold amount based on the taxpayer's filing status.

Employers are responsible for withholding the 0.9% Additional Medicare Tax on an individual's wages paid in excess of $200,000 in a calendar year, without regard to filing status.

An employer is required to begin withholding Additional Medicare Tax in the pay period in which it pays wages in excess of $200,000 to an employee and continue to withhold it each pay period until the end of the calendar year.

There's no employer match for Additional Medicare Tax.

Federal Income Tax Withholding

Taxpayers are not required to withhold federal income tax from wages they pay to a household employee. However, if the employee asks a taxpayer to withhold federal income tax and he or she agrees, he or she will need a completed Form W-4, Employee's Withholding Certificate (PDF) from the employee.

Form W-2, Wage and Tax Statement

If taxpayers must withhold and pay social security and Medicare taxes, or if they withhold federal income tax, they'll need to complete Form W-2, Wage and Tax Statement (PDF) for each employee. They'll also need a Form W-3, Transmittal of Wage and Tax Statement (PDF)

Federal Unemployment Tax Act (FUTA)

If a taxpayer paid cash wages to household employees totaling more than $1,000 in any calendar quarter during the calendar year or the prior year, the taxpayer generally must pay federal unemployment tax (FUTA) tax on the first $7,000 of cash wages paid to each household employee. However, don't count wages paid to the spouse, the child who is under the age of 21, or the parent. Also, don't consider the amounts paid to these individuals as wages subject to FUTA tax.

Generally, taxpayers can take a credit against the FUTA tax liability for amounts paid into state unemployment funds. If a taxpayer paid wages that are subject to the unemployment compensation laws of a credit reduction state, the FUTA tax credit may be reduced. A state that hasn't repaid money it borrowed from the federal government to pay unemployment benefits is a "credit reduction state."

Schedule H (Form 1040 or 1040-SR), Household Employment Taxes. If a taxpayer pays wages subject to FICA tax, FUTA tax, or if he or she withholds federal income tax from the employee's wages, he or she will need to file a Schedule H (Form 1040 or 1040-SR), Household Employment Taxes.

Attach Schedule H to the individual income tax return, Form 1040, U.S. Individual Income Tax Return, Form 1040-SR, U.S. Tax Return for Seniors, Form 1040-NR, U.S. Nonresident Alien Income Tax Return, Form 1040-SS, U.S. Self-Employment Tax Return (Including the Additional Child Tax Credit for Bona Fide Residents of Puerto Rico).

If a taxpayer is not required to file a return, he or she must still file Schedule H to report household employment taxes. However, a sole proprietor who must file Form 940, Employer's Annual Federal Unemployment (FUTA) Tax Return, and Form 941, Employer's QUARTERLY Federal Tax Return, or Form 944, Employer's ANNUAL Federal Tax Return, for business employees, or Form 943, Employer's Annual Federal Tax Return for Agricultural Employees, for farm employees, may report household employee tax information on these forms instead of on Schedule H.

If the taxpayer chooses to report the wages for a household employee on the forms shown above, be sure to pay any taxes due by the date required based on the form, making federal tax deposits if required.

Estimated Tax Payments. If a taxpayer files Schedule H (Form 1040 or Form 1040-SR), he or she can avoid owing taxes with the return if he or she pays enough tax before the taxpayer files the return to cover both the employment taxes for the household employee and the income tax. If the taxpayer is employed, he or she can ask the employer to withhold more federal income tax from the wages during the year. The taxpayer can also make estimated tax payments to the IRS during the year using Form 1040-ES, Estimated Tax for Individuals.

SECTION 199A QUALIFIED BUSINESS INCOME DEDUCTIONS

Section 199A of the Internal Revenue Code provides many owners of sole proprietorships, partnerships, S corporations and some trusts and estates, a deduction of income from a qualified trade or business. The deduction has two components.

- **QBI Component** - This component of the deduction equals 20 percent of QBI from a domestic business operated as a sole proprietorship or through a partnership, S corporation, trust or estate. Depending on the taxpayer's taxable income, the QBI component is subject to multiple limitations including the type of trade or business, the amount of W-2 wages paid by the qualified trade or business and the unadjusted basis immediately after acquisition (UBIA) of qualified property held by the trade or business. It may also be reduced by the patron reduction if the taxpayer is a patron of an agricultural or horticultural cooperative. Income earned through a C corporation or by providing services as an employee is not eligible for the deduction.

- **Real Estate Investment Trust / Publicly Traded Partnership Component** - This component of the deduction equals 20 percent of the combined qualified REIT dividends (including REIT dividends earned through a regulated investment company (RIC)) and qualified PTP income. This component is not limited by W-2 wages or the UBIA of qualified property. Depending on the taxpayer's income, the amount of PTP income that qualifies may be limited depending on the type of business engaged in by the PTP.

The deduction is limited to the lesser of the QBI component plus the REIT/PTP component or 20 percent of the taxpayer's taxable income minus the net capital gain. For details on figuring the deduction, see Q&A 6 and 7. The deduction is available for taxable years beginning after Dec. 31, 2017 and ending before December 31, 2025. Most eligible taxpayers will be able to claim it for the first time when they file their 2018 federal income tax return in 2019. The deduction is available, regardless of whether an individual itemizes their deductions on Schedule A or takes the standard deduction.

The deduction is limited to the lesser of the QBI component plus the REIT/PTP component or 20 percent of the taxable income minus net capital gain.

QBI is the net amount of qualified items of income, gain, deduction and loss from any qualified trade or business, including income from partnerships, S corporations, sole proprietorships, and certain trusts. Generally this includes, but is not limited to, the deductible part of self-employment tax, self-employed health insurance, and deductions for contributions to qualified retirement plans (e.g. SEP, SIMPLE and qualified plan deductions).
QBI does not include items such as:

- Items that are not properly includable in taxable income
- Investment items such as capital gains or losses or dividends
- Interest income not properly allocable to a trade or business
- Wage income
- Income that is not effectively connected with the conduct of business within the United States Commodities transactions or foreign currency gains or losses
- Certain dividends and payments in lieu of dividends
- Income, loss, or deductions from notional principal contracts
- Annuities, unless received in connection with the trade or business
- Amounts received as reasonable compensation from an S corporation Amounts received as guaranteed payments from a partnership
- Payments received by a partner for services other than in a capacity as a partner Qualified REIT dividends
- PTP income

FOREIGN INCOME TAXES

The foreign earned income exclusion, the foreign housing exclusion, and the foreign housing deduction are based on foreign earned income. For this purpose, foreign earned income is income received for services performed in a foreign country in a period during which the tax home is in a foreign country and the taxpayer meets either the bona fide residence test or the physical presence test.

Bona fide residence test: US citizen or US resident alien who is physically present in a foreign country for a continuous year. The physical presence test: Same who is physically present in a foreign country or countries for at minimum 330 full days during a 12-month continuous period. The maximum foreign earned income exclusion is $108,700 (married couples take both per person). Not automatic, taxpayers must file form 2555. Non-resident aliens do not qualify

Earned income is pay for personal services performed, such as wages, salaries, or professional fees.

Classification of Types of Income

Earned Income	Unearned Income	Variable Income
Salaries and wages	Dividends	Business profits
Commissions	Interest	Royalties
Bonuses	Capital Gains	Rents
Professional fees	Gambling winnings	Scholarships and Fellowships
Tips	Alimony	
	Social security benefits	
	Pensions	
	Annuities	

FOREIGN HOUSING EXCLUSION OR DEDUCTION

The foreign housing exclusion applies only to amounts considered paid for with employer-provided amounts, which includes any amounts paid to the taxpayer or paid or incurred on the behalf by the employer that are taxable foreign earned income to the taxpayer for the year (without regard to the foreign earned income exclusion). The housing deduction applies only to amounts paid for with self-employment earnings.

The foreign housing amount is the total of the foreign housing expenses for the year minus the base housing amount. The computation of the base housing amount (line 32 of Form 2555) is tied to the maximum foreign earned income exclusion. The amount is 16% of the maximum exclusion amount divided by 365 (366 if a leap year), then multiplied by the number of days in the qualifying period that fall within the tax year.

Housing expenses include reasonable expenses actually paid or incurred for housing in a foreign country for the taxpayer and (if they lived with the taxpayer) for the spouse and dependents.
Consider only housing expenses for the part of the year that the taxpayer qualifies for the foreign earned income exclusion.
Housing expenses do not include expenses that are lavish or extravagant under the circumstances, the cost of buying property, purchased furniture or accessories, and improvements and other expenses that increase the value or appreciably prolong the life of the property.

If a taxpayer chooses the foreign housing exclusion, he or she must figure it before figuring the foreign earned income exclusion and cannot claim less than the full amount of housing exclusion to which the taxpayer is entitled. Once the taxpayer chooses to exclude foreign housing amounts, he or she can't take a foreign tax credit or deduction for taxes on income that can be excluded. If the taxpayer does take a credit or deduction for any of those taxes, the choice to exclude housing amounts may be considered revoked.

The foreign housing deduction cannot be more than the foreign earned income less the total of (1) the foreign earned income exclusion, plus (2) the housing exclusion, if any. The taxpayer would not have both a foreign housing deduction and a foreign housing exclusion unless during the tax year he or she was both self-employed and an employee.

Although the foreign housing exclusion and/or deduction will reduce the regular income tax, they will not reduce the self-employment tax.

The foreign housing exclusion or deduction is computed in parts VI, VIII, and IX of Form 2555.

FOREIGN TAX CREDIT

Qualifying Foreign Taxes

Taxpayers can claim a credit only for foreign taxes that are imposed on them by a foreign country or U.S. possession. Generally, only income, war profits and excess profits taxes qualify for the credit.

Taken as a deduction, foreign income taxes reduce the U.S. taxable income. Deduct foreign taxes on Schedule A (Form 1040), Itemized Deductions

Taken as a credit, foreign income taxes reduce the U.S. tax liability. In most cases, it is to the advantage to take foreign income taxes as a tax credit.

If a taxpayer chooses to exclude either foreign earned income or foreign housing costs, he or she cannot take a foreign tax credit for taxes on income that can be excluded. If the taxpayer does take the credit, one or both of the choices may be considered revoked.

FIXED, DETERMINABLE, ANNUAL OR PERIODIC (FDAP) INCOME

FDAP income is defined very broadly and generally includes all U.S. sourced income except gains derived from the sale of real or personal property and income specifically excluded from gross income such as tax-exempt interest and qualified scholarship income

FDAP income normally includes income that is:

- fixed or for which the amounts to be paid are known ahead of time; is determinable or there is a basis for figuring the amount to be paid; is annual or paid yearly;
- or is periodic or paid from time to time not specifically in regular intervals

Fixed, Determinable, Annual, or Periodical (FDAP) income is all income, except:

Gains derived from the sale of real or personal property (including market discount and option premiums, but not including original issue discount)

Items of income excluded from gross income, without regard to the U.S. or foreign status of the owner of the income, such as tax-exempt municipal bond interest and qualified scholarship income

Income is fixed when it is paid in amounts known ahead of time. Income is determinable whenever there is a basis for figuring the amount to be paid. Income can be periodic if it is paid from time to time. It does not have to be paid annually or at regular intervals. Income can be determinable or periodic, even if the length of time during which the payments are made is increased or decreased.

GILTI TAX (GLOBAL INTANGIBLE LOW-TAXED INCOME)

GILTI is a newly defined category of foreign income added to corporate taxable income each year. In effect, it is a tax on earnings that exceed a 10 percent return on a company's invested foreign assets. GILTI is subject to a worldwide minimum tax of between
10.5 and 13.125 percent on an annual basis. GILTI is supposed to reduce the incentive to shift corporate profits out of the United States by using intellectual property (IP).

The primary purpose of GILTI is to reduce the incentive for U.S.-based multinational corporations to shift profits out of the United States into low- or zero-tax jurisdictions. This is done by placing a floor on the average foreign tax rate paid by U.S. multinationals of between 10.5 percent and 13.125 percent. The incentive to shift profits from one jurisdiction to another is the function of the difference between the countries' statutory tax rates. That difference is the tax savings a company receives per dollar shifted. Companies subject to GILTI would compare a 21 percent domestic rate with a 10.5 to 13.125 percent rate rather than a zero rate.

GILTI is calculated as follows:

active income of controlled foreign corporation - (depreciable tangible property * 10%) = GILTI

- Congress assumed that foreign firms would earn a return of 10% on depreciable tangible property (e.g., buildings, equipment). Thus, any income over and above that amount is deemed to be GILTI.
- Once you have calculated GILTI, a U.S. corporation would calculate the tax due as follows:

([GILTI - (50% of GILTI)] * corporate income tax rate) - (80% of foreign taxes paid) The U.S. corporate income tax rate as of 2021 is 21%.

Thus, if the foreign company paid no foreign income taxes, the effective tax rate on the GILTI would be 10.5%.

POP QUIZ & ANSWER SHEET

ADDITIONAL TAXES & CREDITS

POP QUIZ

Test your knowledge on Additional Taxes & Credits by answering the questions below. The answer sheet may be found at the end of the Pop Quiz.

Q1: All statements are true about Alternative Minimum Tax, except:

A. It can be triggered by taxpayers who have high household income and significant itemized deductions
B. Taxpayers exercise of incentive stock options
C. Taxpayers who normally take the standard deduction to reduce their tax liability
D. Taxpayer sales a large amount of capital assets including cryptocurrency that resulted in a long term capital gain

Q2: It is a type of income, normally received tax-free, that may trigger the alternative minimum tax (AMT) for taxpayers. It includes interest on private activity municipal-bonds, qualifying exclusions for small business stock, and excess intangible drilling costs for oil and gas - if the amount of these items exceeds 40% of AMT income. It is added to the amount of AMT income in the IRS' tax formula.

A. AMT Preference Items
B. Social Security and Equivalent Railroad Retirement Benefits
C. Passive Activities Credits
D. Capital Gains

Q3: Individuals, Estates and Trusts can use this form to receive a nonrefundable credit for alternative minimum tax paid in a prior year called:

A. Form 8949, Sales and other Dispositions of Capital Assets
B. Form 8801, Credit for Prior Year Minimum Tax Individuals, Estates and Trusts
C. Form 982, Reduction of Tax Attributes Due to Discharge of Indebtedness
D. Schedule B (Form 1040), Interest and Ordinary Dividends

Q4: Taxpayer A is a US citizen who now lives in Canada. Of the income received below, how much can the taxpayer exclude as foreign earned income?
Wages earned in Toronto, Canada: $75,000
US Municipal Bond Interest: $1500
Rental Income from a property in Chicago, Illinois: $24,000

A. $76,500
B. $75,000
C. $99,000
D. $102,000

Q5: Taxpayer A employed household employees and paid them the following:
Nanny- $24,000
Housekeeper-$12,000
How much tax does the household employer have to withhold in Social Security & Medicare?

A. $2592
B. $2100
C. $522
D. $2232

Q6: What are the conditions when filing Tax for Certain Children who have unearned income?

A. Unearned income more than $4,200. Both parents are alive at the end of the tax year. Must not file a tax return for the tax year. Must file a joint return for the year.
B. Unearned income more than $4,400.Both parents alive at the end of the tax year. Must file a tax return for the tax year. Must not file a joint return for the year.
C. Unearned income more than $2,400. At least one of the parents is alive at the end of the tax year. Must file a tax return for the tax year. Must not file a joint return for the year.
D. Unearned income more than $2,200. At least one of the parents was alive at the end of the tax year. Must file a tax return for the tax year. Must not file a joint return for the year.

Q7: If an employer pays cash wages of $2,200 or more for 2021 to any household employee, how much Social Security and Medicare taxes must be withheld?

A. 6.15% of Social Security and 1.50% Medicare taxes (total of 7.65%)
B. 6.20% of Social Security and 1.45% Medicare taxes (total of 7.65%)
C. 6.05% of Social Security and 1.60% Medicare taxes (total of 7.65%)
D. 6.45% of Social Security and 1.20% Medicare taxes (total of 7.65%)

Q8: Taxpayer A received the first time homebuyer credit in 2008 and just sold their home in 2021 to a relative for $250,000. What is the tax consequence of the sale?

A. The first-time home buyer credit balance will be transferred to the relative
B. They can exclude up to $250,000 and waive the repayment of the first-time homebuyer credit
C. Taxpayer A must pay the rest of the unpaid balance of the credit in the current year
D. The taxpayer and the relative will split the first-time homebuyer credit repayment amount

Q9: Salaries and Wages, Commissions, Bonuses and Tips are examples of:

A. Unearned Income
B. Earned Income
C. Invariable Income
D. Variable Income

Q10: Interest, Alimony, Pensions and Annuities are examples of:

A. Unearned Income
B. Earned Income
C. Invariable Income
D. Variable Income

Q11: Taxpayer A is a citizen of a country that does not have a tax treaty with the United States and receives $24,000 in rental income from a property owned in Florida. Taxpayer A's rental income will be taxed at a flat rate of:

A. 10%
B. 20%
C. 30%
D. 40%

ANSWER SHEET

1. Answer is C – Taxpayers who normally take the standard deduction to reduce their tax liability

2. Answer is A – AMT Preference Items

3. Answer is B – Form 8801, Credit for Prior Year Minimum Tax Individuals, Estates and Trusts

4. Answer is B – $75,000

5. Answer is A – $2,592

6. Answer is D – Unearned income more than $2,200. At Least one of the parents was alive at the end of the tax year. Must file a tax return for the tax year. Must not file a joint return for the year.

7. Answer is B – 6.20% of Social Security and 1.45% Medicare taxes (total of 7.65%)

8. Answer is C – Taxpayer A must pay the rest of the unpaid balance of the credit in the current year

9. Answer is B – Earned Income

10. Answer is A – Unearned Income

NON-RECOGNITION PROPERTY TRANSACTIONS

SALE OF MAIN HOME SECTION 121 EXCLUSION AMT PREFERENCE ITEMS

The tax code recognizes the importance of home ownership by allowing to exclude gain when selling the main home. To qualify for the maximum exclusion of gain ($250,000 or $500,000 if married filing jointly) taxpayers must meet the Eligibility Test , explained later. To qualify for a partial exclusion of gain, meaning an exclusion of gain less than the full amount, taxpayers must meet one of the situations listed.

ELIGIBILITY REQUIREMENTS FOR SECTION 121

Eligibility Step 1—Automatic Disqualification

Determine whether any of the automatic disqualifications apply.

- The home sale isn't eligible for the exclusion if ANY of the following are true.
- Individuals acquired the property through a like-kind exchange (1031 exchange), during the past 5 years. See Pub. 544, Sales and Other Dispositions of Assets.
- Individuals are subject to expatriate tax. For more information about expatriate tax, see chapter 4 of Pub. 519, U.S. Tax Guide for Aliens.

Eligibility Step 2—Ownership

Determine whether the taxpayer meets the ownership requirement.

- If a taxpayer owned the home for at least 24 months (2 years) out of the last 5 years leading up to the date of sale (date of the closing), he or she meets the ownership requirement. For a married couple filing jointly, only one spouse has to meet the ownership requirement.

Eligibility Step 3—Residence

Determine whether the taxpayer meets the residence requirement.

- If a taxpayer owned the home and used it as a residence for at least 24 months of the previous 5 years, he or she meets the residence requirement. The 24 months of residence can fall anywhere within the 5-year period, and it doesn't have to be a single block of time. All that is required is a total of 24 months (730 days) of residence during the 5-year period. Unlike the ownership requirement, each spouse must meet the residence requirement individually for a married couple filing jointly to get the full exclusion.
- If a taxpayer was ever away from home, he or she needs to determine whether that time counts towards the residence requirement. A vacation or

other short absence counts as time lived at home (even if the taxpayer rented out the home while gone).

- If taxpayers become physically or mentally unable to care for themselves, and they use the residence as the principal residence for 12 months in the 5 years preceding the sale or exchange, any time spent living in a care facility (such as a nursing home) counts toward the 2-year residence requirement, so long as the facility has a license from a state or other political entity to care for people with the same condition.

Eligibility Step 4—Look-Back

Determine whether individuals meet the look-back requirement.

- If individuals did not sell another home during the 2-year period before the date of sale (or, if they did sell another home during this period, but didn't take an exclusion of the gain earned from it), taxpayers meet the look-back requirement. They may take the exclusion only once during a 2-year period.

Eligibility Step 5—Exceptions to the Eligibility Test

There are some exceptions to the Eligibility Test. If any of the following situations apply, read on to see if they may affect the qualification. If none of these situations apply, skip to Step 6.

- A separation or divorce occurred during the ownership of the home.
- The death of a spouse occurred during the ownership of the home.
- The sale involved vacant land.
- The taxpayer owned a remainder interest, meaning the right to own a home in the future, and he or she sold that right.
- The previous home was destroyed or condemned.
- The taxpayer was a service member during the ownership of the home.
- The taxpayer acquired or is relinquishing the home in a like-kind exchange.
- Eligibility Step 6—Final Determination of Eligibility
- If the taxpayer meets the ownership, residence, and look-back requirements, taking the exceptions into account, then he or she meets the Eligibility Test. The home sale qualifies for the maximum exclusion

DIFFERENT RULES FOR MARRIED HOMEOWNERS

Generally, if an individual transferred the home (or share of a jointly owned home) to a spouse or ex-spouse as part of a divorce settlement, he or she is considered to have no gain or loss. The individual has nothing to report from the transfer. However, there is one exception to this rule. If the spouse or ex-spouse is a nonresident alien, then the individual likely will have a gain or loss from the transfer.

REDUCED EXCLUSIONS

If taxpayers don't meet the Eligibility Test, they may still qualify for a partial exclusion of gain. They can meet the requirements for a partial exclusion if the main reason for the home sale was a change in workplace location, a health issue, or an unforeseeable event.

Even if the situation doesn't match any of the standard requirements described above, taxpayers still may qualify for an exception. Taxpayers may qualify if they can demonstrate the primary reason for sale, based on facts and circumstances, is work related, health related, or unforeseeable. Important factors are:

- The situation causing the sale arose during the time they owned and used the property as their residence.
- The taxpayer sold the home not long after the situation arose.
- The taxpayer couldn't have reasonably anticipated the situation when he or she bought the home.
- The taxpayer began to experience significant financial difficulty maintaining the home.
- The home became significantly less suitable as a main home for the taxpayer and the family for a specific reason.

LIKE-KIND EXCHANGES SECTION 1031 EXCHANGE

Like-kind exchanges -- when individuals exchange real property used for business or held as an investment solely for other business or investment property that is the same type or "like-kind" -- have long been permitted under the Internal Revenue Code. Generally, if individuals make a like-kind exchange, they are not required to recognize a gain or loss under Internal Revenue Code Section 1031.
Under the Tax Cuts and Jobs Act, Section 1031 now applies only to exchanges of real property and not to exchanges of personal or intangible property. An exchange of real property held primarily for sale still does not qualify as a like-kind exchange.

CASH BOOT & MORTGAGE BOOT

If, as part of the like-kind exchange, individuals also receive other (not like-kind) property or money, they must recognize a gain to the extent of the other property and money received. The individuals can not recognize a loss. This includes:

- Any cash paid by the other party;
- The FMV of other (not like-kind) property received, if any; and
- Net liabilities assumed by the other party—the excess, if any, of liabilities (including mortgages) assumed by the other party over the total of (a) any liabilities assumed, (b) cash paid to the other party, and (c) the FMV of the other (not like-kind) property given up.

THE BASIS OF PROPERTY RECEIVED IN A LIKE-KIND EXCHANGE

Basis of like-kind property is the sum of:

- The adjusted basis of the like-kind property given up;

- Exchange expenses, if any (except for expenses used to reduce the amount reported on line 15); and
- Net amount paid to the other party—the excess, if any, of the total of (a) any liabilities assumed, (b) cash paid to the other party, and (c) the FMV of the other (not like-kind) property given up over any liabilities assumed by the other party.

RELATED PARTY TRANSACTIONS

If a gain is recognized on the sale or exchange of property to a related person, the gain may be ordinary income even if the property is a capital asset. It is ordinary income if the sale or exchange is a depreciable property transaction or a controlled partnership transaction.

INVOLUNTARY CONVERSIONS (SECTION 1033 EXCHANGE)

An involuntary conversion occurs when the property is destroyed, stolen, condemned, or disposed of under the threat of condemnation and the taxpayer receives other property or money in payment, such as insurance or a condemnation award. Involuntary conversions are also called involuntary exchanges. Gain or loss from an involuntary conversion of the property is usually recognized for tax purposes unless the property is the taxpayer's main home.

Taxpayers report the gain or deduct the loss on the tax return for the year they realize it. They cannot deduct a loss from an involuntary conversion of property held for personal use unless the loss resulted from a casualty or theft. However, depending on the type of property received, taxpayers may not have to report a gain on an involuntary conversion.

Generally, taxpayers do not report the gain if they receive property that is similar or related in service or use to the converted property. The basis for the new property is the same as the basis for the converted property. This means that the gain is deferred until a taxable sale or exchange occurs.

Section 1.1033(a)-2(c)(1) of the Income Tax Regulations provides:

If property (as a result of its destruction in whole or in part, theft, seizure, or requisition or condemnation or threat or imminence thereof) is compulsorily or involuntarily converted into money or into property not similar or related in service or use to the converted property, the gain, if any, shall be recognized, at the election of the taxpayer, only to the extent that the amount realized upon such conversion exceeds the cost of other property purchased by the taxpayer which is similar or related in service or use to the property so converted . . . if the taxpayer purchased such other property . . . for the purpose of replacing the property so converted and during the period specified in subparagraph (3) of this paragraph.

CONDEMNATIONS AND EMINENT DOMAIN

A condemnation is the process by which private property is legally taken for public use without the owner's consent. The property may be taken by the federal government, a state government, a political subdivision, or a private organization that has the power to legally take it. The owner receives a condemnation award (money or property) in exchange for the property taken. A condemnation is like a forced sale, the owner being the seller and the condemning authority being the buyer.

Gain or Loss from Condemnations

If the property was condemned or disposed of under the threat of condemnation, figure the gain or loss by comparing the adjusted basis of the condemned property with the net condemnation award.

If the net condemnation award is more than the adjusted basis of the condemned property, the taxpayer has a gain. He or she can postpone reporting gain from a condemnation if he or she buys replacement property.

If only part of the property is condemned, the taxpayer can treat the cost of restoring the remaining part to its former usefulness as the cost of replacement property. See Postponement of Gain, later. If the net condemnation award is less than the adjusted basis, the taxpayer has a loss. If the loss is from property held for personal use, the taxpayer cannot deduct it. He or she must report any deductible loss in the tax year it happened.

CONDEMNATION OR DESTRUCTION OF A MAIN HOME

If a taxpayer has a gain because the main home is condemned, generally he or she can exclude the gain from the income as if the taxpayer had sold or exchanged the home. He or she may be able to exclude up to $250,000 of the gain (up to $500,000 if married filing jointly). For information on this exclusion, see Pub.523. If the gain is more than the taxpayer can exclude but he or she buys replacement property, the taxpayer may be able to postpone reporting the rest of the gain.

POP QUIZ & ANSWER SHEET

NON-RECOGNITION PROPERTY TRANSACTIONS

POP QUIZ

Test your knowledge on *Non-Recognition Property Transactions* by answering the questions below. The answer sheet may be found at the end of the Pop Quiz.

Q1: A taxpayer's home sale is eligible for the exclusion of gain, Section 121 exclusion if:

A. Taxpayers acquired the property through a like-kind exchange during the past 5 years.
B. Taxpayers owned the home for at least 24 months (2 years) out of the last 5 years leading up to the date of sale (date of the closing).
C. Taxpayer sold another home during the 2-year period before the date of sale.
D. Taxpayers are subject to expatriate tax.

Q2: Married taxpayers live in a studio apartment they purchased one year ago in Manhattan, New York. The married taxpayers are now expecting twins and sell their studio condo for $550,000. How much could the married taxpayers exclude from the gain of their home, if any?

A. The taxpayers may qualify for a partial exclusion of $125,000
B. The taxpayers can't exclude anything since they don't meet the residence test and lived in the home for at least 2 years.
C. $550,000
D. $250,000

Q3: Mary Kate & Ashley jointly purchased a beachfront property for $550,000 in 2015 and made it their primary residence. In 2021, they decided to sell the property since the real estate market exploded. They sell the home for $985,000. How much gain can each sister exclude on their individual tax return?

A. $985,000
B. $250,000
C. $125,000
D. $500,000

Q4: After owning and living in the home since 2001, Taxpayer A spouse died in 2019. Taxpayer B decided to sell in 2021 for $300,000. How much can the surviving spouse claim as an exclusion?

A. $125,000

B. $250,000
C. $500,000
D. $0

Q5: Taxpayer A exchanged a commercial property with an adjusted basis of $225,000 for an apartment building with a FMV of $175,000. Taxpayer A receives $50,000 cash and pays $10,000 in attorney expenses. What is the taxable gain on the transaction if any?

A. $50,000
B. $60,000
C. $40,000
D. $0

Q6: What is condemnation of property?

A. A condemnation is the process by which private property is illegally taken for public use without the owner's consent.
B. A condemnation is the process by which private property is legally taken for private use without the owner's consent.
C. A condemnation is the process by which private property is legally taken for public use without the owner's consent.
D. A condemnation is the process by which private property is legally taken for public use with the owner's consent.

Q7: If you make a like-kind exchange, you are not required to recognize a gain or loss under Internal Revenue Code ___.

A. Section 1031
B. Section 1040
C. Section 1051
D. Section 1060

Q8: Basis of like-kind property is the sum of:

A. The adjusted basis of the like-kind property you gave up
B. Exchange expenses
C. Net amount paid to the other party
D. All of the above

Q9: Which of the following transactions does not qualify for a section 1031 exchange?

A. Exchange of a commercial property for an apartment building
B. Exchange of a residential property for an undeveloped lot of land
C. Exchange of a developer's land inventory for a house flipper's inventory
D. Exchange of empty farmland for a manufacturing building

Q10: If you have a gain because your main home is condemned, how much gain can you exclude from your income?

A. Up to $ 50,000
B. Up to $100,000
C. Up to $200,000
D. Up to $250,000

ANSWER SHEET

1. Answer is B – Taxpayer owned the home for at least 24 months (2 years) out of the last 5 years leading up to the date of sale (date of the closing).

2. Answer is A – The taxpayers may qualify for a partial exclusion of $125,000

3. Answer is B – $250,000

4. Answer is C – $500,000

5. Answer is C – $40,000

6. Answer is C – A condemnation is the process by which private property is legally taken for public use without the owner's consent.

7. Answer is A – Section 1031

8. Answer is D – All of the above

9. Answer is C – Exchange of a developer's land inventory for a house flipper's inventory

10. Answer is D – Up to $250,000

CALCULATING THE BASIS OF ASSETS

OVERVIEW

To correctly arrive at the net capital gain or loss, capital gains and losses are classified as long-term or short-term.

Generally, if individuals hold the asset for more than one year before they dispose of it, the capital gain or loss is long-term. If they hold it for one year or less, the capital gain or loss is short-term.

If individuals have a net capital gain, a lower tax rate may apply to the gain than the tax rate that applies to the ordinary income. The term "net capital gain" means the amount by which the net long-term capital gain for the year is more than the net short-term capital loss for the year. The term "net long-term capital gain" means long-term capital gains reduced by long-term capital losses including any unused long- term capital loss carried over from previous years.

BASIS IN GENERAL

The basis of property individuals buy is usually its cost. The cost is the amount paid in cash, debt obligations, other property, or services. The cost also includes amounts paid for the following items.

- Sales tax
- Freight
- Installation and testing
- Excise taxes
- Legal and accounting fees (when they must be capitalized)
- Revenue stamps
- Recording fees
- Real estate taxes (if assumed for the seller)
- Individuals may also have to capitalize (add to basis) certain other costs related to buying or producing property

Example:

Maria purchased a beautiful home with amazing views. The cost of this home was $750,000. She financed the home with her local bank. Included in the purchase of her home was property taxes totaling $35,000 for the year the seller was in the home. Maria went right to work building out a luxurious pool that cost $150,000 to complete. What is Maria's basis in her new home?

Answer:

$750,000 purchase price $35,000 was already included in the purchase price so no change here. $150,000 pool addition added.

The math is as follows:

$750,000 + $150,000= $900,000
Maria's basis in her home is $900,000

DEPRECIATION DEDUCTION

Individuals generally can't deduct in one year the entire cost of property they acquired, produced, or improved and placed in service for use either in the trade or business or to produce income if the property is a capital expenditure. Instead, they generally must depreciate such property.

Depreciation is the recovery of the cost of the property over a number of years. Individuals deduct a part of the cost every year until they fully recover its cost.

Individuals may depreciate property that meets all the following requirements:

- It must be owned property.
- It must be used in a business or income-producing activity.
- It must have a determinable useful life.
- It must be expected to last more than one year.
- It must not be an accepted property. Excepted property includes certain intangible property, certain term interests, equipment used to build capital improvements, and property placed in service and disposed of in the same year.

Example:

Amazon pays $1 billion to upgrade its servers around the World. Amazon figures a useful life of 4 years for the servers. Amazon can not deduct the full $1 billion as an expense, instead they must depreciate the amount over 4 years. How much can Amazon depreciate in year one?

Answer:

Servers cost $1 billion Useful life is 4 years

The math:

$1 billion divided by 4= $250,000,000
Amazon can deduct $250 million in the first year as a depreciation deduction.

BASIS OF REAL PROPERTY

Real property, also called real estate, is land and generally anything built on or attached to it. If an individual buys real property, certain fees and other expenses become part of the cost basis in the property.

If an individual pays real estate taxes the seller owed on the bought real property, and the seller didn't reimburse the individual, treat those taxes as part of the basis. Individuals can't deduct them as taxes.

If an individual reimburses the seller for taxes the seller paid, the individual can usually deduct that amount as an expense in the year of purchase. Don't include that amount in the basis of the property. If the taxpayer didn't reimburse the seller, he or she must reduce the basis by the amount of those taxes.

Settlement Cost

The basis includes the settlement fees and closing costs for buying property. Individuals can't include in the basis the fees and costs for getting a loan on property. A fee for buying property is a cost that must be paid even if the property is bought for cash.

The following items are some of the settlement fees or closing costs individuals can include in the basis of the property.

- Abstract fees (abstract of title fees).
- Charges for installing utility services.
- Legal fees (including title search and preparation of the sales contract and deed).
- Recording fees.
- Surveys.
- Transfer taxes.
- Owner's title insurance.
- Any amounts the seller owes that the individual agrees to pay, such as back taxes or interest, recording or mortgage fees, charges for improvements or repairs, and sales commissions
- Settlement costs don't include amounts placed in escrow for the future payment of items such as taxes and insurance.

The following items are some settlement fees and closing costs that individuals can't include in the basis of the property.

1. Casualty insurance premiums.
2. Rent for occupancy of the property before closing.
3. Charges for utilities or other services related to occupancy of the property before closing.
4. Charges connected with getting a loan.
   The following are examples of these charges:
   - Points (discount points, loan origination fees).

- Mortgage insurance premiums.
- Loan assumption fees.
- Cost of a credit report.
- Fees for an appraisal required by a lender.

1. Fees for refinancing a mortgage.

If these costs relate to business property, items (1) through (3) are deductible as business expenses. Items (4) and (5) must be capitalized as costs of getting a loan and can be deducted over the period of the loan.

BASIS OF SECURITIES

The basis of stocks or bonds an individual owns generally is the purchase price plus the costs of purchase, such as commissions and recording or transfer fees. When selling securities, the individual should be able to identify the specific shares the individual is selling.

If the individual **can identify** which shares of stock are sold, the basis generally is:

- What is paid for the shares sold plus any costs of purchase.

If the individual **can't adequately identify** the shares that are sold and the individual bought the shares at various times for different prices, the basis of the stock sold is:

- The basis of the shares acquired first, then the basis of the stock later acquired, and so forth (first-in first-out). Except for certain mutual fund shares and certain dividend reinvestment plans, the individual can't use the average basis per share to figure gain or loss on the sale of stock.

Each security the individual buys is considered a covered security. The broker is required to provide the basic information on the Form 1099-B, Proceeds From Broker and Barter Exchange Transactions. For each sale of a covered security for which the individual receives a Form 1099-B, the broker will provide the following information: the date of acquisition (box 1b), whether the gain or loss is short-term or long-term (box 2), cost or other basis (box 1e), and the loss disallowed due to a wash sale (box 1g) or the amount of accrued market discount (box 1f).

The law requires to keep and maintain records that identify the basis of all capital assets.

STOCK OPTIONS

If a taxpayer receives an option to buy stock as payment for the services, he or she may have income when he or she receives the option, when the taxpayer exercises that option, or when he or she disposes of the option or stock received when exercising the option. There are two types of stock options:

- Options granted under an employee stock purchase plan or an incentive stock option (ISO) plan are statutory stock options.
- Stock options that are granted neither under an employee stock purchase plan nor an ISO plan are non-statutory stock options.

STATUTORY STOCK OPTIONS

If the employer grants a taxpayer a statutory stock option, he or she generally doesn't include any amount in the gross income when received or exercised the option. However, the taxpayer may be subject to alternative minimum tax in the year he or she exercises an ISO.

Individuals have taxable income or deductible loss when they sell the stock bought by exercising the option. They generally treat this amount as a capital gain or loss.

However, if an individual doesn't meet special holding period requirements, he or she has to treat income from the sale as ordinary income. Add these amounts, which are treated as wages, to the basis of the stock in determining the gain or loss on the stock's disposition.
There a two kinds of statutory stock options:

- **Incentive Stock Option -** After exercising an ISO, an individual should receive from the employer a Form 3921 (Exercise of an Incentive Stock Option). This form will report important dates and values needed to determine the correct amount of capital and ordinary income (if applicable) to be reported on the return.
- **Employee Stock Purchase Plan** - After the first transfer or sale of stock acquired by exercising an option granted under an employee stock purchase plan, the taxpayer should receive from the employer a Form 3922. This form will report important dates and values needed to determine the correct amount of capital and ordinary income to be reported on the return.

BASIS OTHER THAN COST

There are many times when taxpayers can't use cost as a basis. The following are examples of situations in which an asset's basis is determined by something other than purchase cost.

- Property Receives as Services
- Taxable Exchanges
- Non-taxable exchanges
- Property Transferred From a Spouse
- Property Received as a Gift
- Inherited Property
- Property Changed to Business or Rental Use

1. Property Receives as Services

If a taxpayer receives property for services, include the property's fair market value (FMV) in income. The amount included in the income becomes the basis. If the services were performed for a price agreed on beforehand, it will be accepted as the FMV of the property if there is no evidence to the contrary.

2. Taxable Exchanges

A taxable exchange is one in which the gain is taxable or the loss is deductible. A taxable gain or deductible loss is also known as a recognized gain or loss. If a taxpayer receives property in exchange for other property in a taxable exchange, the basis of property received is usually its FMV at the time of the exchange. A taxable exchange occurs when the taxpayer receives cash or property not similar or related in use to the property exchanged.

3. Non-taxable Exchanges

A non-taxable exchange is an exchange in which the taxpayer is not taxed on any gain and he or she can't deduct any loss. If the taxpayer receives property in a non-taxable exchange, its basis is usually the same as the basis of the transferred property. A non-taxable gain or loss is also known as an unrecognized gain or loss.

Example:

Grant exchanged real estate with an adjusted basis of $50,00 and an FMV of $80,000 held for investment for other real estate with a fair market value of $80,000 held for investment. What is Grant's basis in the new property?

Answer:

Grant's basis in the new property is the same as the basis of the old property ($50,000).

4. Property Changed to Business or Rental Use

If a taxpayer holds property for personal use and then changes it to business use or uses it to produce rent, he or she must figure its basis for depreciation. An example of changing property held for personal use to business use would be renting out the former main home.

5. Basis for depreciation.

The basis for depreciation is the lesser of the following amounts.

- The FMV of the property on the date of the change, or
- The adjusted basis on the date of the change.

Example:

Several years ago, Jessica paid $160,000 to have her home built on a lot that cost $25,000. She paid $20,000 for permanent improvements to the house. She claimed a $2,000 casualty loss deduction for damage to the house before changing the property to rental use last year. Because land isn't depreciable, she includes only the cost of the house when figuring the basis for depreciation. Her adjusted basis in the house when she changed its use was $178,000 ($160,000 + $20,000 − $2,000). On the same date, the property had an FMV of $180,000, of which $15,000 was for the land and $165,000 was for the house.

BASIS OF PROPERTY TRANSFERS INCIDENT TO DIVORCE

The basis of property transferred to a taxpayer or transferred in trust for the benefit by the spouse (or former spouse if the transfer is incident to divorce) is the same as the spouse's adjusted basis.
However, adjust the basis for any gain recognized by the spouse or former spouse on property transferred in trust. This rule applies only to a transfer of property in trust in which the liabilities assumed, plus the liabilities to which the property is subject, are more than the adjusted basis of the property transferred.

At the time of the transfer, the transferor must give the taxpayer the records necessary to determine the adjusted basis and holding period of the property as of the date of transfer.

Example:

Mark owns land in which his basis is $100,000. He sells it to his ex-wife Jennifer for $190,000, its fair market value. Mark does not report any gain on the sale. Jennifer is the new owner, but her basis is $100,000 (Mark's basis), even though she actually paid $190,000 for it.

THE BASIS OF GIFTED PROPERTY

To figure out the basis of property received as a gift, the taxpayer must know three amounts:

- The adjusted cost basis to the donor just before the donor made the gift.
- The fair market value (FMV) at the time the donor made the gift.
- The amount of any gift tax paid on Form 709.

If the FMV of the property at the time of the gift is less than the donor's adjusted basis, the adjusted basis depends on whether the taxpayer has a gain or loss when he or she disposes of the property.

The basis for figuring a gain is the same as the donor's adjusted basis, plus or minus any required adjustments to the basis while the taxpayer held the property.
The basis for figuring a loss is the FMV of the property when receiving the gift, plus or minus any required adjustments to the basis while the taxpayer held the property.

If the FMV is equal to or greater than the donor's adjusted basis, the basis is the donor's adjusted basis at the time of the gift.

If the taxpayer received a gift, increase the basis by the part of the gift tax paid on it that is due to the net increase in value of the gift. Also, for figuring gain or loss, the taxpayer must increase or decrease the basis by any required adjustments to the basis while holding the property.

THE BASIS OF INHERITED PROPERTY

The basis of property inherited from a decedent is generally one of the following.

- The Fair Market Value (FMV) of the property at the date of the individual's death.
- The FMV on the alternate valuation date if the personal representative for the estate chooses to use alternate valuation.
- The value under the special-use valuation method for real property used in farming or a closely held business if chosen for estate tax purposes.
- The decedent's adjusted basis in land to the extent of the value excluded from the decedent's taxable estate as a qualified conservation easement.

If a federal estate tax return doesn't have to be filed, the basis in the inherited property is its appraised value at the date of death for state inheritance or transmission taxes.

POP QUIZ & ANSWER SHEET

CALCULATING THE BASIS OF ASSETS

POP QUIZ

Test your knowledge on Calculating the Basis of Assets by answering the questions below. The answer sheet may be found at the end of the Pop Quiz.

Q1: If you hold the asset for more than one year before you dispose of it, your capital gain or loss is ___. If you hold it for one year or less, your capital gain or loss is ___.

A. Long term capital gain or loss, short term capital gain or loss
B. Short term capital gain or loss, long term capital gain or loss
C. Temporary gain or loss, Permanent gain or loss
D. More than one year capital gain or loss, Less than on year capital gain or loss

Q2: All of the following will be used to increase the basis of an asset, except:

A. Sales tax paid
B. Installation costs paid
C. Depreciation taken
D. Legal and accounting fees paid

Q3: ___ is the recovery of the cost of the property over a number of years.

A. Appreciation
B. Depreciation
C. Reduction
D. Deduction

Q4: Amazon pays $1 billion to upgrade its servers around the World. Amazon figures a useful life of 4 years for the servers. How much can Amazon depreciate in year one?

A. $1 billion multiplied by 4= $4,000,000,000
B. $1 billion multiplied by 4 divided by 4 = $1,000,000,000
C. $1 billion divided by 4= $250,000,000
D. $1 billion divided by 4 multiplied by 3= $750,000,000

Q5: The following items are some of the settlement fees or closing costs you can include in the basis of your property, except:

A. Recording Fees
B. Surveys
C. Transfer Taxes

D. Loan Assumption Fees

Q6: When a taxpayer sells securities, they will usually receive Form ___ from their broker.

A. 1098-B
B. 1099-B
C. 1099-NEC
D. 1099-MISC

Q7: If you receive an option to buy stock as payment for your services, you may have income when you receive the option, when you exercise the option, or when you dispose of the option or stock received. What are the two types of stock options?

A. Call stock options and put stock options
B. Strike price options and premium price option
C. Statutory stock options and non statutory stock options
D. Stationary stock options and put stock options

Q8: Which of the following scenarios is an asset's basis determined by its Fair Market Value?

A. Real Estate Property Received from an Spouse due to divorce
B. A car gifted by a grandson from his grandmother
C. Single family home given to a daughter and her husband from her father as a newlywed gift
D. Stocks received by a US resident from her deceased grandfather's estate

Q9: Grant exchanged real estate with an adjusted basis of $50,000 and a FMV of $80,000 held for investment for other real estate with a fair market value of $80,000 held for investment. What is Grant's basis in the new property?

A. 30,000
B. 50,000
C. 80,000
D. 130,000

Q10: Several years ago, Taxpayer A paid $160,000 for a home built on a lot that cost $25,000. Taxpayer A paid $20,000 for permanent improvements to the house and claimed a $2,000 casualty loss deduction for damage to the house before changing the property to rental use last year. What is the adjusted basis in the house when the use was changed?

A. 183,000
B. 178,000
C. 165,000
D. 155,000

ANSWER SHEET

1. Answer is A – Long term capital gain or loss, short term capital gain or loss

2. Answer is C – Depreciation taken

3. Answer is B – Depreciation

4. Answer is C – $1 billion divided by 4= $250,000,000

5. Answer is D – Loan Assumption Fees

6. Answer is B – 1099-B

7. Answer is C – Statutory stock options and non-statutory stock options

8. Answer is D – Stocks received by a US resident from her deceased grandfather's estate

9. Answer is B – 50,000

10. Answer is B – 178,000

FOREIGN FINANCIAL PLANNING

OVERVIEW

International Financial Reporting Standards (IFRS) IFRS are designed to bring consistency to accounting language, practices and statements, and to help businesses and investors make educated financial analyses and decisions. The IFRS Foundation sets the standards to "bring transparency, accountability and efficiency to financial markets around the world… fostering trust, growth and long-term financial stability in the global economy." Companies benefit from the IFRS because investors are more likely to put money into a company if the company's business practices are transparent.

FBAR IN GENERAL

Every year, under the law known as the Bank Secrecy Act, individuals must report certain foreign financial accounts, such as bank accounts, brokerage accounts and mutual funds, to the Treasury Department and keep certain records of those accounts. Individuals must report the accounts by filing a Report of Foreign Bank and Financial Accounts (FBAR) on FinCEN Form 114.

Who Must File

A United States person, including a citizen, resident, corporation, partnership, limited liability company, trust and estate, must file an FBAR to report:

- a financial interest in or signature or other authority over at least one financial account located outside the United States if
- the aggregate value of those foreign financial accounts exceeded $10,000 at any time during the calendar year reported.

Generally, an account at a financial institution located outside the United States is a foreign financial account. Whether the account produced taxable income has no effect on whether the account is a "foreign financial account" for FBAR purposes.

But, these foreign financial accounts do not need to be reported:

- Correspondent/Nostro accounts,
- Owned by a governmental entity,
- Owned by an international financial institution,
- Maintained on a United States military banking facility,
- Held in an individual retirement account (IRA) that are owned or are beneficiary of,
- Held in a retirement plan of which the owner is a participant or beneficiary, or

- Part of a trust of which the owner is a beneficiary, if a U.S. person (trust, trustee of the trust or agent of the trust) files an FBAR reporting these accounts.

When to File

The FBAR is an annual report, due April 15 following the calendar year reported.

If an individual is affected by a natural disaster, the government may further extend the FBAR due date. It's important to review relevant FBAR Relief Notices for complete information.

Individuals are allowed an automatic extension to October 15 if they fail to meet the FBAR annual due date of April 15. Individuals don't need to request an extension to file the FBAR.

For certain employees or officers with signature or other authority over, but no financial interest in certain foreign financial accounts, the 2018 FBAR due date is deferred to April 15, 2021.

PENALTIES FOR NON-FILING THE FBAR

Individuals may be subject to civil monetary penalties and/or criminal penalties for FBAR reporting and/or recordkeeping violations. Assertion of penalties depends on facts and circumstances. Civil penalty maximums must be adjusted annually for inflation. Current maximums are as follows:

U.S. Code citation	Civil Monetary Penalty Description	Current Maximum
31 U.S.C. 5321(a)(5)(B)(i)	Foreign Financial Agency Transaction - Non-Willful Violation of Transaction	$12,921
31 U.S.C. 5321(a)(5)(C)	Foreign Financial Agency Transaction - Willful Violation of Transaction	Greater of $129,210, or 50% of the amount per 31 U.S.C.5321(a)(5)(D)
31 U.S.C. 5321(a)(6)(A)	Negligent Violation by Financial Institution or Non-Financial Trade or Business	$1,118
31 U.S.C. 5321(a)(6)(B)	Pattern of Negligent Activity by Financial Institution or Non-Financial Trade or Business	$86,976

OFFSHORE VOLUNTARY DISCLOSURE PROGRAM (OVDP)

The IRS announced Offshore Voluntary Disclosure Programs available to taxpayers with undisclosed foreign assets. They are designed to allow taxpayers to come clean with their previously undisclosed overseas accounts. Taxpayers have the added benefit of receiving a fixed penalty structure for settlement of past non-compliance.

In order to enter into the Offshore Voluntary Disclosure Program, taxpayers must:

- Provide copies of previously filed original (and, if applicable, previously filed amended) federal income tax returns for tax years covered by the voluntary disclosure
- Provide complete and accurate amended federal income tax returns for all tax years covered by the voluntary disclosure;
- File complete and accurate original or amended offshore-related information returns, including Form 114 (Foreign Bank and Financial Accounts "FBAR") for tax years covered by the voluntary disclosure; and
- Cooperate in the voluntary disclosure process, including providing information on offshore financial accounts, institutions and facilitators, and signing agreements to extend the period of time for assessing liabilities and FBAR penalties;

FOREIGN FINANCIAL ACCOUNTS

If the taxpayer is a U.S. "person", he or she is required to complete and file a report of the foreign bank and financial account (FBARs) if:

- The taxpayer had a financial interest in or signature authority over at least 1 financial account located in a foreign country AND
- The total value of all foreign financial accounts exceeded over $10,000 at any time during the calendar year that the accounts are to be reported.

In general, taxpayers do not have to file a FBAR if the assets are with a US military bank operated by an American financial institution or if combined funds in the account(s) are $10,000 or less during the entire Tax Year

Exemptions from filing FBAR

1. IRA owners and beneficiaries
2. Participants in and beneficiaries of tax-qualified retirement plans
3. Certain individuals with signature authority over but no financial interest in a foreign financial account
4. U.S. "persons" included in a consolidated foreign bank and financial account report
5. Foreign financial accounts owned by a government entity
6. Foreign financial accounts owned by an international financial institution
7. Correspondent/nostro accounts
8. Foreign financial accounts maintained on a U.S. military banking facility
9. Certain foreign financial accounts jointly owned by spouses
10. Trust beneficiaries

FORM 3520: REPORTING FOREIGN GIFTS AND BEQUESTS

If a taxpayer is a U.S. person who received foreign gifts of money or other property, he or she may need to report these gifts on Form 3520, Annual Return to Report Transactions with Foreign Trusts and Receipt of Certain Foreign Gifts. Form 3520 is an information return, not a tax return, because foreign gifts are not subject to income tax. However, there are significant penalties for failure to file Form 3520 when it is required.

U.S. citizens and residents who receive gifts or bequests from covered expatriates under IRC 877A may be subject to tax under IRC section 2801, which imposes a transfer tax on

U.S. persons who receive gifts or bequests on or after June 17, 2008, from such former U.S. citizens or former U.S. lawful permanent residents.

Penalties for Failure to File Form 3520

Taxpayers may be penalized if they do not file the Form 3520 on time or if it is incomplete or inaccurate. See the Instructions for Form 3520 for more details on penalties that may be imposed for not timely filing the Form 3520, or if the information is incomplete or incorrect, for failure to report foreign gifts, and/or for undisclosed foreign financial asset understatements

Note: Taxpayers may also be required to file FinCEN Form 114. See Report of Foreign Bank and Financial Accounts (FBAR) for more details.

Filing tips to avoid penalties

- Form 3520
    - Be sure to check Form 3520, Box 1K, and enter the form number of the income tax return if an extension was filed.
- Form 3520-A
    - Filed by the 15th day of the 3rd month after the end of the trust's tax year, the due date may be extended by filing Form 7004, Application for Automatic Extension of Time to File Certain Business Income Tax, Information and Other Returns.
    - Form 7004 must be filed with an Employer Identification Number (EIN) for the foreign trust. Forms 7004 for a foreign trust cannot be processed under an individual's Social Security Number (SSN). Please obtain an EIN for the foreign trust.
    - If the foreign trust will not file a Form 3520-A, the U.S. owner of the foreign trust must file a substitute Form 3520-A by completing a Form 3520-A to the best of their ability and attaching it to a timely filed Form 3520, including extensions (see

Form 3520 Instructions for more information on filing a substitute Form 3520-A). Do not separately file a duplicate Form 3520-A if you are filing a substitute 3520-A.

FORM 8938: STATEMENT OF SPECIFIED FOREIGN FINANCIAL ASSETS

Certain U.S. taxpayers holding specified foreign financial assets with an aggregate value exceeding $50,000 will report information about those assets on new Form 8938, which must be attached to the taxpayer's annual income tax return. Higher asset thresholds apply to U.S. taxpayers who file a joint tax return or who reside abroad.

Form 8938 reporting applies for specified foreign financial assets in which the taxpayer has an interest in taxable years starting after March 18, 2010. For most individual taxpayers, this means they will start filing Form 8938 with their 2011 income tax return.

1. If a taxpayer does not have to file an income tax return for the tax year, he or she does not need to file Form 8938, even if the value of the specified foreign assets is more than the appropriate reporting threshold.
2. If a taxpayer is required to file Form 8938, he or she did not have to report financial accounts maintained by:
    - U.S. payer, the foreign branch of a U.S. financial institution, or the U.S. branch of a foreign financial institution.

Taxpayers must file Form 8938 if:

- A taxpayer is a specified person (either a specified individual or a specified domestic entity). A specified individual is:
    1. A U.S. citizen
    2. A resident alien of the United States for any part of the tax year (see Publication 519 for more information)
    3. A nonresident alien who makes an election to be treated as resident alien for purposes of filing a joint income tax return
    4. A nonresident alien who is a bona fide resident of American Samoa or Puerto Rico (See Publication 570 for definition of a bona fide resident)
- Taxpayers have an interest in specified foreign financial assets required to be reported. A specified foreign financial asset is:
    1. Any financial account maintained by a foreign financial institution, except as indicated above
    2. Other foreign financial assets held for investment that are not in an account maintained by a US or foreign financial institution, namely:
        a. Stock or securities issued by someone other than a U.S. person
        b. Any interest in a foreign entity, and
        c. Any financial instrument or contract that has as an issuer or counterparty that is other than a U.S. person.

- The aggregate value of the specified foreign financial assets is more than the reporting thresholds that applies to the taxpayer:
    1. Unmarried taxpayers living in the US: The total value of the specified foreign financial assets is more than $50,000 on the last day of the tax year or more than $75,000 at any time during the tax year
    2. Married taxpayers filing a joint income tax return and living in the US: The total value of the specified foreign financial assets is more than $100,000 on the last day of the tax year or more than $150,000 at any time during the tax year
    3. Married taxpayers filing separate income tax returns and living in the US: The total value of the specified foreign financial assets is more than $50,000 on the last day of the tax year or more than $75,000 at any time during the tax year.
    4. Taxpayers living abroad.
    5. Specified Domestic Entities

SCHEDULE B, REPORTING FOREIGN ACCOUNTS AND TRUSTS

1. Schedule B is a form that needs to be filed together with the regular income tax by April 15.
2. It is used to identify interest and dividend income.
    - If the total amount earned from all accounts during the year exceeded $1,500.
    - If the amount is less than $1,500, the taxpayer doesn't have to file a Schedule B.
2. It is also used to alert the IRS that a taxpayer has a foreign account/s.
    - There is no dollar threshold to report foreign accounts
    - It is essential to state whether the taxpayer was required to file FinCen Form 114, Report of Foreign Bank and Financial Accounts (FBAR).
    - The taxpayer may also file other forms like a foreign trust, he or she must file IRS Form 3520.
    - If the taxpayer has a foreign business, he or she must file IRS Form 5471.
    - For most taxpayers, the most commonly filed forms are Form 8938 and the FBAR form.

What If a Taxpayer Did Not Properly File Schedule B?

1. The taxpayers should amend the return to disclose the income and pay any tax, interest, and penalties.
2. If the taxpayer had foreign accounts, he or she may be able to amend the tax return to include a proper Schedule B without having to pay any penalties, provided the taxpayer filed any required FBARs and were not required to file Form 8938. However, if the taxpayer was required to file Form 8938 but did not do so, amending Schedule B and including 8938 forms may result in penalties, since the taxpayer would basically be announcing to the IRS that he or she did not disclose the foreign accounts to them before.

3. On the other hand, did the taxpayer filed a Schedule B for the domestic accounts but not disclose the foreign accounts? Did he or she affirmatively answer on Schedule B that the taxpayer did not have any interest or signatory authority over a foreign financial account, when he or she actually did? The IRS would consider this an outright lie, and therefore it will not be as easy to amend the Schedule B.
4. If the taxpayer did not file FBARs and a Schedule B, or did not file the FBAR and misrepresented the foreign accounts on Schedule B, the taxpayer should contact a tax attorney to discuss the potential penalties and courses of action.

Form 5471, Information Return of U.S. Persons With Respect to Certain Foreign Corporations

The purpose of Form 5471 isn't to file tax information, but rather so the IRS has a record of which U.S. citizens and residents have ownership in foreign corporations. The IRS wants to prevent people from hiding overseas assets and being aware of who owns what and in which countries helps it do that. Form 5471 is somewhat similar to Form 1120 (a U.S. corporate income tax return) and requires a lot of the same information and disclosures.

Because this form is an informational form, it most likely doesn't affect how much you have to pay in taxes—unless you fail to file, in which case you'll have to pay a penalty. There are exceptions to this norm—for example, if you are a shareholder of a Controlled Foreign Corporation (CFC) Form 5471may affect your income in the form of the GILTI tax (Global Intangible Low-Taxed Income).
Reporting requirements may be as simple as what percentage of stock the taxpayer owns and company information, to reporting the corporation's entire income from financial statements and balance sheets.

Who files Form 5471?

Any U.S. citizen, corporation, partnership, trust, or estate who has at least 10% ownership in a foreign corporation, needs to file Form 5471.

What is a Controlled Foreign Corporation?

A Controlled Foreign Corporation is a foreign corporation where U.S. shareholders hold more than 50% stock ownership. The IRS defines a foreign corporation as being U.S. controlled if:

- "more than 50% of the total combined voting power of all classes of stock of such corporation entitled to vote, or more than 50% of the value of all its outstanding stock, is owned (directly, indirectly, or constructively) by U.S. shareholders on any day during the foreign corporation's tax year."

If this applies to the taxpayer, they may also be liable for the GILTI tax.

DIFFERENCES BETWEEN THE FBAR VS. FORM 8938

The Form 8938 filing requirement does not replace or otherwise affect a taxpayer's obligation to file FinCEN Form 114 (Report of Foreign Bank and Financial Accounts)

	Form 8938, Statement of Specified Foreign Financial Assets	FinCEN Form 114, Report of Foreign Bank and Financial Accounts (FBAR)
Who Must File?	Specified individuals and specified domestic entities that have an interest in specified foreign financial assets and meet the reporting threshold: * Specified individuals include U.S citizens, resident aliens, and certain non-resident aliens * Specified domestic entities include certain domestic corporations, partnerships, and trusts	U.S. persons, which include U.S. citizens, resident aliens, trusts, estates, and domestic entities that have an interest in foreign financial accounts and meet the reporting threshold
Does the United States include U.S. territories?	No	Yes, resident aliens of U.S territories and U.S. territory entities are subject to FBAR reporting
Reporting Threshold (Total Value of Assets)	Specified individuals living in the US: • Unmarried individual (or married filing separately): Total value of assets was more than $50,000 on the last day of the tax year, or more than $75,000 at any time during the year. * Married individual filing jointly: Total value of assets was more than $100,000 on the last day of the tax year, or more than	Aggregate value of financial accounts exceeds $10,000 at any time during the calendar year. This is a cumulative balance, meaning if you have 2 accounts with a combined account balance greater than $10,000 at any one time, both accounts would have to be reported.

	$150,000 at any time during the year. Specified individuals living outside the US: • Unmarried individual (or married filing separately): Total value of assets was more than $200,000 on the last day of the tax year, or more than $300,000 at any time during the year. • Married individual filing jointly: Total value of assets was more than $400,000 on the last day of the tax year, or more than $600,000 at any time during the year. Specified domestic entities: Total value of assets was more than $50,000 on the last day of the tax year, or more than $75,000 at any time during the tax year.	
When do you have an interest in an account or asset?	If any income, gains, losses, deductions, credits, gross proceeds, or distributions from holding or disposing of the account or asset are or would be required to be reported, included, or otherwise reflected on your income tax return	Financial interest: you are the owner of record or holder of legal title; the owner of record or holder of legal title is your agent or representative; you have a sufficient interest in the entity that is the owner of record or holder of legal title. Signature authority: you have authority to control the disposition of the assets in the account by direct communication with the financial institution maintaining the account.

		See instructions for further details.
What is Reported?	Maximum value of specified foreign financial assets, which include financial accounts with foreign financial institutions and certain other foreign non-account investment assets	Maximum value of financial accounts maintained by a financial institution physically located in a foreign country
How are maximum account or asset values determined and reported?	Fair market value in U.S. dollars in accord with the Form 8938 instructions for each account and asset reported Convert to U.S. dollars using the end of the taxable year exchange rate and report in U.S. dollars.	Use periodic account statements to determine the maximum value in the currency of the account. Convert to U.S. dollars using the end of the calendar year exchange rate and report in U.S. dollars.
When Due?	Form is attached to your annual return and due on the date of that return, including any applicable extensions	Received by April 15 (6-month automatic extension to Oct 15)
Where to File?	File with income tax return pursuant to instructions for filing the return.	File electronically through FinCENs BSA E-Filing System. The FBAR is not filed with a federal tax return.
Penalties	Up to $10,000 for failure to disclose and an additional $10,000 for each 30 days of non-filing after IRS notice of a failure to disclose, for a potential maximum penalty of $60,000; criminal penalties may also apply	Civil monetary penalties are adjusted annually for inflation. For civil penalty assessment prior to Aug 1, 2016, if non-willful, up to $10,000; if willful, up to the greater of $100,000 or 50 percent of account balances; criminal penalties may also apply

POP QUIZ & ANSWER SHEET

FOREIGN FINANCIAL PLANNING

POP QUIZ

Test your knowledge on Foreign Financial Planning by answering the questions below. The answer sheet may be found at the end of the Pop Quiz.

Q1: Under the law known as the ___, you must report certain foreign financial accounts, such as bank accounts, brokerage accounts and mutual funds, to the Treasury Department and keep certain records of those accounts.

A. USA Patriot Act
B. Bank Secrecy Act
C. Anti-Money Laundering Act
D. Foreign Assets Act

Q2: Taxpayer A, a US Citizen is an authorized signer on her grandparent's accounts in Germany. The grandparents keep about $80,000 in the account during the year and only has Taxpayer A as an authorized signer in case something happens to them. Taxpayer A does not withdraw or deposit money into the account. All of the following is true, except:

A. Taxpayer A does not have to file an FBAR since she is just a signer and doesn't take money out
B. Taxpayer A must file an FBAR because she is an authorized signer and the account reached over $10,000
C. Taxpayer A must have the grandparents file the FBAR since the account reached over $10,000
D. None of the above

Q3: All are Foreign Financial Accounts that need not be reported, except:

A. Correspondent/Nostro Accounts
B. Owned by a Governmental Entity
C. Owned by an International Financial Institution
D. Part of a Trust of which you're not a Beneficiary

Q4: When is the annual report of FBAR due?

A. April 15 following the calendar year reported
B. April 15 of the prior calendar year
C. October 15 following the calendar year reported
D. October 15 of the next calendar year

Q5: An automatic extension until ___ is given if a taxpayer fails to meet the FBAR annual due date.

A. June 15th
B. August 15th
C. October 15th
D. December 15th

Q6: Taxpayer A who is a US Citizen receives as a gift a plot of land from his grandfather in Nigeria worth $350,000 USD. What form must taxpayer A use to report this transaction?
A. Form 3520
B. Form 8938
C. FinCEN
D. BSA

Q7: Taxpayer A, an unmarried US Citizen receives $250,000 in foreign stocks from her sister in France. Which form must taxpayer A may be required to file?
A. Form 8865, Return of U.S. Persons With Respect to Certain Foreign Partnerships
B. Form 5471, Information Return of U.S. Persons With Respect to Certain Foreign Corporations
C. Form 8938, Statement of Specified Foreign Foreign Financial Assets
D. Form 3520: Reporting Foreign Gifts and Bequests

Q8: This form is used by U.S. persons who have an interest in a foreign partnership.
A. Schedule B, Reporting Foreign Accounts and Trusts
B. Form 8865, Return of U.S. Persons With Respect to Certain Foreign Partnerships
C. Form 8938: Statement of Specified Foreign Financial Assets
D. Form 5471, Information Return of U.S. Persons With Respect to Certain Foreign Corporations

Q9: The IRS uses this form as a record of which U.S. citizens and residents have ownership in foreign corporations:
A. Form 5471, Information Return of U.S. Persons With Respect to Certain Foreign Corporations
B. Form 8865, Return of U.S. Persons With Respect to Certain Foreign Partnerships
C. Schedule B, Reporting Foreign Accounts and Trusts
D. Form 8938: Statement of Specified Foreign Financial Assets

ANSWER SHEET

1. Answer is B – Bank Secrecy Act

2. Answer is B – Taxpayer A must file an FBAR because she is an authorized signer and the account reached over $10,000

3. Answer is D – Part of a Trust of which you're not a Beneficiary

4. Answer is A – April 15 following the calendar year reported

5. Answer is C – October 15th

6. Answer is A – Form 3520

7. Answer is C – Form 8938, Statement of Specified Foreign Financial Assets

8. Answer is B – Form 8865, Return of U.S. Persons With Respect to Certain Foreign Partnerships

9. Answer is A – Form 5471, Information Return of U.S. Persons With Respect to Certain Foreign Corporations

ESTATE & GIFT TAXES

PERSONAL REPRESENTATIVE OR EXECUTOR

The term "executor" includes the executor, personal representative, or administrator of the decedent's estate. If none of these is appointed, qualified, and acting in the United States, every person in actual or constructive possession of any property of the decedent is considered an executor and must file a return.

Executors must provide documentation proving their status. Documentation will vary but may include documents such as a certified copy of the will or a court order designating the executor(s). A statement by the executor attesting to their status is insufficient.

FINAL INCOME TAX RETURN (FORM 1040)

In general, the final individual income tax return of a decedent is prepared and filed in the same manner as when they were alive. All income up to the date of death must be reported and all credits and deductions to which the decedent is entitled may be claimed. File the return using Form 1040 or 1040-SR or, if the decedent qualifies, one of the simpler forms in the 1040 series (Forms 1040 or 1040- SR, A).

INCOME IN RESPECT OF A DECEDENT (IRD)

The method of accounting used by the decedent at the time of death determines the income to include and the deductions to take on the final return. Most individuals use the cash receipts and disbursements method. Under this method, the final individual return should show only the items of income the decedent actually or constructively received, that were credited to his or her account, or that were made available to him or her without restriction before death.

Generally, the final individual return can claim deductions for expenses the decedent paid before death.

THE ESTATE TAX RETURN (FORM 706)

Purpose of Form 706

The executor of a decedent's estate uses Form 706 to figure the estate tax imposed by Chapter 11 of the Internal Revenue Code. This tax is levied on the entire taxable estate and not just on the share received by a particular beneficiary.

Form 706 is also used to figure the generation-skipping transfer (GST) tax imposed by Chapter 13 on direct skips (transfers to skip persons of interests in property included in the decedent's gross estate).

Which Estates Must File

For decedents who died in 2021, Form 706 must be filed by the executor of the estate of every U.S. citizen or resident:

- Whose gross estate, plus adjusted taxable gifts and specific exemption, is more than $11,700,000 in 2021; or
- Whose executor elects to transfer the DSUE amount to the surviving spouse, regardless of the size of the decedent's gross estate.

When to File

Taxpayers must file Form 706 to report estate and/or GST tax within 9 months after the date of the decedent's death. If they are unable to file Form 706 by the due date, they may receive an extension of time to file. Use Form 4768, Application for Extension of Time To File a Return and/or Pay U.S. Estate (and Generation-Skipping Transfer) Taxes, to apply for an automatic 6-month extension of time to file.

Portability Election

An executor can only elect to transfer the DSUE amount to the surviving spouse if the Form 706 is filed timely; that is, within 9 months of the decedent's date of death or, if the taxpayer has received an extension of time to file, before the 6-month extension period ends.

FORM 1041, ANNUAL TAX RETURNFOR ESTATES & TRUSTS

The fiduciary of a domestic decedent's estate, trust, or bankruptcy estate uses Form 1041 to report:

- The income, deductions, gains, losses, etc. of the estate or trust;
- The income that is either accumulated or held for future distribution or distributed currently to the beneficiaries;
- Any income tax liability of the estate or trust;
- Employment taxes on wages paid to household employees; and
- Net Investment Income Tax. See Schedule G, Part I, line 5, and the Instructions for Form 8960.

THE ESTATE TAX

The estate tax is a tax on the individuals' right to transfer property at their death. The fair market value of these items is used, not necessarily what the individuals paid for them or what their values were when they acquired them. It consists of an accounting of everything the individuals own or have certain interests in at the date of death refer to form 706

The total of all of these items is the individuals' "gross estate." the includible property may consist of cash and securities, real estate, insurance, trusts, annuities, business interests and other assets.

THE GROSS ESTATE

The gross estate includes all property in which the decedent had an interest (including real property outside the United States). It also includes:

- Certain transfers made during the decedent's life without an adequate and full consideration in money or money's worth,
- Annuities,
- The includible portion of joint estates with right of survivorship (see the instructions for Schedule E), The includible portion of tenancies by the entirety (see the instructions for Schedule E),
- Certain life insurance proceeds (even though payable to beneficiaries other than the estate) (see the instructions for Schedule D),
- Property over which the decedent possessed a general power of appointment, Dower or curtesy (or statutory estate) of the surviving spouse, and
- Community property to the extent of the decedent's interest as defined by applicable law.

DEDUCTIONS FROM THE GROSS ESTATE

Marital Deduction

One of the primary deductions for married decedents is the Marital Deduction. All property that is included in the gross estate and passes to the surviving spouse is eligible for the marital deduction. The property must pass "outright." In some cases, certain life estates also qualify for the marital deduction.

Charitable Deduction

- If the decedent leaves property to a qualifying charity, it is deductible from the gross estate.
- Mortgages and Debt.
- Administration expenses of the estate.
- Losses during estate administration.

SPECIAL RULE FOR MEDICAL EXPENSES

Medical expenses paid before death by the decedent are deductible, subject to limits, on the final income tax return if deductions are itemized. This includes expenses for the decedent, as well as for the decedent's spouse and dependents.

Election for decedent's expenses. Medical expenses not paid before death are liabilities of the estate and are shown on the federal estate tax return (Form 706). However, if medical expenses for the decedent are paid out of the estate during the 1-

year period beginning with the day after death, individuals can elect to treat all or part of the expenses as paid by the decedent at the time they were incurred.

THE MARITAL DEDUCTION

The marital deduction is authorized by section 2056 for certain property interests that pass from the decedent to the surviving spouse. Taxpayers may claim the deduction only for property interests that are included in the decedent's gross estate (Schedules A through I).

Note. The marital deduction generally is not allowed if the surviving spouse is not a U.S. citizen.

Item number	Description of property interests passing to surviving spouse. For securities, give the CUSIP number. If trust, partnership, or closely held entity, give EIN	Amount
B1	All other property: One-half the value of a house and lot, 256 South West Street, held by decedent and surviving spouse as joint tenants with right of survivorship under deed dated July 15, 1975 (Schedule E, Part I, item 1) .	$182,500
B2	Proceeds of Metropolitan Life Insurance Company Policy No. 104729, payable in one sum to surviving spouse (Schedule D, item 3)	200,000
B3	Cash bequest under Paragraph Six of will	100,000

DECEASED SPOUSAL UNUSED EXCLUSION (DSUE)

Section 303 of the Tax Relief, Unemployment Insurance Reauthorization, and Job Creation Act of 2010 authorized estates of decedents dying after December 31, 2010, to elect to transfer any unused exclusion to the surviving spouse. The amount received by the surviving spouse is called the deceased spousal unused exclusion, or DSUE, amount. If the executor of the decedent's estate elects transfer, or portability, of the DSUE amount, the surviving spouse can apply the DSUE amount received from the estate of his or her last deceased spouse (defined later) against any tax liability arising from subsequent lifetime gifts and transfers at death.
A timely filed and complete Form 706 is required to elect portability of the DSUE amount to a surviving spouse.

INHERITANCES

Property received as a gift, bequest, or inheritance isn't included in the income. However, if the received property in this manner later produces income, such as interest, dividends, or rents, that income is taxable to the taxpayer.

The income from property donated to a trust that is paid, credited, or distributed to the taxpayer is taxable income. If the gift, bequest, or inheritance is the income from property, that income is taxable.

THE BASIS OF ESTATE PROPERTY

The basis of property inherited from a decedent is generally one of the following:

- The FMV of the property on the date of the individual's death.
- The FMV on the alternate valuation date (discussed in the Instructions for Form 706) if elected by the personal representative.
- The value under the special-use valuation method for real property used in farming or other closely held business (see Special-use valuation, later), if elected by the personal representative.
- The decedent's adjusted basis in land to the extent of the value excluded from the decedent's taxable estate as a qualified conservation easement (discussed in the Instructions for Form 706).

GENERATION SKIPPING TRANSFER TAX (GST)

The generation-skipping transfer (GST) tax may apply to gifts during the decedent's life or transfers occurring at the decedent's death, called bequests, made to skip persons.

A skip person is a person who belongs to a generation that is two or more generations below the generation of the donor. For instance, the decedent's grandchild will generally be a skip person to the decedent and his or her spouse.

The GST tax is figured on the amount of the gift or bequest transferred to a skip person, after subtracting any GST exemption allocated to the gift or bequest at the maximum gift and estate tax rates. Each individual has a GST exemption equal to the basic exclusion amount, as indexed for inflation, for the year the gift or bequest was made.

The GST exemption is 11.58 million (same as the Estate exemption) and the GST tax rate is also set at the estate tax rate with a max of 40%. The GST is imposed separately and in addition to the estate and gift taxes.

GSTs have three forms: direct skip, taxable distribution, and taxable termination.

Payments for tuition or medical expenses on behalf of a skip person that are made directly to an educational or medical institution are exempt from gift tax and GST. There is no reporting requirement for this type of gift, regardless of the dollar amount

THE GIFT TAX

The gift tax applies to lifetime transfers of property from one person (the donor) to another person (the donee). A gift is made if tangible or intangible property (including money), the use of property, or the right to receive income from property is given without expecting to receive something of at least equal value in return. If something is sold for less than its full value or if a loan is made without interest or with reduced (less than market rate) interest, a gift may have been made.
The general rule is that any gift is a taxable gift. However, there are many exceptions to this rule.

The Gift Tax Exclusions

The gift tax annual exclusion for 2021 is $15,000 per donee. Generally, the following gifts aren't taxable gifts

- Tuition or medical expenses paid directly to an educational or medical institution for someone else.
- Gifts to the spouse, if the spouse is a United States citizen.
- Gifts to a political organization for its use.
- Gifts to certain exempt organizations described in 501(c)(4), 501(c)(5), and 501(c) (6).
- Gifts to charities

GIFT SPLITTING BY MARRIED COUPLES

If the decedent or his or her spouse made a gift to a third party, the gift can be considered as made one-half by the decedent and one-half by the decedent's spouse. This is known as gift splitting.
Both spouses must be United States citizens or residents, must agree to split the gift and in the case of a deceased spouse, the personal representative will act on behalf of the decedent.

If there is consent to split the gift, both spouses can apply the annual exclusion to one-half of the gift. For gifts made in 2021, gift splitting allows married couples to give up to $30,000 to a person without making a taxable gift.

If a gift is split, both spouses must file a gift tax return to show an agreement to use gift splitting. Form 709 must be filed even if half of the split gift is less than the annual exclusion.

THE BASIS OF PROPERTY RECEIVED AS A GIFT

The general rule is that the basis in the property is the same as the basis of the donor. For example, if a taxpayer was given stock that the donor had purchased for $10 per share (and that was his/her basis), and he or she later sold it for $100 per share, he or she would pay income tax on a gain of $90 per share. (Note: The rules are different for property acquired from an estate.)

THE UNIFIED CREDIT (THE APPLICABLE CREDIT)

- The unified tax credit gives a set dollar amount that an individual can gift during their lifetime before any estate or gift taxes apply.
- The tax credit unifies both the gift and estate taxes into one tax system which decreases the tax bill of the individual or estate, dollar to dollar.
- Since some people prefer to use the unified tax credits to save on estate taxes after their deaths, the unified tax credit may not be used for reducing gift taxes while still alive, and may instead be used on the inheritance amount bequeathed to beneficiaries after death.

LIFE INSURANCE & INDIVIDUAL RETIREMENT ACCOUNTS

Life insurance proceeds contribute to the value of a decedent's taxable estate if the decedent was the owner of the policy or if the decedent transferred ownership within three years of death, such as into an irrevocable living trust.

A decedent's estate is liable for federal estate taxes if it's valued at more than $11.7 million as of 2021. Any balance of value over this threshold is taxable.

- An inherited IRA, also known as a beneficiary IRA, is an account that is opened when an individual inherits an IRA or employer-sponsored retirement plan after the original owner dies.
- Additional contributions may not be made to an inherited IRA.
- Rules vary for spousal and non-spousal beneficiaries of inherited IRAs.
- The SECURE Act mandated that non-spousal beneficiaries must empty inherited IRAs within a decade.

Rules for Spouses

Spouses have more flexibility in how to handle an inherited IRA. For one, they can roll over the IRA, or a part of the IRA, into their own existing individual retirement accounts; the big advantage of this is the ability to defer required minimum distributions (RMDs) of the funds until they reach the age of 72.

They have 60 days from receiving a distribution to roll it over into their own IRAs as long as the distribution is not a required minimum distribution.

Spousal heirs can also set up a separate inherited IRA account, as described above. How they deal with this IRA depends on the age of the deceased account holder.

If the original owner had already begun receiving RMDs at the time of death, the spousal beneficiary must continue to receive the distributions as calculated or submit a new schedule based on their own life expectancy. If the owner had not yet committed to an RMD schedule or reached their required beginning date (RBD)—the age at which they had to begin RMDs—the beneficiary of the IRA has a five-year window to withdraw the funds, which would then be subject to income taxes.

Rules for NON-Spouses

Non-spouse beneficiaries may not treat an inherited IRA as their own. That is, they may not make additional contributions to the account, nor can they transfer funds into an existing IRA account they have in their own names. Non-spouses may not leave assets in the original IRA. They must set up a new inherited IRA account unless they want to distribute the assets immediately via a lump-sum payment.

It is in the realm of distributions that the SECURE Act most drastically affects non-spouse inheritors of IRAs. Previously, these beneficiaries could handle RMDs pretty much as spousal heirs could; in particular, they could recalculate them based on their own life expectancy—which often significantly decreased the annual amount that had to be withdrawn and the tax due on them (in the case of traditional IRAs).

No longer. The SECURE Act dictates that, for accounts inherited after Dec. 31, 2019, non-spouse beneficiaries typically must cash out the account within 10 years of the original owner's death. Some heirs are exempted: those whose age is within a decade of the deceased's, disabled or chronically ill individuals, or minor children. However, these minors must be direct descendants (no grandchildren, in other words), and, once they reach majority age, the 10-year rule kicks in for them too. There's no particular timetable for the withdrawals; they can be taken annually or all at once.

POP QUIZ & ANSWER SHEET

ESTATE & GIFT TAXES

POP QUIZ

Test your knowledge on *Estate & Gift Taxes* by answering the questions below. The answer sheet may be found at the end of the Pop Quiz.

Q1: The final individual income tax return of a decedent is prepared and filed in the same manner as when they were alive. All income up to the date of death must be reported and all credits and deductions to which the decedent is entitled may be claimed. What form must one file for a final individual income tax return?

A. Form 1040
B. Form 1040-NR
C. 1040-X
D. 1040-V

Q2: Form 706 must be filed on behalf of a deceased U.S. citizen or resident whose gross estate, adjusted taxable gifts, and specific exemptions exceed __________ for deaths in 2021:

A. $11 million
B. $11.7 million
C. $15 million
D. $0

Q3: What is the purpose of Form 706?

A. Helps executors determine the overall value of an estate prior to distributing any assets to beneficiaries as outlined in the decedent's will or trust.
B. Used by an executor of an estate to calculate the amount of tax owed on estates valued at more than $11,700,000 for deaths in 2021.
C. Both A & B
D. None of the Above

Q4: When do you file Form 706?

A. You must file it within 30 days after the date of the decedent's death.
B. You must file it within 3 months after the date of the decedent's death.
C. You must file it within 6 months after the date of the decedent's death.
D. You must file it within 9 months after the date of the decedent's death.

Q5: **The fiduciary of a domestic decedent's estate, trust, or bankruptcy estate uses** Form 1041 to report all of the following, except:

A. Net Investment Income Tax
B. The income, deductions, gains, losses, etc. of the estate or trust
C. The income that is either accumulated or held for future distribution or distributed currently to the beneficiaries
D. Income in respect of a decedent

Q6: **___ is a tax on taxpayers right to transfer property at their death:**

A. Income Tax
B. Estate Tax
C. Progressive Tax
D. Sales Tax

Q7: **The gross estate includes all property in which the decedent had an interest** (including real property outside the United States). It does not include:

A. Property over which the decedent does not possess a general power of appointment.
B. Dower or courtesy (or statutory estate) of the surviving spouse.
C. Community property to the extent of the decedent's interest as defined by applicable law.
D. Certain transfers made during the decedent's life without an adequate and full consideration in money or money's worth.

Q8: **What is not a deduction from the Gross Estate?**

A. Mortgages & Debt
B. Administration Expenses of the Estate
C. Losses During Estate Administration
D. Annuities

Q9: **All are basis of property inherited from a decedent, except:**

A. The FMV of the property on the date of the individual's death.
B. The adjusted basis of real estate, vehicles, and stocks.
C. The value under the special-use valuation method for real property used in farming or other closely held business, if elected by the personal representative.
D. The FMV on the alternate valuation date if elected by the personal representative.

Q10: **A ___ is a person who belongs to a generation that is two or more** generations below the generation of the donor.

A. Boomers
B. Gen Z
C. Skip Person
D. Lost Person

ANSWER SHEET

1. Answer is A – Form 1040

2. Answer is B – $11.7 million

3. Answer is C – Both A & B

4. Answer is D – You must file it within 9 months after the date of the decedent's death.

5. Answer is D – Income in respect of a decedent

6. Answer is B – Estate Tax

7. Answer is A – Property over which the decedent does not possess a general power of appointment.

8. Answer is D – Annuities

9. Answer is B – The adjusted basis of real estate, vehicles, and stocks.

10. Answer is C – Skip Person

INDIVIDUAL RETIREMENT ACCOUNTS

OVERVIEW

IRAs allow taxpayers to make tax-deferred investments to provide financial security when they retire.

Contributions to the individual retirement accounts (IRAs) that are Traditional IRAs or Roth IRAs are generally limited to a certain annual dollar amount or the compensation that is includible in the gross income for the tax year.

TRADITIONAL IRA RULES

The maximum annual contribution limit for 2021, 2020 and 2019 is $6,000 (or $7,000 if the taxpayer is age 50 or older). Contributions may be tax-deductible in the year they are made. Investments within the account grow tax deferred. Withdrawals in retirement are taxed as ordinary income.

The IRS requires individuals to begin taking money out of the account at age 72. (people who turned 70½ in 2019 or earlier were required to start distributions then.) Nonqualified withdrawals before age 59½ may trigger a 10% early withdrawal penalty and income taxes.

IRA Contribution Rules

Having earned income is a requirement for contributing to a traditional IRA, and the annual contributions to an IRA cannot exceed what is earned that year. Otherwise, for 2021, 2020 and 2019 the annual contribution limit is $6,000 for those younger than 50 and $7,000 for those 50 and older.

IRA Deduction Rules

The answer to the deductibility question is based on the income and whether the taxpayer or his or her spouse is covered by an employer-sponsored retirement plan, such as a 401(k). If neither of them has access to a workplace savings plan, they can deduct all of the contributions (remember, the maximum contribution is $6,000, or $7,000 if taxpayers are 50 or older)

IRA Withdrawal Rules

Age 59½ may not be widely considered a milestone birthday, but in IRS circles it is notable for being the age at which individuals are allowed to start making withdrawals from their IRAs. Tapping the account before that age can trigger a 10% early withdrawal penalty and additional income taxes.

Age 72 is another one to mark on the calendar. This is when investors who have saved in a traditional IRA are required to start taking required minimum distributions, or RMDs. (Note: Until the end of 2019, 70½ was the age when minimum distributions were required to start.)

IRA CONTRIBUTION LIMITS

The 2021 combined annual contribution limit for Roth and traditional IRAs is $6,000 ($7,000 if the taxpayer is age 50 or older)—unchanged from 2020.

Roth IRA contribution limits are reduced or eliminated at higher incomes. Traditional IRA contributions are deductible, but the amount that can be deducted may be reduced or eliminated if the taxpayer or his or her spouse is covered by a retirement plan at work. Lower-income taxpayers may be eligible for the "saver's credit" if they contribute to an IRA.

IRA FAQs – Contributions

How much can a taxpayer contribute to an IRA?

The annual contribution limit for 2021 is $6,000, or $7,000 if the taxpayer is age 50 or older (same as 2020 limit). The annual contribution limit for 2015, 2016, 2017 and 2018 is $5,500, or $6,500 if the taxpayer is age 50 or older. The Roth IRA contributions may also be limited based on the filing status and income.

Is the IRA contribution deductible on the tax return?

If neither the taxpayer or his or her spouse is covered by a retirement plan at work, the deduction is allowed in full. For contributions to a traditional IRA, the amount that can be deducted may be limited if the taxpayer or his or her spouse is covered by a retirement plan at work and the income exceeds certain levels. Roth IRA contributions aren't deductible.

Can a taxpayer contribute to a traditional or Roth IRA if they are covered by a retirement plan at work?

Yes, a taxpayer can contribute to a traditional and/or Roth IRA even if he or she participates in an employer-sponsored retirement plan (including a SEP or SIMPLE IRA plan). If the taxpayer or his or her spouse is covered by an employer-sponsored retirement plan and the income exceeds certain levels, he or she may not be able to deduct the entire contribution.

A taxpayer wants to set up an IRA for their spouse. How much can he or she contribute?

If a taxpayer files a joint return and has taxable compensation, together with his or her spouse they can both contribute to their own separate IRAs. The total contributions to both the taxpayer's IRA and his or her spouse's IRA may not exceed the joint taxable income or the annual contribution limit on IRAs times two, whichever is less. It doesn't matter which spouse earned the income. Roth IRAs and IRA deductions have other income limits.

Does a taxpayer report the nondeductible Roth IRA contributions on Form 8606?

Do not use Form 8606, Nondeductible IRAs (PDF), Nondeductible IRAs, to report nondeductible Roth IRA contributions. However, the taxpayer should use Form 8606 to report amounts that he or she converted from a traditional IRA, a SEP, or Simple IRA to a Roth IRA.

SPLITTING IRA CONTRIBUTIONS BETWEEN MULTIPLE ACCOUNTS

Having multiple IRAs can help the taxpayer to tweak the tax strategy and increase the investment choices and increased account insurance. Here's how:

Tax diversification: Having multiple IRA's gives the taxpayer an immediate tax deduction, allowing the taxpayer to delay what he or she owes the IRS until he or she starts removing the savings from the account in retirement. With a Roth IRA, there's no upfront tax break on contributions, but qualified withdrawals are completely tax-free.

Investment diversification: Having IRAs at multiple financial firms can give the taxpayer coverage to diverse types of investments and even diverse investing policies.

Flexibility on withdrawals: In addition to the variances in how the savings are taxed, traditional and Roth IRAs have dissimilar rules about withdrawals both before and during retirement. Roth IRA contributions (not earnings) can be withdrawn tax- and penalty-free at any time and for any reason. Traditional IRAs have less leeway, although they do allow early withdrawals (before age 59½) without penalty in certain circumstances. And unlike the Roth, withdrawals from a traditional IRA become mandatory after age 72. There are no mandatory minimum withdrawals with the Roth.

More insurance coverage for cash and investments: In the questionable event the brokerage or bank that holds the IRA fails, SIPC and FDIC insurance on investment and deposit accounts can cover the losses. Coverage is generally capped at $500,000 (SIPC) and $250,000 (FDIC) for a single account holder at a single institution, but there are ways to increase the coverage through multiple accounts.

Simplified estate planning: Naming beneficiaries is part of the procedure of opening an IRA. While the taxpayer can name more than one beneficiary per IRA (a primary and contingency), having diverse people named on separate accounts can mitigate beneficiary tiffs after he or she retires to the great beyond.

DEDUCTIBILITY OF TRADITIONAL IRA CONTRIBUTIONS

A traditional IRA has many benefits, including the ability to save and invest money for retirement on a tax-deferred basis, meaning the interest and capital gains from the market grow tax-free. Also, traditional IRAs offer a tax deduction in the tax year of the contribution or deposit.

If the tax filing status is single, the maximum tax-deductible contribution starts shrinking once the income reaches $65,000 and $75,000.

If an individual is married and neither he or she nor the spouse is an active participant in a qualified plan, the taxpayer can deduct the full contribution amount.

If one of the spouses is an active participant, then the income and tax filing status determines whether or not they can deduct the contribution.

REQUIRED MINIMUM DISTRIBUTIONS (RMDS)

Required Minimum Distributions (RMDs) generally are minimum amounts that a retirement plan account owner must withdraw annually starting with the year that he or she reaches 72 (70 ½ if you reach 70 ½ before January 1, 2020), if later, the year in which he or she retires.
Retirement plan participants and IRA owners, including owners of SEP IRAs and SIMPLE IRAs, are responsible for taking the correct amount of RMDs on time every year from their accounts, and they face stiff penalties for failure to take RMDs.

How is the amount of the required minimum distribution calculated?

- Generally, a RMD is calculated for each account by dividing the prior December 31 balance of that IRA or retirement plan account by a life expectancy factor that IRS publishes in Tables in Publication 590-B, Distributions from Individual Retirement Arrangements (IRAs)

Can an account owner just take a RMD from one account instead of separately from each account?

- An IRA owner must calculate the RMD separately for each IRA that he or she owns, but can withdraw the total amount from one or more of the IRAs.
- However, RMDs required from other types of retirement plans, such as 401(k) and 457(b) plans have to be taken separately from each of those plan accounts.

Who calculates the amount of the RMD?

- Although the IRA custodian or retirement plan administrator may calculate the RMD, the IRA or retirement plan account owner is ultimately responsible for calculating the amount of the RMD.
- What happens if a person does not take a RMD by the required deadline?

- If an account owner fails to withdraw a RMD, fails to withdraw the full amount of the RMD, or fails to withdraw the RMD by the applicable deadline, the amount not withdrawn is taxed at 50%. The account owner should file Form 5329, Additional Taxes on Qualified Plans (Including IRAs) and Other Tax-Favored Accounts, with his or her federal tax return for the year in which the full amount of the RMD was not taken.

Contribution Deadline

IRA contributor donations for a specific tax year must be made by April 15 of the following year, the date that taxes for the previous year are due. If April 15 falls on a weekend or other holiday, the deadline is the next business day. For the tax year 2022, taxpayers can contribute toward their 2021 tax year limit of $6,000 until May 17. Contributions postmarked on or before May 17 are made by the deadline.

Making The Contribution After Filing the Tax Return

The IRA contribution for the tax year can be made at any time between January 1 of that year and April 15 the following year.

Taxpayers can donate to an IRA even if they filed the income tax return before the April 15 tax deadline. If they decide to make the contribution after they file the tax return, they need to notify their tax professional so that if the contribution was not included on the return, an amended return that includes the contribution can be filed.

Indicate the Tax Year on Check

Many taxpayers may mark an IRA contribution for the previous tax year by taking advantage of the 3½-month extension for the deadline on April 15 (the following year) or the 6½-month extension in 2021 with the July 15 deadline.

TAXABILITY OF IRA DISTRIBUTIONS

The withdrawals from a Roth IRA are tax free as long as the taxpayers are 59 ½ or older and the account is at least five years old.

Withdrawals from traditional IRAs are taxed as regular income, based on the tax bracket for the year in which taxpayers make the withdrawal.

IRA FAQs - Distributions (Withdrawals)

1. Distributions while still working

Can individuals take money from their traditional IRA, or my SEP or SIMPLE IRA, while they are still working?

Taxpayers can take distributions from the IRA (including the SEP-IRA or SIMPLE-IRA) at any time. There is no need to show a hardship to take a distribution. However, the distribution will be includible in the taxable income and it may be subject to a 10% additional tax if a taxpayer is under age 59 1/2.

The following, though not exhaustive, are exceptions to the 10% additional tax: Corrective distributions, Death, Total & Permanent Disability, Qualified Education expenses, first time homebuyers up to $10k, IRS Levy, Military called to active duty, Separation of service from employer.

If individuals withdraw money from the IRA before they are 59 1/2, which forms do they need to fill out?

Regardless of their age, individuals will need to file a Form 1040 and show the amount of the IRA withdrawal. Since they took the withdrawal before they reached age 59 1/2, unless they met one of the exceptions, individuals will need to pay an additional 10% tax on early distributions on the Form 1040. Taxpayers may need to complete and attach a Form 5329, Additional Taxes on Qualified Plans (Including IRAs) and Other Tax-Favored Accounts (PDF), to the tax return. Certain distributions from Roth IRAs are not taxable.

Can individuals deduct the 10% additional early withdrawal tax as a penalty on early withdrawal of savings?

Yes. Unless the individuals qualify for an exception, they must still pay the 10% additional tax for taking an early distribution from the traditional IRA even if they take it to satisfy a divorce court order (Internal Revenue Code section 72(t)). The 10% additional tax is charged on the early distribution amount that must be included in the income and is in addition to any regular income tax from including this amount in income. Unlike distributions made to a former spouse from a qualified retirement plan under a Qualified Domestic Relations Order, there is no comparable exception. The only divorce-related exception for IRAs is if a taxpayer transfers the interest in the IRA to a spouse or former spouse, and the transfer is under a divorce or separation instrument (see IRC section 408(d)(6)). However, the transfer must be done by: changing the name of the IRA from the name to that of the former spouse (if transferring the entire interest in that IRA), or a trustee-to-trustee transfer from the IRA to one established by the former spouse. Note: an indirect rollover doesn't qualify as a transfer to the former spouse even if the distributed amount is deposited into the former spouse's IRA within 60-days.

QUALIFIED CHARITABLE DISTRIBUTIONS

What is a qualified charitable distribution?

Generally, a qualified charitable distribution is an otherwise taxable distribution from an IRA (other than an ongoing SEP or SIMPLE IRA) owned by an individual who is age 72 or over that is paid directly from the IRA to a qualified charity. See Publication

590-B, Distributions from Individual Retirement Arrangements (IRAs) for additional information.

Can a qualified charitable distribution satisfy the required minimum distribution from an IRA?

Yes, the qualified charitable distributions can satisfy all or part the amount of the required minimum distribution from the IRA. For example, if the 2018 required minimum distribution was $10,000, and a taxpayer made a $5,000 qualified charitable distribution for 2018, he would have had to withdraw another $5,000 to satisfy the 2014 required minimum distribution.

How are qualified charitable distributions reported on Form 1099-R?

Charitable distributions are reported on Form 1099-R for the calendar year the distribution is made.

How do individuals report a qualified charitable distribution on the income tax return?

To report a qualified charitable distribution on the Form 1040 tax return, taxpayers generally report the full amount of the charitable distribution on the line for IRA distributions. On the line for the taxable amount, enter zero if the full amount was a qualified charitable distribution. Enter "QCD" next to this line. See the Form 1040 instructions for additional information.

Individuals must also file Form 8606, Nondeductible IRAs, if:

- the individuals made the qualified charitable distribution from a traditional IRA in which they had basis and received a distribution from the IRA during the same year, other than the qualified charitable distribution; or
- The qualified charitable distribution was made from a Roth IRA.

Generally, a qualified charitable distribution is an otherwise taxable distribution from an IRA (other than an ongoing SEP or SIMPLE IRA) owned by an individual who is age 72 or over that is paid directly from the IRA to a qualified charity. See Publication 590-B, Distributions from Individual Retirement Arrangements (IRAs) for additional information.

Charitable distributions are reported on Form 1099-R for the calendar year the distribution is made. To report a qualified charitable distribution on the Form 1040 tax return, taxpayers generally report the full amount of the charitable distribution on the line for IRA distributions. On the line for the taxable amount, enter zero if the full amount was a qualified charitable distribution.

10% PENALTY ON EARLY DISTRIBUTIONS AND PENALTY EXCEPTIONS

Most retirement plan distributions are subject to income tax and may be subject to an additional 10% tax. The amounts an individual removes from an IRA or retirement plan before reaching age 59½ are called "early" or "premature" distributions. Individuals must pay an additional 10% early withdrawal tax unless an exception applies.

Below are eight situations which may qualify taxpayers for an exception to the IRA penalty tax on withdrawals

- Medical Expenses
    - Taxpayers qualify for an exclusion from the IRA penalty tax if they used the IRA early withdrawal to pay medical expenses that are more than 7.5% of the adjusted gross income
- Healthcare Insurance
    - If a taxpayer is unemployed, and used the IRA early withdrawal to pay for the medical insurance
- Disability
    - If a taxpayer is disabled, plan on a doctor's verification to qualify for an exception to the penalty tax.

4. Inherited IRA

Individuals Inherit an IRA in the following ways:

- If an individual inherits an IRA from a non-spouse, even if the IRA owner was under age 59 1/2, he or she will not have to pay the penalty tax on amounts withdrawn. The taxpayer will still have to include any IRA withdrawal in the adjusted gross income (AGI).
- If an individual inherits an IRA from a spouse, and he or she chooses to treat it as his or her own IRA, then any IRA early withdrawal received will be subject to the 10% penalty tax.
- If an individual inherits an IRA from a spouse, but he or she chooses to title the IRA as an "inherited IRA," then he or she would be eligible to receive IRA early withdrawals without paying the 10% penalty tax.

5. Qualified Higher Education Expenses

IRA early withdrawals used to pay qualified higher education expenses on behalf of the taxpayer, his or her spouse, or the children or grandchildren of the taxpayer or the spouse, are exempt from the 10% penalty tax if they were paid to an eligible educational institution.

6. First-Time Home Purchase If both the taxpayer and his or her spouse qualify as first-time home buyers, then each of them could withdraw $10,000 from each of the respective IRAs without paying the 10% penalty tax.

7. Qualified Reservist Distributions

A qualified reservist distribution is not subject to the penalty tax on IRA early withdrawals.

ROTH IRA VS. TRADITIONAL IRA

This chart highlights some of their similarities and differences.

Features	Traditional IRA	Roth IRA
Who can contribute?	You can contribute if you (or your spouse if filing jointly) have taxable compensation. Prior to January 1, 2020, you were unable to contribute if you were age 70½ or older.	You can contribute at any age if you (or your spouse if filing jointly) have taxable compensation and your modified adjusted gross income is below certain amounts (see 2020 and 2021 limits).
Are my contributions deductible?	You can deduct your contributions if you qualify.	Your contributions aren't deductible.
How much can I contribute?	The most you can contribute to **all** of your traditional and Roth IRAs is the smaller of: • For 2019, $6,000, or $7,000 if you're age 50 or older by the end of the year; or • your taxable compensation for the year. • For 2020, $6,000, or $7,000 if you're age 50 or older by the end • of the year; or • your taxable compensation for the year. • For 2021, $6,000, or $7,000 if you're age 50 or older by the end of the year; or • your taxable compensation for the year.	
What is the deadline to make contributions?	Your tax return filing deadline (not including extensions). For example, you can make 2021 IRA contributions until April 15, 2022..	
When can I withdraw money?	You can withdraw money anytime.	
Do I have to take required minimum distributions?	You must start taking distributions by April 1 following the year in which you turn age 72 (70 1/2 if you reach the age of 70 ½ before	Not required if you are the original owner.

	January 1, 2020) and by December 31 of later years.	
Are my withdrawals and distributions taxable?	Any deductible contributions and earnings you withdraw or that are distributed from your traditional IRA are taxable. Also, if you are under age 59 ½ you may have to pay an additional 10% tax for early withdrawals unless you qualify for an exception.	None if it's a qualified distribution (or a withdrawal that is a qualified distribution). Otherwise, part of the distribution or withdrawal may be taxable. If you are under age 59 ½, you may also have to pay an additional 10% tax for early withdrawals unless you qualify for an exception.

IRA ROLLOVERS

When taxpayers roll over a retirement plan distribution, they generally don't pay tax on it until they withdraw it from the new plan. By rolling over, taxpayers are saving for their future and their money continues to grow tax deferred.

If taxpayers don't roll over their payment, it will be taxable (other than qualified Roth distributions and any amounts already taxed) and taxpayers may also be subject to additional tax unless they are eligible for one of the exceptions to the 10% additional tax on early distributions

How to complete a rollover?

Direct rollover – If taxpayers are getting a distribution from a retirement plan, they can ask the plan administrator to make the payment directly to another retirement plan or to an IRA. Contact the plan administrator for instructions. The administrator may issue the distribution in the form of a check made payable to the new account. No taxes will be withheld from the transfer amount.

Trustee-to-trustee transfer – If taxpayers are getting a distribution from an IRA, they can ask the financial institution holding the IRA to make the payment directly from the IRA to another IRA or to a retirement plan. No taxes will be withheld from the transfer amount.

60-day rollover – If a distribution from an IRA or a retirement plan is paid directly to the taxpayer, he or she can deposit all or a portion of it in an IRA or a retirement plan within 60 days. Taxes will be withheld from a distribution from a retirement plan (see below), so the taxpayer will have to use other funds to roll over the full amount of the distribution.

ROLLOVER RULES

Taxpayers generally cannot make more than one rollover from the same IRA within a 1-year period. They also cannot make a rollover during this 1-year period from the IRA to which the distribution was rolled over.

Taxpayers can make only one rollover from an IRA to another (or the same) IRA in any 12-month period, regardless of the number of IRAs owned.

The one-per year limit does not apply to:

- rollovers from traditional IRAs to Roth IRAs (conversions)
- trustee-to-trustee transfers to another IRA
- IRA-to-plan rollovers
- plan-to-IRA rollovers
- plan-to-plan rollovers

Once this rule takes effect, the tax consequences are:

- Taxpayers must include in gross income any previously untaxed amounts distributed from an IRA if they made an IRA-to-IRA rollover (other than a rollover from a traditional IRA to a Roth IRA) in the preceding 12 months, and
- Taxpayers may be subject to the 10% early withdrawal tax on the amount they include in gross income.

Which types of distributions can taxpayers roll over?

Retirement plans: Taxpayers can roll over all or part of any distribution of the retirement plan account except:

- Required minimum distributions,
- Loans treated as a distribution,
- Hardship distributions,
- Distributions of excess contributions and related earnings,
- A distribution that is one of a series of substantially equal payments,
- Withdrawals electing out of automatic contribution arrangements,
- Distributions to pay for accident, health or life insurance,
- Dividends on employer securities, or
- S corporation allocations treated as deemed distributions.

Will taxes be withheld from the distribution?

If individuals have not elected a direct rollover, in the case of a distribution from a retirement plan, or they have not elected out of withholding in the case of a distribution from an IRA, the plan administrator or IRA trustee will withhold taxes from the distribution. If individuals later roll the distribution over within 60 days, they must use other funds to make up for the amount withheld.

Example:

Jordan, age 42, received a $10,000 eligible rollover distribution from her 401(k) plan. Her employer withheld $2,000 from her distribution.

If Jordan later decides to roll over the $8,000, but not the $2,000 withheld, she will report $2,000 as taxable income, $8,000 as a nontaxable rollover, and $2,000 as taxes paid. Jordan must also pay the 10% additional tax on early distributions on the $2,000 unless she qualifies for an exception.

If Jordan decides to roll over the full $10,000, she must contribute $2,000 from other sources. Jordan will report $10,000 as a nontaxable rollover and $2,000 as taxes paid.

ROLLOVER AFTER THE DEATH OF AN IRA OWNER

A beneficiary can be any person or entity the owner chooses to receive the benefits of a retirement account or an IRA after he or she dies. Beneficiaries of a retirement account or traditional IRA must include in their gross income any taxable distributions they receive.

IRA Beneficiaries

Inherited from spouse. If a traditional IRA is inherited from a spouse, the surviving spouse generally has the following three choices:

- Treat it as his or her own IRA by designating himself or herself as the account owner.
- Treat it as his or her own by rolling it over into a traditional IRA, or to the extent it is taxable, into a:
    - Qualified employer plan,
    - Qualified employee annuity plan (section 403(a) plan),
    - Tax-sheltered annuity plan (section 403(b) plan),
    - Deferred compensation plan of a state or local government (section 457(b) plan), or
- Treat himself or herself as the beneficiary rather than treating the IRA as his or her own.

If a surviving spouse receives a distribution from his or her deceased spouse's IRA, it can be rolled over into an IRA of the surviving spouse within the 60-day time limit, as long as the distribution is not a required distribution, even if the surviving spouse is not the sole beneficiary of his or her deceased spouse's IRA.

Inherited from someone other than a spouse?

If the inherited traditional IRA is from anyone other than a deceased spouse, the beneficiary cannot treat it as his or her own. This means that the beneficiary cannot make any contributions to the IRA or roll over any amounts into or out of the inherited IRA. However, the beneficiary can make a trustee-to-trustee transfer as long as the IRA into which amounts are being moved is set up and maintained in the name of the deceased IRA owner for the benefit of the beneficiary.

10-year rule.

The 10-year rule requires the IRA beneficiaries who are not taking life expectancy payments to withdraw the entire balance of the IRA by December 31st of the year containing the 10th anniversary of the owner's death. For example, if the owner died in 2021, the beneficiary would have to fully distribute the plan by December 31, 2031.. The beneficiary is allowed, but not required, to take distributions prior to that date.

Like the original owner, the beneficiary generally will not owe tax on the assets in the IRA until he or she receives distributions from it.

Generally, the entire interest in a Roth IRA must be distributed by the end of the fifth calendar year after the year of the owner's death unless the interest is payable to a designated beneficiary over the life or life expectancy of the designated beneficiary.

If paid as an annuity, the entire interest must be payable over a period not greater than the designated beneficiary's life expectancy and distributions must begin before the end of the calendar year following the year of death. Distributions from another Roth IRA cannot be substituted for these distributions unless the other Roth IRA was inherited from the same decedent.

If the sole beneficiary is the spouse, he or she can either delay distributions until the decedent would have reached age 72 or treat the Roth IRA as his or her own.

Beneficiaries of Qualified Plans

Generally, a beneficiary reports pension or annuity income in the same way the plan participant would have reported it. However, some special rules apply.

- A beneficiary of an employee who was covered by a retirement plan can exclude from income a portion of nonperiodic distributions received that totally relieve the payer from the obligation to pay an annuity. The amount that the beneficiary can exclude is equal to the deceased employee's investment in the contract (cost).
- If the beneficiary is entitled to receive a survivor annuity on the death of an employee, the beneficiary can exclude part of each annuity payment as a tax-free recovery of the employee's investment in the contract. The beneficiary must figure the tax-free part of each payment using the method that applies as if he or she were the employee.
- Benefits paid to a survivor under a joint and survivor annuity must be included in the surviving spouse's gross income in the same way the retiree would have included them in gross income.

CONVERSION OF A TRADITIONAL IRA TO A ROTH IRA

A Roth IRA conversion lets taxpayers change a traditional IRA into a Roth IRA. Taxpayers will instantly be indebted of taxes due on the converted amount, but qualified withdrawals in retirement will then be tax-free.

A conversion makes the most sense if taxpayers imagine being in a higher tax bracket in the future. Because of the tax laws passed in 2017, a conversion can no longer be overturned to a traditional IRA.

Benefits of Roth IRAs

Money that is withdrawn from a Roth is tax free, assuming that the taxpayer is 59 ½ years old and the initial contribution to a Roth was 5 years ago.

Traditional IRA owners must start taking the required minimum distributions (RMDs) from their accounts by April 1 of the year following the calendar year they turn 72.

Traditional IRA owners who qualify get a tax break for the money they invested into their accounts. Roth owners do not, they deposit post tax money into their account.

The Case for Roth IRA Conversions

1. Taxpayers save on taxes in the long run
    - When taxpayers convert some or all of the money in the traditional IRA to a Roth, they have to pay income tax the year it was converted.
    - After taxpayers have paid tax on that money, they will enjoy tax free transactions
2. Taxpayers might avoid RMDs and harsh penalties
    - With traditional IRAs, taxpayers must start taking RMDs at age 72. Or else, they'll face a big tax penalty—50% of the amount they did not withdraw.
3. It could be the only way to get one.
    - If taxpayers want a Roth, for inheritance or other purposes, but earn too much to contribute to one, converting the money they already have in a traditional IRA is the only option.
4. Taxpayers might end up paying more taxes in the long run.
    - Taxpayers are most likely to be in a lower tax bracket later on, as many people are after they retire, they would do better to wait.

1. Taxpayers might end up facing a big tax bill
    - If they plan to cover the taxes by withdrawing extra money from the traditional IRA, they'll generally be subject to a 10% early withdrawal penalty if they are under 59½.

RECHARACTERIZATION

A recharacterization allows individuals to treat a regular contribution made to a Roth IRA or to a traditional IRA as having been made to the other type of IRA. So basically, taxpayers can convert a traditional IRA to a Roth IRA or vice versa.

How do individuals recharacterize a regular IRA contribution?

To recharacterize a regular IRA contribution, individuals tell the trustee of the financial institution holding the IRA to transfer the amount of the contribution plus earnings to a different type of IRA (either a Roth or traditional) in a trustee-to-trustee transfer or to a different type of IRA with the same trustee. If this is done by the due date for filing the tax return (including extensions), individuals can treat the contribution as made to the second IRA for that year (effectively ignoring the contribution to the first IRA).

Can individuals recharacterize a rollover or conversion to a Roth IRA?

Pursuant to the Tax Cuts and Jobs Act a conversion from a traditional IRA, SEP or SIMPLE to a Roth IRA cannot be recharacterized. The new law also prohibits recharacterizing amounts rolled over to a Roth IRA from other retirement plans, such as 401(k) or 403(b) plans.

Excise Tax on Excess IRA Contributions

If taxpayers exceed the 2021 IRA contribution limit, they may withdraw excess contributions from the account by the due date of the tax return (including extensions). Otherwise, they must pay a 6% tax each year on the excess amounts left in the account.

How can an excess contribution happen?

An excess contribution is generally one that surpasses the IRA contribution limit. A superfluous contribution can occur in an IRA for a variety of reasons including the following:

- Contribution is more than the annual contribution limit
- Contribution is more than the earned income
- Contribution made on behalf of an individual after date of death
- Required minimum distribution (RMD) is rolled over
- Making an ineligible rollover contribution
- Contribution to a Roth IRA and the modified adjusted gross income (MAGI) exceeded the income limit
- Unable to deduct a Traditional IRA contribution; this is truly not an excess contribution because being unable to deduct does not mean that the individual wasn't able to contribute

Prohibited Transactions

Prohibited transactions are certain transactions between a retirement plan and a disqualified person. If individuals are a disqualified person who takes part in a prohibited transaction, they must pay a tax.

Prohibited transactions in a qualified plan

Prohibited transactions generally include the following transactions:

- A disqualified person's transfer of plan income or assets to, or use of them by or for his or her benefit
- A fiduciary's act by which he or she deals with plan income or assets in his or her own interest
- A fiduciary's receipt of consideration for his or her own account in a transaction that involves plan income or assets from any party dealing with the plan
- Any of the following acts between the plan and a disqualified person:
    - Selling, exchanging, or leasing property
    - Lending money or extending credit
    - Furnishing goods, services or facilities

Prohibited Transactions in an IRA

Generally, a prohibited transaction in an IRA is any improper use of an IRA account or annuity by the IRA owner, his or her beneficiary or any disqualified person.

Disqualified persons include the IRA owner's fiduciary and members of his or her family (spouse, ancestor, lineal descendant, and any spouse of a lineal descendant).

The following are examples of possible prohibited transactions with an IRA.

- Borrowing money from it
- Selling property to it
- Using it as security for a loan
- Buying property for personal use (present or future) with IRA funds

Prohibited transactions generally include the following transactions:

- A disqualified person's transfer of plan income or assets to, or use of them by or for his or her benefit
- A fiduciary's act by which he or she deals with plan income or assets in his or her own interest
- A fiduciary's receipt of consideration for his or her own account in a transaction that involves plan income or assets from any party dealing with the plan

Any of the following acts between the plan and a disqualified person:

- Selling, exchanging, or leasing property

- Lending money or extending credit
- Furnishing goods, services or facilities

Exempt Transactions

The law exempts some transactions from being prohibited transactions. For example, if a taxpayer is a disqualified person and receives any benefit to which he or she is entitled as a plan participant or beneficiary (such as a participant loan), this is not considered a prohibited transaction. However, the benefit must be on the same terms as for all other participants and beneficiaries.

RETIREMENTS PLANS FOR BUSINESSES

Retirement plans can provide a significant source of income at retirement by allowing employers to set aside money in retirement accounts for themselves and their employees.

Eligible Employee – An eligible employee is an employee who:

- Is at least age 21, and
- Has performed service for the taxpayer in at least 3 of the last 5 years.
- All eligible employees must participate in the plan, including part-time employees, seasonal employees, and employees who die or terminate employment during the year.

Types of Retirement Plans

1. SEP plans

SEP plans provide a simplified method for taxpayers to make contributions to a retirement plan for themselves and for their employees.

Instead of setting up a profit-sharing or money purchase plan with a trust, taxpayers can adopt a SEP agreement and make contributions directly to a traditional individual retirement account or a traditional individual retirement annuity (SEP-IRA) set up for themselves and each eligible employee.

2. SIMPLE plans

Generally, if taxpayers had 100 or fewer employees who received at least $5,000 in compensation last year, they can set up a SIMPLE IRA plan.

Under a SIMPLE plan, employees can choose to make salary reduction contributions rather than receiving these amounts as part of their regular pay. In addition, individuals will contribute matching or nonelective contributions.

The two types of SIMPLE plans are the SIMPLE IRA plan and the SIMPLE 401(k) plan.

3. Qualified plans

The qualified plan rules are more complex than the SEP plan and SIMPLE plan rules.

However, there are advantages to qualified plans, such as increased flexibility in designing plans and increased contribution and deduction limits in some cases.

QUALIFIED RETIREMENT PLANS

A sole proprietor or a partnership can set up one of these plans. A common-law employee or a partner can't set up one of these plans.

The plan must be for the exclusive benefit of employees or their beneficiaries. These qualified plans can include coverage for a self-employed individual.

The plans described here can also be set up and maintained by employers that are corporations. All of the rules discussed here apply to corporations except where specifically limited to the self-employed.

As an employer, individuals can usually deduct, subject to limits, contributions they make to a qualified plan, including those made for their own retirement. The contributions (and earnings and gains on them) are generally tax free until distributed by the plan.

Kinds of Plans

There are two basic kinds of qualified plans—defined contribution plans and defined benefit plans—and different rules apply to each

DEFINED BENEFIT PLAN

A defined-benefit plan is an employer-based program that pays aids based on elements such as length of employment and salary history. Pensions are defined-benefit plans. Unlike defined-contribution plans, the employer, not the employee, is accountable for all of the planning and investment risk of a defined-benefit plan. Aids can be dispersed as fixed-monthly payments like an annuity or in one lump-sum payment. The surviving spouse is often eligible for benefits if the employee passes away.

Examples of Defined-Benefit Plan Payouts

It assurances a precise benefit or payout upon retirement. The employer naturally funds the plan by paying a regular amount, usually a percentage of the employee's pay, into a tax-deferred account.

The employer may decide for a fixed benefit or one calculated according to a formula that factors in years of service, age, and average salary. Upon retirement, the plan might pay monthly payments during the course of the employee's lifetime or as a lump-sum payment.

Annuity vs. Lump-Sum Payments

Payment options are:

A. single-life annuity, which provides a fixed monthly benefit until death;
B. a qualified joint and survivor annuity, which offers a fixed monthly benefit until death and allows the surviving spouse to continue receiving benefits thereafter;
C. or a lump-sum payment, which pays the entire value of the plan in a single payment.

DEFINED CONTRIBUTION PLAN

A defined contribution plan provides an individual account for each participant in the plan. It provides benefits to a participant largely based on the amount contributed to that participant's account. Benefits are also affected by any income, expenses, gains, losses, and forfeitures of other accounts that may be allocated to an account.

A defined contribution plan can be either a profit-sharing plan or a money purchase pension plan

1. Profit-sharing plan

Individuals don't actually have to make a business profit for the year in order to make a contribution (except for themselves if they are self-employed, as discussed under Self-employed individuals, later).

A profit-sharing plan can be set up to allow for discretionary employer contributions, meaning the amount contributed each year to the plan isn't fixed.

An employer may even make no contribution to the plan for a given year

2. Money purchase pension plan

Contributions to a money purchase pension plan are fixed and aren't based on the business profits.

For example, a money purchase pension plan may require that contributions be 10% of the participants' compensation without regard to whether the taxpayer has profits (or the self-employed person has earned income).

RESTRICTED LOANS FROM QUALIFIED PLANS

A qualified plan may, but is not required to provide for loans. If a plan provides for loans, the plan may limit the amount that can be taken as a loan.

The maximum amount that the plan can permit as a loan is (1) the greater of $10,000 or 50% of the vested account balance, or (2) $50,000, whichever is less.

Example:

If a participant has an account balance of $40,000, the maximum amount that he or she can borrow from the account is $20,000. A participant may have more than one outstanding loan from the plan at a time. However, any new loan, when added to the outstanding balance of all of the participant's loans from the plan, cannot be more than the plan maximum amount. In determining the plan maximum amount in that case, the $50,000 is reduced by the difference between the highest outstanding balance of all of the participant's loans during the 12-month period ending on the day before the new loan and the outstanding balance of the participant's loans from the plan on the date of the new loan.

Things to Remember

1. A plan may require the spouse of a married participant to consent to a plan loan.
2. A plan that provides for loans must specify the procedures for applying for a loan and the repayment terms for the loan. Repayment of the loan must occur within 5 years, and payments must be made in substantially equal payments that include principal and interest and that are paid at least quarterly. Loan repayments are not plan contributions
3. A loan that is taken for the purpose of purchasing the employee's principal residence may be able to be paid back over a period of more than 5 years.
4. A plan may suspend loan repayments for employees performing military service.
5. A plan also may suspend loan repayments during a leave of absence of up to one year. However, upon return, the participant must make up the missed payments either by increasing the amount of each monthly payment or by paying a lump sum at the end, so that the term of the loan does not exceed the original 5-year term.
6. Loans are not dependent upon hardship. Some plans may provide for hardship withdrawals,
7. The participant's relationship to the plan (e.g., being an owner of the plan sponsor) does not affect the participant's ability to take a loan, as long as all participants are equally able to take loans under the plan's loan provisions.
8. Loans are not taxable distributions unless they fail to satisfy the plan loan rules of the regulations with respect to amount, duration and repayment terms, as described above. In addition, a loan that is not paid back according to the repayment terms is treated as a distribution from the plan and is taxable as such.

HARDSHIP DISTRIBUTIONS AND QUALIFIED DISASTER DISTRIBUTIONS

A retirement plan may, but is not required to, provide for hardship distributions. Many plans that provide for elective deferrals provide for hardship distributions. Thus, 401(k) plans, 403(b) plans, and 457(b) plans may permit hardship distributions.

If a 401(k) plan provides for hardship distributions, it must provide the specific criteria used to make the determination of hardship. Thus, for example, a plan may provide that a distribution can be made only for medical or funeral expenses, but not for the purchase of a principal residence or for payment of tuition and education expenses.

In determining the existence of a need and of the amount necessary to meet the need, the plan must specify and apply nondiscriminatory and objective standards.

Under the provisions of the Pension Protection Act of 2006, the need of the employee also may include the need of the employee's non-spouse, non-dependent beneficiary.
Certain expenses are deemed to be immediate and heavy, including:

- certain medical expenses;
- costs relating to the purchase of a principal residence;
- tuition and related educational fees and expenses;
- payments necessary to prevent eviction from, or foreclosure on, a principal residence;
- burial or funeral expenses; and
- certain expenses for the repair of damage to the employee's principal residence that would qualify for the casualty deduction under IRC Section 165

The proposed regulations modify the safe harbor list of expenses for which distributions are deemed to be made on account of an immediate and heavy financial need by:

- Adding "primary beneficiary under the plan" as an individual for whom qualifying medical, educational, and funeral expenses may be incurred;
- modifying the expense relating to damage to a principal residence that would qualify for a casualty deduction under Section 165 to provide that for this purpose the new limitations in Section 165(h)(5) do not apply; and
- adding a new type of expense to the list, relating to expenses incurred as a result of certain disasters.

A hardship distribution may not exceed the amount of the employee's need. However, the amount required to satisfy the financial need may include amounts necessary to pay any taxes or penalties that may result from the distribution.

POP QUIZ & ANSWER SHEET

INDIVIDUAL RETIREMENT ACCOUNTS

POP QUIZ

Test your knowledge on *Individual Retirement Accounts* by answering the questions below. The answer sheet may be found at the end of the Pop Quiz.

Q1: Which of the following is not true about traditional IRA Rules?

A. The maximum annual contribution limit for 2021 and 2022 is $6,000 for those younger than 50.
B. Contributions may be tax deductible in the year they are made.
C. Investment within the account grows tax-deferred.
D. Withdrawals in retirement are non-taxable.

Q2: When a taxpayer makes a nondeductible contribution to a traditional IRA, they must attach which form to their 1040 return?

A. Form 8606, Nondeductible IRAs
B. Form 8948, Preparer Explanation for Not Filing Electronically
C. Form 9645 Installment Agreement Request
D. None of the Above

Q3: What is the requirement to avail a 10% penalty free withdrawal from a Traditional IRA?

A. You need to be 59 ½ or older and your account is at least three years old.
B. You need to be 59 ½ or older and your account is at least five years old.
C. You need to be 70 ½ or older and your account is at least five years old.
D. You need to be 70 ½ or older and your account is at least five years old.

Q4: Taxpayer A files their return March 15, 2022. What is the latest date that the taxpayer can make a traditional IRA contribution for the 2021 tax year?

A. March 30, 2022
B. April 15, 2022
C. May 15, 2022
D. October 15, 2022

Q5: Aside from income tax, how much additional tax must be paid by individuals for early withdrawal of retirement plans?

A. 5%
B. 10%
C. 15%
D. 20%

Q6: Which of the following situations may qualify for an exception to the IRA penalty tax on withdrawals?

A. Qualified Higher Education Expenses
B. First-Time Home Purchase
C. Qualified Reservist Distributions
D. All of the Above

Q7: Taxpayer A is 55 and single. The taxpayer earned $43,000 in wages and has a Roth IRA and a Traditional IRA. In 2021 the taxpayer contributes $3,000 to the traditional IRA. What is the maximum amount the taxpayer can contribute to the Roth IRA?

A. $3000
B. $3500
C. $4000
D. $4500

Q8: Taxpayers must take a required minimum distribution (RMD) from their Roth IRA at what age?

A. Age 59 ½
B. Age 70 ½
C. Age 72
D. Not required

Q9: If a traditional IRA is inherited from a late spouse, the surviving spouse generally has the following choices, except:

A. Treat it as his or her own IRA by designating himself or herself as the account owner.
B. Empty the IRA within 10 years
C. Treat himself or herself as the beneficiary rather than treating the IRA as his or her own.
D. Treat it as his or her own by rolling it over into a traditional IRA.

Q10: Taxpayer A wants to convert a traditional IRA to a Roth IRA. Which of the following is true?

A. The taxpayer can convert the traditional IRA to a Roth IRA and income tax must be paid on the conversion
B. The taxpayer has to wait until age 59 1/2 to convert their traditional IRA to a Roth IRA
C. Taxpayer can convert the traditional IRA to a Roth IRA tax free
D. None of the above

ANSWER SHEET

1. Answer is D – Withdrawals in retirement are non-taxable.

2. Answer is A – Form 8606, Nondeductible IRAs

3. Answer is B –You need to be 59 ½ or older and your account is at least five years old.

4. Answer is B – April 15, 2021

5. Answer is B – 10%

6. Answer is D – All of the Above

7. Answer is C – $4,000

8. Answer is D – Not required

9. Answer is B – Empty the IRA within 10 years

10. Answer is A – The taxpayer can convert the traditional IRA to a Roth IRA and income tax must be paid on the conversion.

33
RENTAL & ROYALTY INCOME

OVERVIEW

In most cases, individuals must include in the gross income all amounts received as rent. Rental income is any payment received for the use or occupation of property. It isn't limited to amounts received as normal rental payments.

When individuals have to report rental income on the tax return generally depends on whether they are a cash or an accrual basis taxpayer. Most individual taxpayers use the cash method.

An individual is a cash basis taxpayer if he or she reports income on the return in the year he or she actually or constructively received it, regardless of when it was earned. An individual constructively receives income when it is made available to the taxpayer, for example, by being credited to the bank account.
If an individual is an accrual basis taxpayer, he or she generally reports income when it's earned, rather than when it's received. The taxpayer generally deducts the expenses when he or she incurs them, rather than when he or she pays them.

If a taxpayer owns rental real estate, he or she should be aware of the federal tax responsibilities. All rental income must be reported on the tax return, and in general the associated expenses can be deducted from the rental income.

If a taxpayer is a cash basis taxpayer, he or she reports rental income on the return for the year he or she receives it, regardless of when it was earned. As a cash basis taxpayer the individual generally deducts the rental expenses in the year he or she paid them. If the taxpayer uses an accrual method, he or she generally reports income when it's earned, rather than when it's received and he or she can deduct the expenses when they are incurred, rather than when they are paid. Most individuals use the cash method of accounting.

RENTAL INCOME DEFINED

Taxpayers generally must include in the gross income all amounts received as rent. Rental income is any payment received for the use or occupation of property. Taxpayers must report rental income for all the properties.

In addition to amounts that are received as normal rent payments, there are other amounts that may be rental income and must be reported on the tax return.

Advance rent is any amount received before the period that it covers. Include advance rent in the rental income in the year that is received regardless of the period covered or the method of accounting that is used. For example, a taxpayer signs a 10-year lease to rent his property. In the first year, he receives $5,000 for the first year's rent and $5,000 as rent for the last year of the lease. He must include $10,000 in the income in the first year.

Security deposits used as a final payment of rent are considered advance rent. It needs to be included in the income when it's received. Do not include a security deposit in the income when it's received if the taxpayer plans to return it to the tenant at the end of the lease. But if the taxpayer keeps part or all of the security deposit during any year because the tenant does not live up to the terms of the lease, include the amount kept in the income in that year.

Payment for canceling a lease occurs if the tenant pays to cancel a lease. The amount that is received is rent. Include the payment in the income in the year that it's received regardless of the method of accounting.

Expenses paid by the tenant occur if the tenant pays any of the expenses. The taxpayer must include them in the rental income. The taxpayer can deduct the expenses if they are deductible rental expenses. For example, the tenant pays the water and sewage bill for the rental property and deducts it from the normal rent payment. Under the terms of the lease, the tenant does not have to pay this bill. Include the utility bill paid by the tenant and any amount received as a rent payment in the rental income.

Property or services received, instead of money, as rent, must be included as the fair market value of the property or services in the rental income. For example, the tenant is a painter and offers to paint the rental property instead of paying rent for two months. If the taxpayer accepts the offer, include in the rental income the amount the tenant would have paid for two months' worth of rent.

Lease with option to buy occurs if the rental agreement gives the tenant the rights to buy the rental property. The payments the taxpayer receives under the agreement are generally rental income.

If the taxpayer owns a part interest in rental property, he or she must report the part of the rental income from the property.

DEPRECIATION OF RENTAL PROPERTY

The taxpayer can recover the cost of income-producing property through yearly tax deductions. This can be done by depreciating the property; that is, by deducting some of the cost each year on the tax return.

Three factors determine how much depreciation a taxpayer can deduct each year:

- The basis in the property
- The recovery period for the property
- The depreciation method used. A taxpayer can't simply deduct the mortgage or principal payments, or the cost of furniture, fixtures, and equipment, as an expense.

The taxpayer can recover the cost of income-producing property through yearly tax deductions. This can be done by depreciating the property; that is, by deducting some of the cost each year on the tax return.

Three factors determine how much depreciation a taxpayer can deduct each year:

- The basis in the property
- The recovery period for the property
- The depreciation method used. A taxpayer can't simply deduct the mortgage or principal payments, or the cost of furniture, fixtures, and equipment, as an expense.

Taxpayers can deduct depreciation only on the part of the property used for rental purposes. Depreciation reduces the basis for figuring gain or loss on a later sale or exchange. Taxpayers may have to use Form 4562 to figure and report the depreciation. See Which Forms To Use in chapter 3. Also, see Pub. 946.

Alternative minimum tax (AMT). If a taxpayer uses accelerated depreciation, he or she may be subject to the AMT. Accelerated depreciation allows you to deduct more depreciation earlier in the recovery period than the taxpayer could deduct using a straight line method (same deduction each year).

The prescribed depreciation methods for rental real estate aren't accelerated, so the depreciation deduction isn't adjusted for the AMT. However, accelerated methods are generally used for other properties connected with rental activities (for example, appliances and wall-to-wall carpeting). To find out if the taxpayer is subjected to the AMT, see the Instructions for Form 6251.

Taxpayers can depreciate the property if it meets all the following requirements.

- The taxpayer owns the property.
- The taxpayer uses the property in the business or income-producing activity (such as rental property).
- The property has a determinable useful life.
- The property is expected to last more than one year.

1. Owned property

To claim depreciation, the taxpayer must usually be the owner of the property. He or she is considered to be the owner of property even if it's subject to a debt.

2. Rented property

Generally, if the taxpayer pays rent for property, he or she can't depreciate that property. Usually, only the owner can depreciate it. However, if the taxpayer makes permanent improvements to leased property, he or she may be able to depreciate the improvements.

3. Cooperative apartments

If the taxpayer is a tenant-stockholder in a cooperative housing corporation and rents the cooperative apartment to others, he or she can depreciate the stock in the corporation. Property having a determinable useful life. To be depreciable, the property must have a determinable useful life. This means that it must be something that wears out, decays, gets used up, becomes obsolete, or loses its value from natural causes.

When Does Depreciation and End?

Taxpayers can begin to depreciate the rental property when they place it in service for the production of income. They stop depreciating it either when they have fully recovered the cost or other basis, or when they retire it from service, whichever happens first.

Placed in Service - Taxpayers can place property in service in a rental activity when it is ready and available for a specific use in that activity. Even if they aren't using the property, it is in service when it is ready and available for its specific use.

Retired From Service - Taxpayers stop depreciating property when they retire it from service, even if they haven't fully recovered its cost or other basis. They retire property from service when they permanently withdraw it from use in a trade or business or from use in the production of income because of any of the following events:
They sell or exchange the property.
They convert the property to personal use.
They abandon the property.
The property is destroyed.

Depreciation Methods

Generally, individuals must use the Modified Accelerated Cost Recovery System (MACRS) to depreciate residential rental property placed in service after 1986.

If a taxpayer placed rental property in service before 1987, he or she is using one of the following methods:

- Accelerated Cost Recovery System (ACRS) for property placed in service after 1980 but before 1987.
- Straight line or declining balance method over the useful life of property placed in service before 1981.

Basis of Depreciable Property

The basis of property used in a rental activity is generally its adjusted basis when the taxpayer places it in service in that activity. This is its cost or other basis when it's acquired, adjusted for certain items occurring before it's placed in service in the rental activity.

If a taxpayer depreciates the property under MACRS, he or she may also have to reduce the basis by certain deductions and credits with respect to the property.

Basis and adjusted basis are explained in the following discussions.

If a taxpayer used the property for personal purposes before changing it to rental use, its basis for depreciation is the lesser of its adjusted basis or its fair market value when the taxpayer changes it to rental use.

Cost Basis

The basis of property a taxpayer buys is usually its cost. The cost is the amount paid for it in cash, in debt obligation, in other property, or in services.

The cost also includes amounts paid for sales tax charged on the purchase (but see Exception next), Freight charges to obtain the property, and Installation and testing charges.

Adjusted Basis

To figure the property's basis for depreciation, the taxpayer may have to make certain adjustments (increases and decreases) to the basis of the property for events occurring between the time the property is acquired and the time it's placed in service for business or the production of income. The result of these adjustments to the basis is the adjusted basis.
Increases to basis. Individuals must increase the basis of any property by the cost of all items properly added to a capital account. These include the following.

- The cost of any additions or improvements made before placing the property into service as a rental that have a useful life of more than 1 year.
    - Amounts spent after a casualty to restore the damaged property.
    - The cost of extending utility service lines to the property.
    - Legal fees, such as the cost of defending and perfecting title, or settling zoning issues.
- Decreases to basis - Taxpayers must decrease the basis of the property by any items that represent a return of the cost. These include the following.
    - Insurance or other payment received as the result of a casualty or theft loss.
    - Casualty loss not covered by insurance for which the taxpayer took a deduction.
    - Amount(s) received for granting an easement.

  - Residential energy credits allowed before 1986 or after 2005 if the taxpayer added the cost of the energy items to the basis of the home.
  - Exclusion from income of subsidies for energy conservation measures.
  - Special depreciation allowance or a section 179 deduction claimed on qualified property.
  - Depreciation deducted or that could have been deducted on the tax returns under the method of depreciation the taxpayer had chosen. If he or she didn't deduct enough or deducted too much in any year, see Depreciation under Decreases to Basis in Pub. 551.

If the rental property was previously used as the main home, the taxpayer must also decrease the basis by the following.

- Gains, postponed from the sale of the main home before May 7, 1997, if the replacement home was converted to the rental property.
  - District of Columbia first-time homebuyer credit allowed the purchase of the main home after August 4, 1997, and before January 1, 2012.
  - Amount of qualified principal residence indebtedness discharged on or after January 1, 2007.

Special Depreciation Allowance

For 2019, some properties used in connection with residential real property activities may qualify for a special depreciation allowance.

This allowance is figured before the taxpayer figures the regular depreciation deduction. See Pub. 946, chapter 3, for details.
Also, see the instructions for Form 4562, line 14.
If the taxpayer qualifies for, but chooses not to take, a special depreciation allowance, he or she must attach a statement to the return. The details of this election are in Pub. 946, chapter 3, and the instructions for Form 4562, line 14.

MACRS Depreciation

Most business and investment property placed in service after 1986 is depreciated using MACRS. This section explains how to determine which MACRS depreciation system applies to the property. It also discusses other information taxpayers need to know before they can figure depreciation under MACRS. This information includes the property's:

- Recovery class
- Applicable recovery period
- Convention
- Placed-in-service date
- Basis for depreciation

- Depreciation method

Depreciation Systems

MACRS consists of two systems that determine how individuals depreciate the property—the General Depreciation System (GDS) and the Alternative Depreciation System (ADS). Individuals must use GDS unless they are specifically required by law to use ADS or they elect to use ADS.

- Figuring The Depreciation
    - Taxpayers can figure the MACRS depreciation deduction in one of two ways. The deduction is substantially the same both ways. They can figure the deduction using either:
        - The depreciation method and convention that apply over the recovery period of the property, or
        - The percentage from the MACRS percentage tables. In this publication, we will use the percentage tables. For instructions on how to compute the deduction, see chapter 4 of Pub. 946.

Claiming the Correct Amount of Depreciation

- Taxpayers should claim the correct amount of depreciation each tax year. If they didn't claim all the depreciation they were entitled to deduct, they must still reduce the basis in the property by the full amount of depreciation that they could have deducted. For more information, see Depreciation under Decreases to Basis in Pub. 551.
- If taxpayers deducted an incorrect amount of depreciation for property in any year, they may be able to make a correction by filing Form 1040-X, Amended U.S. Individual Income Tax Return. If they aren't allowed to make the correction on an amended return, they may be able to change the accounting method to claim the correct amount of depreciation. See How Do You Correct Depreciation Deductions in Pub. 946 for more information.

DEPRECIATION OF RENTAL ESTATE

Basis Other Than Cost

- Individuals can't use cost as a basis for property that they received:
- In return for services they performed;
- In an exchange for other property;
- As a gift;
- From the spouse, or from the former spouse as the result of a divorce; or
- As an inheritance.

If the individual received property in one of these ways, see Pub. 551 for information on how to figure the basis.

DEPRECIATION OF RENTAL INCOME

Examples of expenses that taxpayers may deduct from the total rental income include:

- Depreciation – Allowances for exhaustion, wear and tear (including obsolescence) of property. Taxpayers can begin to depreciate the rental property when they place it in service. They can recover some or all of the original acquisition cost and the cost of improvements by using Form 4562, Depreciation and Amortization (PDF) (to report depreciation) beginning in the year the rental property is first placed in service, and beginning in any year the taxpayer makes improvements or adds furnishings.
- Repair Costs – Expenses to keep the property in good working condition but that don't add to the value of the property.
- Operating Expenses – Other expenses are necessary for the operation of the rental property, such as the salaries of employees or fees charged by independent contractors (groundskeepers, bookkeepers, accountants, attorneys, etc.) for services provided. If an individual is a cash basis taxpayer, he or she can't deduct uncollected rents as an expense because he or she has not included those rents in income. Repair costs, such as materials, are usually deductible.

  To claim depreciation, taxpayers must usually be the owner of the property. They are considered as owning property even if it is subject to a debt.

  Example 1. A taxpayer made a down payment to purchase rental property and assumed the previous owner's mortgage. He owns the property and he can depreciate it.

  Example 2. A taxpayer bought a new van that he will use only for the courier business. He will be making payments on the van over the next 5 years. He owns the van and he can depreciate it.

  - Leased property - Taxpayers can depreciate leased property only if they retain the incidents of ownership in the property (explained below). This means they bear the burden of exhaustion of the capital investment in the property.

Therefore, if a taxpayer leases property from someone to use in the trade or business or for the production of income, generally he or she cannot depreciate its cost because the taxpayer does not retain the incidents of ownership. The taxpayer can, however, depreciate any capital improvements made to the property. If a taxpayer leases property to someone, he or she can generally depreciate its cost even if the lessee (the person leasing) has agreed to preserve, replace, renew, and maintain the property. However, if the lease provides that the lessee is to maintain the property and return to the taxpayer the same property or its equivalent in value at the expiration of the lease in as good condition and value as when leased, the taxpayer cannot depreciate the cost of the property. Incidents of ownership. Incidents of ownership in property include the following:

- The legal title to the property

- The legal obligation to pay for the property.
- The responsibility to pay maintenance and operating expenses.
- The duty to pay any taxes on the property.
- The risk of loss if the property is destroyed, condemned, or diminished in value through obsolescence or exhaustion.
- Life tenant. Generally, if the taxpayer holds business or investment property as a life tenant, he or she can depreciate it as if he or she was the absolute owner of the property.

- Cooperative apartments. If the taxpayer is a tenant–stockholder in a cooperative housing corporation and uses the cooperative apartment in the business or for the production of income, the taxpayer can depreciate the stock in the corporation, even though the corporation owns the apartment. Figure the depreciation deduction as follows.
    1. Figure the depreciation for all the depreciable real property owned by the corporation in which the taxpayer has a proprietary lease or right of tenancy. If the taxpayer bought the cooperative stock after its first offering, figure the depreciable basis of this property as follows.
        1. Multiply the cost per share by the total number of outstanding shares, including any shares held by the corporation.
        2. Add to the amount figured in (a) any mortgage debt on the property on the date the stock was bought.
        3. Subtract from the amount figured in (b) any mortgage debt that is not for the depreciable real property, such as the part for the land.

2. Subtract from the amount figured in (1) any depreciation for space owned by the corporation that can be rented but cannot be lived in by tenants–stockholders.
    1. Divide the number of the shares of stock by the total number of outstanding shares, including any shares held by the corporation.
    2. Multiply the result of (2) by the percentage figured in (3). This is the depreciation on the stock. The depreciation deduction for the year cannot be more than the part of the adjusted basis in the stock of the corporation that is allocable to the business or income-producing property. The taxpayer must also reduce the depreciation deduction if only a portion of the property is used in a business or for the production of income

Example:

A taxpayer figures the share of the cooperative housing corporation's depreciation to be $30,000. The adjusted basis in the stock of the corporation is $50,000. The taxpayer uses one half of the apartment solely for business purposes. The depreciation deduction for the stock for the year cannot be more than $25,000 (1/2 of $50,000).

Change to business use. If the taxpayer changes the cooperative apartment to business use, figure the allowable depreciation as explained earlier. The basis of all the depreciable real property owned by the cooperative housing corporation is the smaller of the following amounts.

- The fair market value of the property on the date a taxpayer changes the apartment to business use. This is considered to be the same as the corporation's adjusted basis minus straight line depreciation, unless this value is unrealistic.
- The corporation's adjusted basis in the property on that date. Do not subtract depreciation when figuring the corporation's adjusted basis.

If a taxpayer bought the stock after its first offering, the corporation's adjusted basis in the property is the amount figured in (1) above. The fair market value of the property is considered to be the same as the corporation's adjusted basis figured in this way minus straight line depreciation, unless the value is unrealistic.

New Section 179 Rules For Certain Types of Rental Property

The section 179 deduction is a means of recovering part or all of the cost of certain qualifying property in the year a taxpayer places the property in service. It is separate from the depreciation deduction. See chapter 2 of Pub. 946 for more information about claiming this deduction. For 2021 the maximum Section 179 deduction is $1,050,000,

To qualify for the section 179 deduction, the property must meet all the following requirements.

- It must be eligible property.
- It must be acquired for business use.
- It must have been acquired by purchase.
- It must not be property.

Eligible Property

To qualify for the section 179 deduction, the property must be one of the following types of depreciable property.

- Tangible personal property.
- Other tangible property (except buildings and their structural components) used as:
    - An integral part of manufacturing, production, or extraction, or of furnishing transportation, communications, electricity, gas, water, or sewage disposal services;
    - A research facility used in connection with any of the activities in (a) above; or
    - A facility used in connection with any of the activities in (a) for the bulk storage of fungible commodities.
- Single-purpose agricultural (livestock) or horticultural structures. See chapter 7 of Pub. 225 for definitions and information regarding the use requirements that apply to these structures.

- Storage facilities (except buildings and their structural components) used in connection with distributing petroleum or any primary product of petroleum.
- Off-the-shelf computer software.
- Qualified section 179 real property (described below).

Tangible personal property

Tangible personal property is any tangible property that is not real property. It includes the following property.

- Machinery and equipment.
- Property contained in or attached to a building (other than structural components), such as refrigerators, grocery store counters, office equipment, printing presses, testing equipment, and signs.
- Gasoline storage tanks and pumps at retail service stations.
- Livestock, including horses, cattle, hogs, sheep, goats, and mink and other fur bearing animals.
- Portable air conditioners or heaters placed in service by the taxpayer in tax years beginning after 2015.
- Certain property used predominantly to furnish lodging or in connection with the furnishing of lodging (except as provided in section 50(b)(2)).

The treatment of property as tangible personal property for the section 179 deduction is not controlled by its treatment under local law. For example, property may not be tangible personal property for the deduction even if treated so under local law, and some property (such as fixtures) may be tangible personal property for the deduction even if treated as real property under local law.

What Property Does Not Qualify?

Excepted Property

Even if the requirements explained earlier under What Property Qualifies are met, taxpayers cannot elect the section 179 deduction for the following property.

- Certain property leased to others (if the taxpayer is a noncorporate lessor).
- Property used predominantly outside the United States, except property described in section 168(g)(4) of the Internal Revenue Code.
- Property used by certain tax-exempt organizations, except property used in connection with the production of income subject to the tax on unrelated trade or business income.
- Property used by governmental units or foreign persons or entities, except property used under a lease with a term of less than 6 months.
- Leased property

Generally, individuals cannot claim a section 179 deduction based on the cost of property they lease to someone else. This rule does not apply to corporations.

However, they can claim a section 179 deduction for the cost of the following property.

- Property individuals manufacture or produce and lease to others.
- Property individuals purchase and lease to others if both the following tests are met.
    - The term of the lease (including options to renew) is less than 50% of the property's class life
    - For the first 12 months after the property is transferred to the lessee, the total business deductions individuals are allowed on the property (other than rents and reimbursed amounts) are more than 15% of the rental income from the property.

REPAIRS VS. IMPROVEMENTS TO RENTAL PROPERTY

How Repairs and Improvements Are Treated

If a taxpayer improves depreciable property, he or she must treat the improvement as separate depreciable property. Improvement means an addition to or partial replacement of property that is a betterment to the property, restores the property, or adapts it to a new or different use. See section 1.263(a)-3 of the regulations.

Taxpayers generally deduct the cost of repairing business property in the same way as any other business expense.

However, if the cost is for a betterment to the property, to restore the property, or to adapt the property to a new or different use, individuals must treat it as an improvement and depreciate it.

Example:

A person repairs a small section on one corner of the roof of a rental house. He deducts the cost of the repair as a rental expense. However, if he completely replaces the roof, the new roof is an improvement because it is a restoration of the building. He depreciates the cost of the new roof.

Individuals can depreciate permanent improvements made to business property rented from someone else.

DEDUCTIBLE RENTAL LOSSES

Rental Expenses

Examples of expenses that taxpayers may deduct from the total rental income include:

- Depreciation – Allowances for exhaustion, wear and tear (including obsolescence) of property. A taxpayer can begin to depreciate the rental

property when he or she places it in service. The taxpayer can recover some or all of the original acquisition cost and the cost of improvements by using Form 4562, Depreciation and Amortization (PDF) (to report depreciation) beginning in the year the rental property is first placed in service, and beginning in any year the taxpayer makes improvements or add furnishings.
- Repair Costs – Expenses to keep the property in good working condition but that don't add to the value of the property.
- Operating Expenses – Other expenses necessary for the operation of the rental property, such as the salaries of employees or fees charged by independent contractors (groundskeepers, bookkeepers, accountants, attorneys, etc.) for services provided.
- In most cases, the expenses of renting the property, such as maintenance, insurance, taxes, and interest, can be deducted from the rental income.
- Personal use of rental property. If a taxpayer sometimes uses the rental property for personal purposes, he or she must divide the expenses between rental and personal use. Also, the rental expense deductions may be limited. See chapter 5, Personal Use of Dwelling Unit (Including Vacation Home).
- Part interest. If the taxpayer owns a part interest in rental property, he or she can deduct expenses paid according to the percentage of ownership.

Example:

Roger owns a one-half undivided interest in a rental house. Last year he paid$968 for necessary repairs on the property. Roger can deduct $484 (50% × $968) as a rental expense. He is entitled to reimbursement for the remaining half from the co-owner.

When To Deduct

Taxpayers generally deduct the rental expenses in the year they pay them.

Types of Expenses:

Listed below are the most common rental expenses.

- Advertising
- Auto and travel expenses
- Cleaning and maintenance
- Commissions
- Depreciation
- Insurance
- Legal and other professional fees
- Interest (other)
- Local transportation expenses
- Management fees
- Mortgage interest paid to banks, etc
- Points

- Rental payments
- Repair
- Taxes
- Utilities

Depreciation

Depreciation is a capital expense. It is the mechanism for recovering the cost in an income-producing property and must be taken over the expected life of the property. Taxpayers can begin to depreciate rental property when it is ready and available for rent.

Insurance Premiums Paid in Advance

If a taxpayer pays an insurance premium for more than one year in advance, he or she can't deduct the total premium in the year it is paid. For each year of coverage, the taxpayer can deduct only the part of the premium payment that applies to that year. See chapter 6 of Pub. 535 for information on deductible premiums.

Interest Expense

Taxpayers can deduct mortgage interest they pay on the rental property. When they refinance a rental property for more than the previous outstanding balance, the portion of the interest allocable to loan proceeds not related to rental use generally can't be deducted as a rental expense.

Certain expenses individuals pay to obtain a mortgage on their rental property can't be deducted as interest. These expenses, which include mortgage commissions, abstract fees, and recording fees, are capital expenses that are part of the basis in the property

Form 1098, Mortgage Interest Statement. If a taxpayer paid $600 or more of mortgage interest on the rental property to any one person, he or she should receive a Form 1098 or similar statement showing the interest paid for the year.

If the taxpayer and at least one other person (other than the spouse if they file a joint return) were liable for, and paid interest on, the mortgage, and the other person received the Form 1098, report the share of the interest on Schedule E (Form 1040 or 1040-SR), line 13.

Attach a statement to the return showing the name and address of the other person. On the dotted line next to line 13, enter "See attached."

Legal and Other Professional Fees

Taxpayers can deduct, as a rental expense, legal and other professional expenses such as tax return preparation fees paid to prepare Schedule E, Part I. For example, on the 2021 Schedule E the taxpayer can deduct fees paid in 2021 to prepare Part I of the

2021 Schedule E. The taxpayer can also deduct, as a rental expense, any expense (other than federal taxes and penalties) paid to resolve a tax underpayment related to the rental activities.

Local Benefit Taxes

In most cases, the taxpayer can't deduct charges for local benefits that increase the value of the property, such as charges for putting in streets, sidewalks, or water and sewer systems. These charges are - capital expenditures and must be added to the basis of the property. However, the taxpayer can deduct local benefit taxes that are for maintaining, repairing, or paying interest charges for the benefits.

Local Transportation Expenses

Taxpayers may be able to deduct their ordinary and necessary local transportation expenses if they incur them to collect rental income or to manage, conserve, or maintain the rental property. However, transportation expenses incurred to travel between the home and a rental property generally constitute non-deductible commuting costs unless the taxpayer uses the home as the principal place of business. See Pub. 587, Business Use of Your Home, for information on determining if the home office qualifies as a principal place of business.

Generally, if a taxpayer uses the personal car, pickup truck, or light van for rental activities, he or she can deduct the expenses using one of two methods: actual expenses or the standard mileage rate. For 2021, the standard mileage rate for business use is 56 cents a mile. For more information, see chapter 4 of Pub. 463.

Special $25,000 Loss Allowance For Real Estate Rental Activities Exception for Rental Real Estate With Active Participation

If the taxpayer or the spouse actively participated in a passive rental real estate activity, he or she may be able to deduct up to $25,000 of loss from the activity from the non-passive income. This special allowance is an exception to the general rule disallowing losses in excess of income from passive activities. Similarly, the taxpayer may be able to offset credits from the activity against the tax on up to $25,000 of non-passive income after taking into account any losses allowed under this exception.

Example:

Jane is single and has $40,000 in wages, $2,000 of passive income from a limited partnership, and $3,500 of passive loss from a rental real estate activity in which she actively participated. $2,000 of Jane's $3,500 loss offsets her passive income. The remaining $1,500 loss can be deducted from her $40,000 wages.

The special allowance isn't available if the taxpayer was married, lived with the spouse at any time during the year, and is filing a separate return.

Maximum special allowance. The maximum special allowance is:

- $25,000 for single individuals and married individuals filing a joint return for the tax year,
- $12,500 for married individuals who file separate returns for the tax year and lived apart from their spouses at all times during the tax year, and
- $25,000 for a qualifying estate reduced by the special allowance for which the surviving spouse qualified.

If the modified adjusted gross income (MAGI) is $100,000 or less ($50,000 or less if married filing separately), the taxpayer can deduct the loss up to the amount specified above. If the MAGI is more than $100,000 (more than $50,000 if married filing separately), the special allowance is limited to 50% of the difference between $150,000 ($75,000 if married filing separately) and the MAGI.

Generally, if the MAGI is $150,000 or more ($75,000 or more if the taxpayer is married filing separately), there is no special allowance.

RENTING ONLY PART OF THE PROPERTY

If a taxpayer rents part of the property, he or she must divide certain expenses between the part of the property used for rental purposes and the part of the property used for personal purposes, as though he or she actually had two separate pieces of property.

Taxpayers can deduct the expenses related to the part of the property used for rental purposes, such as home mortgage interest, mortgage insurance premiums, and real estate taxes, as rental expenses on Schedule E (Form 1040 or 1040-SR). Taxpayers can also deduct as rental expenses a portion of other expenses that are normally nondeductible personal expenses, such as expenses for electricity or painting the outside of the house.

There is no change in the types of expenses deductible for the personal-use part of the property. Generally, these expenses may be deducted only if the taxpayer itemizes the deductions on Schedule A (Form 1040 or 1040-SR).

Taxpayers can't deduct any part of the cost of the first phone line even if the tenants have unlimited use of it.

Taxpayers don't have to divide the expenses that belong only to the rental part of the property. For example, if a taxpayer paints a room that he or she rents or pays premiums for liability insurance in connection with renting a room in the home, the entire cost is a rental expense. If the taxpayer installs a second phone line strictly for the tenant's use, all the cost of the second line is deductible as a rental expense. Taxpayers can deduct depreciation on the part of the house used for rental purposes as well as on the furniture and equipment used for rental purposes.

How To Divide Expenses

If an expense is for both rental use and personal use, such as mortgage interest or heat for the entire house, the taxpayer must divide the expense between rental use and personal use. The taxpayer can use any reasonable method for dividing the expense. It may be reasonable to divide the cost of some items (for example, water) based on the number of people using them. The two most common methods for dividing an expense are (1) the number of rooms in the home, and (2) the square footage of the home.

Example:

A taxpayer rents a room in his house. The room is 12 × 15 feet, or 180 square feet. The entire house has 1,800 square feet of floor space. He can deduct as a rental expense 10% of any expense that must be divided between rental use and personal use. If the heating bill for the year for the entire house was $600, $60 ($600 × 0.10) is a rental expense. The balance, $540, is a personal expense that can't be deducted.

Duplex

A common situation is the duplex where a taxpayer lives in one unit and rents out the other. Certain expenses apply to the entire property, such as mortgage interest and real estate taxes, and must be split to determine rental and personal expenses. Example. Jordan owns a duplex and lives in one half, renting the other half. Both units are approximately the same size. Last year, he paid a total of $10,000 mortgage interest and $2,000 real estate taxes for the entire property. He can deduct $5,000 mortgage interest and $1,000 real estate taxes on Schedule E. If he itemize his deductions, include the other $5,000 mortgage interest and $1,000 real estate taxes when figuring the amount he can deduct on Schedule A

PERSONAL USE OF A DWELLING UNIT

If a taxpayer has any personal use of a dwelling unit (including a vacation home) that he or she rents, he or she must divide the expenses between rental use and personal use. In general, the rental expenses will be no more than the total expenses multiplied by a fraction, the denominator of which is the total number of days the dwelling unit is used and the numerator of which is the total number of days actually rented at a fair rental price. Only the rental expenses may be deducted on Schedule E (Form 1040 or 1040-SR). Some of the personal expenses may be deductible on Schedule A (Form 1040 or 1040-SR) if the taxpayer itemizes the deductions.

Taxpayers must also determine if the dwelling unit is considered a home. The amount of rental expenses that they can deduct may be limited if the dwelling unit is considered a home. Whether a dwelling unit is considered a home depends on how many days during the year are considered to be days of personal use. There is a special rule if the taxpayer used the dwelling unit as a home and he or she rented it for less than 15 days during the year.

A dwelling unit includes a house, apartment, condominium, mobile home, boat, vacation home, or similar property. It also includes all structures or other property belonging to the dwelling unit. A dwelling unit has basic living accommodations, such as sleeping space, a toilet, and cooking facilities.

A dwelling unit doesn't include property (or part of the property) used solely as a hotel, motel, inn, or similar establishment. Property is used solely as a hotel, motel, inn, or similar establishment if it is regularly available for occupancy by paying customers and isn't used by an owner as a home during the year.

Example:

Matt rents a room in his home that is always available for short-term occupancy by paying customers. He doesn't use the room himself and he allows only paying customers to use the room. This room is used solely as a hotel, motel, inn, or similar establishment and isn't a dwelling unit.

PARTIAL RENTAL ACTIVITY (WITH A PROFIT MOTIVE)

If the taxpayer uses a dwelling unit for both rental and personal purposes, divide the expenses between the rental use and the personal use based on the number of days used for each purpose.

When dividing the expenses, follow these rules.

- Any day that the unit is rented at a fair rental price is a day of rental use even if the taxpayer used the unit for personal purposes that day. (This rule doesn't apply when determining whether he or she used the unit as a home.)
- Any day that the unit is available for rent but not actually rented isn't a day of rental use.

Fair Rental Price

A fair rental price for the property is generally the amount of rent that a person who isn't related to the taxpayer would be willing to pay. The rent the taxpayer charges isn't a fair rental price if it is substantially less than the rents charged for other properties that are similar to the property in the area.

Ask the following questions when comparing another property with the one of the taxpayer.

- Is it used for the same purpose?
- Is it approximately the same size?
- Is it in approximately the same condition?
- Does it have similar furnishings?
- Is it in a similar location?

If any of the answers are no, the properties probably aren't similar.

Example:

Maggie's beach cottage was available for rent from June 1 through August 31 (92 days). Except for the first week in August (7 days), when she was unable to find a renter, she rented the cottage at a fair rental price during that time. The person who rented the cottage for July allowed her to use it over the weekend (2 days) without any reduction in or refund of rent. Her family also used the cottage during the last 2 weeks of May (14 days). The cottage wasn't used at all before May 17 or after August 31.

The taxpayers can figure the part of the cottage expenses to treat as rental expenses as follows.

- The cottage was used for rental a total of 85 days (92 − 7). The days it was available for rent but not rented (7 days) aren't days of rental use. The July weekend (2 days) Maggie used it for rental use because she received a fair rental price for the weekend.
- She used the cottage for personal purposes for 14 days (the last 2 weeks in May).
- The total use of the cottage was 99 days (14 days personal use + 85 days rental use). The rental expenses are 85/99 (86%) of the cottage expenses.

Note. When determining whether Maggie used the cottage as a home, the July weekend (2 days) she used it is considered personal use even though she received a fair rental price for the weekend. Therefore, she had 16 days of personal use and 83 days of rental use for this purpose. Because she used the cottage for personal purposes for more than 14 days and more than 10% of the days of rental use (8 days), she used it as a home. If she has a net loss, she may not be able to deduct all of the rental expenses.

NOT FOR PROFIT RENTALS AND BELOW MARKET RENTALS

If taxpayers don't rent a property to make a profit, they can't deduct rental expenses in excess of the amount of the rental income. They can't deduct a loss or carry forward to the next year any rental expenses that are more than the rental income for the year.

Where to report. Report the not-for-profit rental income on Schedule 1 (Form 1040 or 1040-SR), line 8, or Form 1040-NR, line 21. If the taxpayers itemize the deductions, include the mortgage interest and mortgage insurance premiums (if they use the property as their main home or second home), real estate taxes, and casualty losses from the not-for-profit rental activity when figuring the amount that can be deducted on Schedule A.

Presumption of profit. If the rental income is more than the rental expenses for at least 3 years out of a period of 5 consecutive years, individuals are presumed to be renting the property to make a profit.

Postponing decision. If a taxpayer is starting a rental activity and doesn't have 3 years showing a profit, he or she can elect to have the presumption made after he or she has the 5 years of experience required by the test. The taxpayer may choose to postpone the decision of whether the rental is for profit by filing Form 5213. He or she must file Form 5213 within 3 years after the due date of the return (determined without extensions) for the year in which the taxpayer first carried on the activity or, if earlier, within 60 days after receiving written notice from the Internal Revenue Service proposing to disallow deductions attributable to the activity.

MINIMAL RENTAL USE – 15 DAY RULE

If a taxpayer rents a dwelling unit to others that he or she also uses as a residence, limitations may apply to the rental expenses that can be deducted. The taxpayer is considered to use a dwelling unit as a residence if he or she uses it for personal purposes during the tax year for more than the greater of 14 days, or 10% of the total days he or she rents it to others at a fair rental price.

It's possible that the taxpayer uses more than one dwelling unit as a residence during the year. For example, if he or she lives in the main home for 11 months, the home is a dwelling unit used as a residence. If the taxpayer lives in the vacation home for the other 30 days of the year, the vacation home is also a dwelling unit used as a residence unless he or she rents the vacation home to others at a fair rental value for 300 or more days during the year in this example.

A day of personal use of a dwelling unit is any day that it's used by:

- The taxpayer or any other person who has an interest in it, unless he or she rents the interest to another owner as his or her main home and the other owner pays a fair rental price under a shared equity financing agreement
- A member of the family or of a family of any other person who has an interest in it, unless the family member uses it as his or her main home and pays a fair rental price
- Anyone under an agreement that lets the taxpayer uses some other dwelling unit
- Anyone at less than fair rental price.

Minimal rental use. If a taxpayer uses the dwelling unit as a home and he or she rents it less than 15 days during the year, that period isn't treated as rental activity. See Used as a home but rented less than 15 days later, for more information.

Used as a home but rented less than 15 days. If a taxpayer uses a dwelling unit as a home and he or she rents it less than 15 days during the year, its primary function isn't considered to be rental and it shouldn't be reported on Schedule E (Form 1040 or 1040-SR). The taxpayer isn't required to report the rental income and rental expenses from this activity. The expenses, including mortgage interest, property taxes, and any qualified casualty loss will be reported as normally allowed on Schedule A (Form 1040 or 1040-SR).

Used as a home and rented for 15 days or more. If a taxpayer uses a dwelling unit as a home and rents it 15 days or more during the year, include all the rental income in the income. Since the taxpayer used the dwelling unit for personal purposes, he or she must divide the expenses between the rental use and the personal use as described earlier in this chapter under Dividing Expenses. The expenses for personal use aren't deductible as rental expenses.

EXCEPTION FOR REAL ESTATE PROFESSIONALS

Real estate professionals

If a taxpayer is a real estate professional, complete line 43 of Schedule E. He or she qualifies as a real estate professional for the tax year if he or she meets both of the following requirements. More than half of the personal services performed in all trades or businesses during the tax year are performed in real property trades or businesses in which the taxpayer materially participates. The taxpayer performs more than 750 hours of services during the tax year in real property trades or businesses in which he or she materially participates.

If the taxpayer qualifies as a real estate professional, rental real estate activities in which he or she materially participated aren't passive activities. For purposes of determining whether he or she materially participated in the rental real estate activities, each interest in rental real estate is a separate activity unless the taxpayer elects to treat all the interests in rental real estate as one activity.

Don't count personal services the taxpayer performed as an employee in real property trades or businesses unless he or she is a 5% owner of the employer. The taxpayer is a 5% owner if he or she owns(or are considered to own) more than 5% of the employer's outstanding stock, or capital or profits interest.

Real property trades or businesses

A real property trade or business is a trade or business that does any of the following with real property.

- Develop or re-develops it.
- Constructs or reconstructs it.
- Acquires it.
- Convert it.
- Rents or leases it.
- Operates or manages it.
- Brokers it.

Choice to treat all interests as one activity

If a taxpayer was a real estate professional and had more than one rental real estate interest during the year, he or she can choose to treat all the interests as one activity. The taxpayer can make this choice for any year that he or she qualifies as a real estate professional. If the taxpayer forgoes making the choice for one year, he or she can still make it for a later year.

If the taxpayer makes the choice, it is binding for the tax year he or she makes it and for any later year that he or she is a real estate professional. This is true even if the taxpayer is not a real estate professional in any intervening year. (For that year, the exception for real estate professionals won't apply in determining whether the activity is subject to the passive activity rules.)

HOTELS, MOTELS, BED AND BREAKFAST

If a taxpayer is a real estate dealer who receives income from renting real property or an owner of a hotel, motel, etc., who provides services (maid services, etc.) for guests, report the rental income and expenses on Schedule C. If the taxpayer is not a real estate dealer or the kind of owner described in the preceding sentence, report the rental income and expenses on Schedule E. For more information, see Pub. 527, Residential Rental Property (Including Rental of Vacation Homes).

Real estate dealer

A taxpayer is a real estate dealer if he or she is engaged in the business of selling real estate to customers with the purpose of making a profit from those sales. Rent received from real estate held for sale to customers is subject to SE tax. However, rent received from real estate held for speculation or investment is not subject to SE tax.

Hotels, boarding houses, and apartments

Rental income received for the use or occupancy of hotels, boarding houses, or apartment houses is subject to SE tax if the taxpayer provides services for the occupants.

Generally, a taxpayer is considered to provide services for the occupants if the services are primarily for their convenience and are not services normally provided with the rental of rooms for occupancy only. An example of a service that is not normally provided for the convenience of the occupants is maid service. However, providing heat and light, cleaning stairways and lobbies, and collecting trash are services normally provided for the occupants' convenience.

ROYALTY INCOME

File Form 1099-MISC for each person to whom the taxpayer has paid during the year: At least $10 in royalties or broker payments in lieu of dividends or tax-exempt interest.

At least $600 in:

- Rents.
- Services performed by someone who is not the employee.
- Prizes and awards.
- Other income payments.
- Medical and health care payments.
- Crop insurance proceeds.
- Cash payments for fish (or other aquatic life) purchased from anyone engaged in the trade or business of catching fish.
- Generally, the cash paid from a notional principal contract to an individual, partnership, or estate.
- Payments to an attorney.
- Any fishing boat proceeds.

In addition, use Form 1099-MISC to report that the taxpayer made direct sales of at least $5,000 of consumer products to a buyer for resale anywhere other than a permanent retail establishment.

Royalties from copyrights, patents, and oil, gas and mineral properties are taxable as ordinary income.

Taxpayers generally report royalties in Part I of Schedule E (Form 1040 or Form 1040-SR), Supplemental Income and Loss. However, if they hold an operating oil, gas, or mineral interest or are in business as a self-employed writer, inventor, artist, etc., report the income and expenses on Schedule C.

Royalties from copyrights, patents, and oil, gas, and mineral properties are taxable as ordinary income. In most cases, taxpayers need to report royalties on Schedule E.

POP QUIZ & ANSWER SHEET

RENTAL & ROYALTY INCOME

POP QUIZ

Test your knowledge on *Rental & Royalty* Income by answering the questions below. The answer sheet may be found at the end of the Pop Quiz.

Q1: Common rental expenses include all of the following, except:

A. Cleaning fees
B. Facebook ads to market the rental
C. Roof replacement
D. Liability insurance

Q2: Which of the following factors does not determine how much depreciation of rental property you can deduct each year:

A. The basis in the property
B. The size of the property
C. The recovery period for the property
D. The depreciation method used

Q3: All of the following will stop depreciation of a property, except:

A. When the taxpayer sells or exchanges the property
B. When the taxpayer converts the property to personal use
C. When the taxpayer abandons the property
D. When the taxpayer has three years left on a depreciation schedule

Q4: What method is typically used to depreciate residential rental property placed in service?

A. Modified Accelerated Cost Recovery System (MACRS)
B. Accelerated Cost Recovery System (ACRS)
C. Straight Line or Declining Balance Method
D. None of the Above

Q5: If a tenant pays to cancel a lease the amount received for the cancellation is considered?

A. Rental expense
B. Rental income
C. Depreciation
D. Capital improvement

Q6: Taxpayer A owns a commercial building. Taxpayer B owns a janitorial business that rents out space for $3500 per month in Taxpayer A's commercial building. Both taxpayers agree to let Taxpayer B clean the commercial building for 6 months in exchange for rent.
How much must taxpayer A recognize as income for services in lieu of rent?

A. $3,500
B. $20,000
C. $21,000
D. $7,000

Q7: To qualify for the section 179 deduction, your property must meet all the following requirements, except:

A. It must be eligible property.
B. It must be acquired for business use.
C. Property used by governmental units or foreign persons or entities for long term use.
D. It must have been acquired by purchase.
E. It must have been acquired by purchase.

Q8: Royalties from patents, copyrights, oil, gas, and mineral properties are taxable as ordinary income and reports on ___

A. 1099-NEC
B. 1099-MISC
C. 1098-C
D. 1099-INT

Q9: Examples of improvements include all of the following, except:

A. New plumbing
B. Installing a new roof
C. Adding a deck
D. Repairing a leaky kitchen sink faucet

Q10: Operators of bed and breakfasts, hotels, or boarding houses must report their income on Schedule___

A. Sch E
B. Sch C
C. Sch F
D. Sch B

ANSWER SHEET

1. Answer is C – Roof replacement

2. Answer is B – The size of the property

3. Answer is D – When the taxpayer has three years left on a depreciation schedule

4. Answer is A – Modified Accelerated Cost Recovery System (MACRS)

5. Answer is B – Rental income

6. Answer is C – $21,000

7. Answer is C – Property used by governmental units or foreign persons or entities for long term use.

8. Answer is B – 1099-MISC

9. Answer is D – Repairing a leaky kitchen sink faucet

10. Answer is B – Sch C

Made in the USA
Middletown, DE
02 June 2022